The
Devil of Today

(1906)

His Play Between the False and the Good

Rev. I. Mench Chambers

ISBN 0-7661-0498-2

Request our FREE CATALOG of over 1,000
Rare Esoteric Books
<u>Unavailable Elsewhere</u>

Freemasonry * Akashic * Alchemy * Alternative Health * Ancient Civilizations * Anthroposophy * Astral * Astrology * Astronomy * Aura * Bacon, Francis * Bible Study * Blavatsky * Boehme * Cabalah * Cartomancy * Chakras * Clairvoyance * Comparative Religions * Divination * Druids * Eastern Thought * Egyptology * Esoterism * Essenes * Etheric * Extrasensory Perception * Gnosis * Gnosticism * Golden Dawn * Great White Brotherhood * Hermetics * Kabalah * Karma * Knights Templar * Kundalini * Magic * Meditation * Mediumship * Mesmerism * Metaphysics * Mithraism * Mystery Schools * Mysticism * Mythology * Numerology * Occultism * Palmistry * Pantheism * Paracelsus * Parapsychology * Philosophy * Plotinus * Prosperity & Success * Psychokinesis * Psychology * Pyramids * Qabalah * Reincarnation * Rosicrucian * Sacred Geometry * Secret Rituals * Secret Societies * Spiritism * Symbolism * Tarot * Telepathy * Theosophy * Transcendentalism * Upanishads * Vedanta * Wisdom * Yoga * *Plus Much More!*

KESSINGER PUBLISHING, LLC

http://www.kessingerpub.com

email: books@kessingerpub.com

The DEVIL OF TO-DAY

HIS PLAY BETWEEN THE FALSE AND *the* GOOD

¶ Being A SEARCHING ALLEGORY on the subtle intrigues of the Devil within The Church, The Home, and Modern Society.

By
REV. I. MENCH CHAMBERS, A. M.
Author of "At the Beautiful Gate," "On the Sunny Side,"
"Harold Payson," etc.

WITH AN INTRODUCTION BY
REV. J. R. MILLER, D. D.

Pictures by J. FRANCIS HART

Copyright 1906, by
W. R. SCULL.

Copyright, 1903, by
I. MENCH CHAMBERS

CAUTION
Notice is hereby given that the entire contents of this book are fully protected by copyrights. The Story is original; the Illustrations are original; the Title has been conceived especially for this book; and any infringements on proprietary rights will be prosecuted to the full extent and penalty of the law.

Dedication

To all brave and courageous souls, who, by godly life and devoted service, are seeking to destroy the works of the Devil, and bring to mankind the gospel of the divine life, this volume is affectionately dedicated by

The Author.

"The good book of the hour. then,—I do not speak of the bad ones—is simply the useful or pleasant talk of some person whom you cannot otherwise converse with, printed for you. Very useful often, telling you what you need to know; very pleasant often, as a sensible friend's present talk would be."

—Ruskin.

PREFACE

*Men don't believe in the Devil now, as their
      fathers used to do;
They've forced the door of the broadest creed
      to let His Majesty through.
There is n't a print of his cloven foot or a fiery
      dart from his brow
To be found in earth or air to-day, for the
      world has voted so.*

*Who dogs the steps of the toiling saint and
      digs the pits for his feet?
Who sows the tares in the fields of time.
      Wherever God sows his wheat?
The Devil is voted not to be, and, of course,
      the thing is true;
But who is doing the kind of work the Devil
      alone can do?*

*We are told that he does not go about as a roaring
      lion now;
But whom shall we hold responsible for the
      everlasting row*

PREFACE

*To be heard in home, in church and state, to
    the earth's remotest bound,
If the Devil by a unanimous vote is nowhere to
    be found?*

*Won't somebody step to the front forthwith
    and make their bow and show
How the frauds and crimes of a single day
    spring up? We want to know.
The Devil was fairly voted out, and, of course,
    the Devil's gone;
But simple people would like to know who
    carries the business on.*
—REV. ALFRED J. HOUGH.

A Word from the Publishers

To-day, men seem to be drifting, in many ways, away from the teachings of Jesus. The Story of the Cross does not thrill them now. They camp on debatable ground; follow debatable occupations; live debatable lives. There is a message for them in these pages.

From time to time, one happens upon a book which has been written because the author had no choice but to write it. So it is with this scathing arraignment of modern conditions in the Home, the Church, the State, and Society. Our author had no rest, day or night, so soon as the book was complete in his mind, until he sat down to write it, and then he wrote at white heat.

For years he has been brooding over these and cognate subjects, while studying an old book—a simple, unpretending old book—in which are printed stories by men who saw and heard things, and then told them to others. He, too, has seen and heard things, and his message to the world is in this volume.

Four of these men were plain and unlettered, but they had

known and loved One "who lifted with His pierced hands empires off their hinges, turned the stream of centuries out of its channel, and still governs the ages." Their stories have changed the face of the world. Another was a man whose hands grew hard in making tents of goats' hair; whose limbs and body bore marks of prison chains and rods and scourges. From his writings, men and women have gained inspiration and a hope of Eternal Life.

It is not easy to think of any book published for many years that is likely to make a greater sensation than this work. Its author is withholding nothing of the large measure of knowledge he has received from the teachings of the Master. He is sharing it with the world, and when Time has done its winnowing, it shall be seen that the world is richer and sweeter for his work.

The author is not a conscious theologian, but his is the theology of civilization, or, rather, the sort of theology that concerns every human being. He does not discuss latter-day religions—the religious vagaries of the day—but, from his high point of view, shows that the world is presided over by goodness; that there are veritable ideas and standards of morality; that the world is, as a whole, steadily growing better; and, best of all, perhaps, that it is worth while to struggle for its continuous betterment.

THE PUBLISHERS.

Contents

CHAPTER I

The Bridge of Sighs

A Guardian Angel Meets the Antagonist of Souls—A Vast Company Cross the Bridge—The Pilgrims' Song—The Angel Chorus—Satan Appears Again—The Angel Denounces Him—The Gates of Hell Shall Not Prevail—The Angel Passes to Her Ministry—A Society Function—Miss Sincere is Led into Temptation—Modern Delilahs and Samsons—Mr. Hypocrite's Creed and Aims—A Sense of Condemnation—A Soul is Won from Sin—What Will It Matter? 29

CHAPTER II

The Cross on the Lonely Hill

A Prayer for an Enlarged Vision—The Path to the Cross—Satan's Hordes Destroy It—Satan and Mr. Hypocrite Meet—A Mist Hides the Hill-top—Satan Secretes Himself—Mr. Hypocrite Meets Determination—The Pilgrims' Song Again—The Pilgrims Sink in the Mire—The Angel Appears—The Glass of Faith—Every Day is a Fresh Beginning—Up-to-date Religious Literature—Mr. Hypocrite and Miss Sincere—Miss Sincere's Faith is Shaken—The Angel Exposes Mr. Hypocrite—Miss Sincere Turns to the Bible—Satan Instructs His Workers—Satan Congratulates Mr. Hypocrite—Onward, Christian Soldiers. 41

CONTENTS

CHAPTER III

The Broken-down Altars

Evangelist Comes from the Eastern Hills—He Accepts Hospitality—He Tells His Mission—Satan in His Council-chamber—Satan Calls Upon Mr. Hypocrite—Prayer Heals the Sick—Hypocrite and Miss Sincere Discuss the Situation—Evangelist and the Faithful Few—Satan's Latest Plan—He Counsels Hypocrite—A Day of Victory—Evangelist Scores Hypocrite—The Seventy Return With Joy, ... 56

CHAPTER IV

Hypocrite in the Pew

Each Church Has Its Judas—Satan Sets More Snares—Minister Good is Attacked from Behind—Hypocrite and His Fellow-plotters Meet—Miss Sincere Appeals to the Angel—Evangelist Scores Hypocrite Again—Satan and His Helpers Discuss the Matter—The Angel Comforts Minister Good, ... 74

CHAPTER V

The Modern Thirst for Gold

Avarice Breaks All of the Commandments—The Thirst for Riches a Disease of the Times—The Lessons and Obligations of Wealth—The Tempter and the Tempted—Hypocrite Has a Troublesome Dream—Satan Hears Good News—Evangelist and the Minister Discuss Municipal Government—Hypocrite is "Taken Care of"—Hypocrite "In the Hands of His Friends"—Man-of-the-World Writes a Letter—The Angel Reveals a Plot to Evangelist, ... 95

CHAPTER VI

The House of Selfishness

Whole-soul and Determination Seek the Hills—The Charmed Path—Self-love Appears—Deception Comes on the Scene—Man-of-the-World and Hypocrite Take Their Ease—The Story of Miser—The House of Selfishness is Doomed—The Hills of Delusion—Determination Defies the Devil—There is a Grander Life—Evangelist Leads a Pilgrimage—The Seed Called Heart's Desire—The Barren Hills—Satan Curses His Tools, ...119

CONTENTS

CHAPTER VII

The Path of the Primrose

The City of Sin—A Great Light Falls Upon It—The Pleasant Beginnings of Vice—The Angel Pleads for the City—Determination Proposes to Reform the City—Satan's Army of Quiet Workers—The Angel Goes with Miss Sincere—The Path of the Primrose—Hypocrite Treads upon Thorns—The Pit of Death—A Note of Warning, ... 139

CHAPTER VIII

Judas in Twentieth-Century Clothes

The Price of a Vote—Satan's Skillful Disguise—His School of Modern Methods—In Satan's Schoolrooms—The Darkened Windows—Modern Business Methods—The Hill of Prospect—Satan's Liberality to His Tools—The Real Things of Life—Mr. Man-of-the-World is Duped—The Downfall of Artful—The Good Angel Saves Him, ... 156

CHAPTER IX

In with the Priests

Satan's Plan Miscarries—He Flies Into a Rage—He Overhears Evangelist Denounce Him—The Communion Under the Cedar—Satan Visits Hypocrite—Miss Sincere and Her Mission—Hypocrite Banters Satan—Satan Plots Against the Ministers—Man-of-the-World Joins in the Plot—A Day of Recreation—The "League" Offers a Bribe—Evangelist Denounces the Plot—Who Pays the Bills? 173

CHAPTER X

Butterflies in Vacation Time

The Stagnant Pool—The Dream Interpreted—The Foolish Trio—The City by the Sea—Satan Very Busy—Man-of-the-World Entertains—The "Boardwalk"—Religion is Left at Home—A John the Baptist is Needed—The Rev. Mr. Please-all—Satan in the Best of Spirits—The Prayer-meeting on the Beach—The Rescue of a Magdalen, ... 191

CONTENTS

CHAPTER XI
Running Past the Signals

Satan Sets Up False Signals—He Visits His Workshop—He Makes the Ink with which Bad Books and Pictures are Printed—The Home of Lies—Lies Made to Order—The Murder of the Innocents—Race Suicide is Fostered—Three Successful Fiends—The Purity League—The Devil's Rapid-fire Guns—The Angel Points Out His Slimy Track—Modern Showbills—The Angel Slays a Company of Fiends, ... 210

CHAPTER XII
The Broken Cogs

Satan Keeps a List of the Churches—He Knows the Weak Ones—His Untiring Plots—He Has His Dupes Among Church Officers—He Attends a Church Meeting, but is Detected There—His Plan Fails—He Sends for Heresy—Satan Issues His Orders—The Bible is to be Attacked—The Church Machinery is to be Disabled—He Introduces Professor Philosophy—Man's Knowledge is Cold Ashes—The Old Book, ... 232

CHAPTER XIII
The Devil's Laboratory

The Green Liquor of Envy—Jealousy is its Twin Poison—Satan Mixes the Ingredients Himself—Narrow Escape of the Widow Faith—Satan's Serpents Use Their Cruel Fangs—Evangelist Has a Timely Message for the Children—The Angel Again Defeats Satan's Plans—Satan Sends for Faultfinder—Love the Antidote of all Venom—Determination Captures and Destroys the Poison—Satan's Fury at His Loss, ... 250

CHAPTER XIV
The Devil's Poisoned Arrows

Satan's Grim Castle—How the Arrows are Made—How the Arrows are Used—The Venom of Cruel Words—Bitterness in Church Societies—The Crime of Reckless Speech—Faultfinder and His Band—Satan Makes a Tour of Inspection—Paying Off Old Scores—Satan is Disgusted—Three Gates of Gold—Hypocrite and Man-of-the-World Discuss Matters—Satan Falls Into a Rage—Miss Sincere and Mrs. Hypocrite, ... 269

CONTENTS

CHAPTER XV

The Divorce Bureau

Satan and Belial Confer—A Letter from Faultfinder—Divorce is Popular—Its Moral Side—Private Marriage Bureaus—Platonic Friendships—Anything to Destroy the Home—The Angel Enters the Castle—She Overhears Satan's Plans—Moral and Political decay—The Hidden Cage—God's Law Regarding Divorce—Belial and Faultfinder Attack a Home—Hypocrite's Wedding Anniversary—The Divorce Mills—They are Destroyed—The Lord Laughs at Satan, ... 292

CHAPTER XVI

The Worship of Other Gods

Glory in the Highest—Thou Shalt Have no Other Gods—The Pulpit and the Pew—Satan's New Pitfalls—A Jealous God—The Christian Goes on Singing—The Church of the Holy Passion—Rev. Mr. Please-all—The Juggernaut of Fashion—Church Festivals—The Cross is Kept in the Background—Sunday Amusements—The Bars of Zion are Let Down—The Path of the Wicked—Evangelist Scores the City—The False Gods—Deception Invents Excuses for Christians—Him Have I Pierced, . . 312

CHAPTER XVII

Wrecks Along the Shore

The Sea of Social Swirl—The Merciless Tides and Their Victims—Pleasure and Death Hand in Hand—Presumption and Ignorance are Lost—Satan Laughs at His Victims—The Hosts of Heaven Gather—Man-of-the-World in the Whirlpool of Wine—Determination Rescues Him—Evangelist Points Him to the Cross—The Dangers of the Wine-cup—Satan's Gilded Traps for Youth—The Secret Path to the Whirlwool—The Angel Gives Determination the Light of Truth—He Turns it on Saloons and Gambling Den—The Banquet of the Select, ... 336

CHAPTER XVIII

His Majesty's Charity Fund.

Hypocrite and Evangelist Discourse on the Love of Money—The Dream of the Vault—Some Riches Come from the Devil—The Gray

Prophet and Minister Good Discuss Philanthropy—Man-of-the-World Endows a Museum of Art—Satan and Deception Plot to Regain Control of Hypocrite—Evangelist Warns Hypocrite—Hypocrite's Confession—The Crusade for Consecrated Wealth—Covering up Great Thefts by Generosity—The Thralldom of Greed, ... 357

CHAPTER XIX
The Pilgrim's Scars

Hypocrite Meets His Greatest Sorrow—Evangelist Comforts the Stricken Man—Satan Torments Hypocrite—The Angel Comforts Him—"Get Thee Behind Me, Satan"—The Enemy of Souls is Abashed—The Unseen Battlefield—Each Pilgrim Has His Scars—Man-of-the-World and Rev. Mr. Please-all Laugh at Hypocrite's Conversion—Satan Sneers at the "Unique Disciple"—The Crack in Satan's Castle Walls—Man-of-the-World Loses His Wealth, ... 378

CHAPTER XX
The Good Angel's Pity

The Cry from Earth to Heaven—Angelic Ministrants—A Great Stir in Satan's Castle—The Challenge—The Breath of Selfishness—Fires of Compassion Are Kindled—The Demons Defy Jehovah—Their Horrible Death—God's Purpose Always Prevails—The Angel's Touch—The Archfiend Blasphemes—The "Bureau of Lies" is Damaged—Satan Exhorts His Hosts—Consecrated Wealth—Hypocrite Consecrates His Life to the Master—The Tree of Pity—Its Story—Satan Cannot Blast It—The Almighty Goeth By—Satan in Dismay, ... 394

CHAPTER XXI
Man-of-the-World Under the Light

The Once Prosperous Mr. Man-of-the-World Soliloquizes—The Pinch of Poverty—Evangelist Shows Man-of-the-World Three Lights—Past, Present, and Future—The Gate of opportunity—The King's Highway—The Tree of Pity Again—The Road of Sacrifice—Satan Hears Man-of-the-World Pray—Hypocrite is a Comforter—The Window of Revelation—The Marys of the New Era—A Magdalen is Saved—The Present Alone is Ours—The Law of Christian Brotherhood—Another Season at Longshore—Mr. Please-all Takes up His Cross, ... 413

CONTENTS xix

CHAPTER XXII

SAVED AS BY FIRE

The Passion of the Pit—Evangelist's Message Falls upon Dull Ears—The Devoted Band Leave the City—A Strange Light Appears—The Day of the Millennium—The Refining Fire Falls upon the City of Worldliness—The Curse of Iniquity is Removed—None to Molest—Satan is Foiled by Grace—He Defies God—The Avenging Angel Overpowers Satan—Satan is Thrown into a Pit—Prophecy is Fulfilled—The Gladness of the World—Satan's Castle in Ruins, ... 428

CHAPTER XXIII

THE OPENING OF THR HEAVENLY GATES

The Light Breaks—The Heavy Cross Seems Small—Minister Good Passes to Higher Service—Easter Morning—The Redeemed City—The Motionless Past—The Oblivion of God's Mercy—The Angel Brings Good Tidings—Christ Shall Come—A Watch-tower Arises—The Advancing Age—Regions of Serene Grace—At the Home of Widow Faith—The Glorified Christ Comes—The Company in White Robes—The City of Peace, ... 440

Principal Characters in the Allegory

SATAN—The archfiend, the enemy of man.
A GUARDIAN ANGEL—On business for the King of Heaven.
MISS SINCERE—A rich young woman, devoted to church work.
MR. HYPOCRITE—Mayor of the City of Worldliness.
EVANGELIST—A servant of God.
MR. MAN-OF-THE-WORLD—Political boss of the City of Worldliness.
REV. MR. GOOD—Pastor of the "Church of the Disciples."
REV. MR. PLEASE-ALL—Pastor of the "Church of the Redeemer."
DETERMINATION—A leader of pilgrims.
WHOLE-SOUL—A fellow-worker with Determination.
LIGHT HEART
PRESUMPTION } An empty-headed trio.
INCREDULOUS
MISS FAITHFUL—A friend of Miss Sincere.
MRS. HYPOCRITE—Wife of Mr. Hypocrite.
MRS. MAN-OF-THE-WORLD—Wife of Mr. Man-of-the-World.
WIDOW FAITH—An earnest worker in the church.
MRS. GOOD—Wife of Rev. Mr. Good.
DECEPTION
BELIAL } Satan's most trusted helpers.
FAULTFINDER
HERESY

Illustrations

"'Get thee behind me, thou Evil One.'" *Frontispiece.*
"Miss Sincere was utterly out of sympathy with her surroundings,"
"An army of laborers destroying the way to the Cross,"
"A man of kindly demeanor and patriarchal appearance,"
"'I see nothing to do but to get rid of him,' said Hypocrite,"
"Grind, grind, grind at the 'Mill of Fortune,'"
"'What can he do?' replied Mrs. Hypocrite,"
"An imposing edifice in the midst of a handsome park,"
"'The three laughed and hurried on,"
"'Thou art weighed in the balances and art found wanting,'"
"'Fifty thousand dollars for one vote!' exclaimed Minister Good,"
"The home of the Adversary crowned the summit of a ragged cliff,"
"The procession arrived at the 'Pavilion of Pleasure,'"
"Thousands spent their time on the 'Boardwalk,'"
"The Archfiend stepped into the 'Home of Lies,'"
"'Halt!' the Angel cried. 'Ye cannot pass!'"
"Then a dozen others were on their feet at once,"
"No hands but his own can mix the death-dealing potions,"
"The entire band of fiends rushed back to the castle,"
"Vile and grotesque beasts lifted their slimy heads,"
"Miss Sincere in the midst of her bitterest enemies,"
"'I saw Belial and Fault-finder approach a home,'"

ILLUSTRATIONS

"'The court has decided to grant a bill of divorcement,'" . . . . .
"'Knees are calloused from the worship of other gods,'" . . . . . .
"'Tis Man-of-the-World !' Determination cried. 'He calls for help !'"
"Tireless fiends sorted and labeled bribes," . . . .
"With face buried in the pillow, he wept bitterly," . . . .
"But now an host of shining guards surrounded it," . . . .
"'I behold the Cross !' cried Man-of-the-World," . . . .
"The fire of His refining burst upon the City of Worldliness," . . .
"'For a thousand years thou shalt await the day of thy doom,'" . .
"The lowly home where the glorified Christ had deigned to come." .
"'I saw that His hands were uplifted in benediction,'" . . . .

"'Get thee behind me, thou Evil One.'"

Introduction

The author of this volume is a writer who has won hosts of friends and admirers by his excellent work, especially by his poems, which are widely read. After reading his gentle verse one would scarcely think of him in connection with a subject so matter-of-fact, and withal requiring so robust treatment, as the title of this book suggests. But poets have the gift of seeing deeply into things, and it is not incongruous to think of Mr. Chambers, even in his quiet and serene life, as capable of seeing a good deal of the evil there is in the world.

That there is such evil no one will deny. The devil is not dead, nor has he withdrawn from activity in the affairs of the world. We are not to suppose that the title in this remarkable allegory, given to the Prince of Evil, implies that the devil who is in the field now is a new one as to his personality; the thought is that he is modernized as to his methods of activity. He is thoroughly up-to-date. He does not belong to that class of conservatives who believe that the old order never should be changed, that things should be done in the twentieth century precisely as they were in the nineteenth, that innovations are essentially heresies. He believes in progress, in doing old work in new ways, in using new methods in these new years. So the modern devil of this volume is the familiar devil of history, who keeps in touch with the times.

The book is a most serious one, treating its subject as one of grave importance. We dare not shut our eyes to the evil that is in the world. Nor may we keep ourselves out of the battle. We must be unquestionably on the right side in the conflict, and must strike valiant blows for the truth and for God, if we would not be disloyal to our Christian manhood and to Him whose we are and whom we serve.

J. R. MILLER, D. D.,
Editor of "Forward."

"Miss Sincere was utterly out of sympathy with her surroundings."

Satan is at Work in Every Walk of Life

CHAPTER I

The Bridge of Sighs

"O may I join the choir invisible
　Of those immortal dead who live again
　In minds made better by their presence: live
　In pulses stirred to generosity,
　In deeds of daring rectitude, in scorn
　For miserable aims that end with self,
　In thoughts sublime that pierce the night like stars,
　And with their mild persistence urge man's search
　To vaster issues."

—*George Eliot.*

IT was near the close of a day spent amid the evils of the world, that I walked in the fields, seeking rest from care and its attendant worry and fear. At length, I came to a place where the soft air invited to rest and peace. Sleep, Death's twin, fell upon me like a benediction, and in that sleep I dreamed.

Let me, with halting words, tell the strange and wonderful vision which came to me there.

I seemed to stand beside the bridge which separates Earth from the world invisible. Its majestic span stretched far across the abyss and lost itself in the shadows of the farther side.

A GUARDIAN ANGEL FACES THE ANTAGONIST OF SOULS

As in my dream I gazed along the bridge, my eyes beheld an angel of majestic form, clothed in glittering apparel, and with a face more beautiful than I had ever seen. Then, in the light which streamed from this radiant form, I saw, lost in the deep shadows which lay beyond, a second presence as dark and menacing as the first was bright and glowing. Sinister and threatening, it seemed a veritable son of gloom, framed in darkness, and a shudder ran through me as I knew it for Satan, the Adversary, the Antagonist of Souls.

"Who art thou, and what is thy errand here?" demanded the Angel in clear, stern tones, as she stood erect and fearless before the shadowy terror. From the darkness there came in reply a voice at whose depth my whole frame shuddered.

"Once I was known in Heaven as the Angel of Light," it said. "Here, on Earth, men call me Satan. Dost thou know me now? Whatever thy purpose may be, I am here to be thy adversary, for the Earth is mine, and men are my slaves and subjects."

As I gazed, the darkness vanished and I saw the two standing in the shadow of a little knoll laced by shrubbery, behind which were hills and trees. A wind came through the tops of the trees

"A man of kindly demeanor and patriarchal appearance."

and bent them and let in from above a light which bathed both and cast its sheen along the grass touching their very feet. Then a great awe stole over me, and my breath came slowly as I opened my mind and gave my soul again to see and hear.

"Get thee behind me, thou Evil One! Our paths must lie separate!" came from the lips of the Angel.

"Separate!" responded Satan, with a sinister laugh. "Thou hast not learned thy lesson well. Our paths shall lie together, and thou canst not escape my companionship. Shall I tell thee whither thy footsteps tend? It is towards the Hill-lands of Faith."

"Such is my destination, Son of the Pit. But thy days are numbered, for the Lord of Heaven and Earth has decreed thy destruction and that thy dire purpose shall in no way prosper. It is mine to be the guardian angel of the good; it is mine to help them in their troubles, and to answer in the name of the King for all the promises he has made concerning those who walk in His ways."

Shadows fell around me, and the Shining One and the Tempter vanished from my sight. I was alone with a new sense of tears and joy in things earthly.

A VAST COMPANY CROSS THE BRIDGE

A faint light now shone upon the bridge, and dimly I saw what seemed an endless multitude crossing its span and losing itself in the shadows which lay beyond. Ministering angels peopled this shadowy realm and their low-breathed sighs of pity for the woes of human hearts had baptized this, the very threshold of their ministry, "The Bridge of Sighs."

"Whence journey this vast throng?" I cried aloud, for I scarcely realized the realm in which my life now seemed to have a part; and a voice, coming I knew not whence, replied:

"These are the souls of those whose term on Earth has ended, and who are crossing the bridge under the escort of spirit guides."

"Why do they wear robes of white?" I asked.

"That is the mark of the kingdom to which they now belong. The All-father, having wrought their deliverance, has given to each this emblem; to them has come victory. Having laid down the burden of life, they are going to receive the crown," was the reply.

Leaning forward, I peered into the distance to see who composed this multitude, but was powerless to behold aught save the moving procession and in its midst the Shining One, for it was she who had answered me.

"Kind Angel," I asked, "who compose this throng?"

"Seest thou not?" she replied.

"Yes," I answered, "but not clearly."

"The aged, and those of middle years, and even little children are there," was the reply: "and to many of them the touch of the world was unkind," she added.

"Whence came they?"

"They have been gathered from all lands and all peoples."

As she spoke I heard a sudden burst of jubilant song, and listened to learn its source and theme.

"This is the Pilgrims' song," said the Angel.

To those of Earth the volume of this mighty chorus was lost, but to me, in my vision, it rolled on and on, and thrilled and throbbed with hallowed melody, and then died away in silence and was lost in the immeasurable distance beyond. Echo and re-echo vibrated in harmony, and as I listened to catch the song, the Angel repeated to me the words of praise.

THE PILGRIMS' SONG

" 'Thou art worthy to take the book, and to open the seals thereof: for thou wast slain, and hast redeemed us to God by thy blood out of every kindred, and tongue, and people, and nation; and hast made us unto our God kings and priests: and we shall reign on the earth.' "

"The Angel Chorus are answering," said the ministering spirit. "Hark!"

Such music as the world has not heard since Christ was born in Bethlehem, now greeted my ears. It came from the vast distance beyond the abyss, as from an abode of heavenly delight; a pealing antiphon from a myriad of holy voices.

THE ANGEL CHORUS

" 'Worthy is the Lamb that was slain to receive power, and riches, and wisdom, and strength, and honor, and glory, and blessing.'

" '——These are they which came out of great tribulation.

and have washed their robes, and made them white in the blood of the Lamb.' "

SATAN APPEARS AGAIN

As I listened with straining ears, the flood of song sank, and a shadow fell over bridge and shore, but ere it closed around me, the form of Satan appeared again, and with his the dim figures of other demons met my eyes. They spoke in low tones, but my ears were opened to hear their words.

"The task before me is no light one," said Satan with a gleam of evil in his eyes. "The messenger from above is strong with the power of the Most High, and her work will be difficult to overcome. She is here to rescue one whom I would give much to win. We shall have to be as wise as serpents and wear a guise as fair as her own, if we would succeed."

As he spoke I saw the Guardian Angel take a roll from her girdle, from which she read:

" '——To open their eyes, and to turn them from darkness to light, and from the power of Satan unto God, that they may receive forgiveness of sins, and inheritance among them which are sanctified by faith that is in me.' "

The Prince of Darkness listened with frowning brow.

" 'Heaven and earth shall pass away: but my words shall not pass away,' " she continued.

A pallor covered the face of the Antagonist, and a trembling seized his form as these words fell upon his ears. He and his followers seemed to shrink deeper into the shadows, and from their depths I heard him, in tones of deepest malevolence, swear

"'I see nothing to do but to get rid of him,' said Mr. Hypocrite."

to thwart the mission of the God-sent messenger. Then he advanced towards her with a threatening gesture.

THE ANGEL DENOUNCES SATAN

Offended by his approach, the Angel thrust forth her hand as though to brush aside a loathsome presence, and cried out:

"Demon of evil and of guile, thou art a coward in the light of virtue and of truth. With all thy show of power, thou art weak and impotent against the purposes of the Almighty.

"I know thee and thy vile aims, and say to thee in the name of the King of Heaven, that all thy evil designs shall be as chaff driven before the winds of His might. Do what thou wilt, thou canst not win from me those to whom I have come. I abhor and detest thee."

Looking into his evil eyes, the Guardian Angel extended her right arm towards him as one pronouncing a sentence of doom.

"The word of my God is established. The Church of the Redeemed is safe, for the very gates of Hell shall not prevail against it. Neither shall a single believing soul be won by thee; for the Saviour said: '——No man is able to pluck them out of my Father's hand.' "

With her arm still extended, her form towered above the shrinking demon as she cried:

"Begone! Rest assured that those committed to my charge shall receive counsel concerning thee, and of them all, not one shall fail of an entrance at last into the City of God."

THE ANGEL PASSES TO HER MINISTRY

As the night deepened, I saw the Guardian Angel pass on, and upon her fell a light which spread through the darkness, outlining the Hill-lands of Faith, while it clothed this ministrant with a brightness above that of the sun. As she moved onward, a number, also in shining array, joined her, and crossing a hill that lay before them, the company came to a great city, in the midst of which the Guardian Angel pitched her invisible tent. In that city dwelt the human soul for whose guidance she had come.

A SCENE OF TEMPTING REVELRY

In my dream, which heretofore had led me into the presence of angels and demons and of souls whose way lay across the Bridge of Sighs, I was now taken to earthly scenes and shown men and women. The forms of the Guardian Angel and the Prince of Evil were still visible at intervals, but those whom I now beheld knew not that the powers of Heaven and Hell were contending for the mastery of their souls.

Before me rose a splendid mansion in that part of the city into which the Angel had made her way. Though the night was far advanced, a brilliant light streamed from its windows, while the sound of music and revelry could be heard within. Men and women, richly dressed, whirled through the dance, or sat at card-tables, or, on pleasure bent, passed and repassed through the well-appointed rooms.

Satan was present, invisibly tempting those who shrank from

the wine-cup or other enticements of the scene. To my dreaming eyes he was plainly visible, now whispering in the ear of one who held back from his evil suggestions, now lightly pressing the arm of one whose hand withdrew reluctantly from the sparkling wine, in every way leading and instigating to evil and vice. There were those present who required the dance and the wine-cup, the pleasings of sensuous music, and the play of light and color over all, to stimulate their jaded senses; and others were there who would have blushed for shame to have had the world know they had been participants in the evening's festivities.

Liquors and cordials were pressed upon the guests by attentive servants, and men and women tempted each other to further sin, with wine that creamed in amber light, or sparkled blood-red as some modern Delilah pledged her chosen Samson; or Faust, in twentieth-century evening dress, peered into the blue of Marguerite's eyes. None saw the leer of Satan as he regarded his tools and their victims.

Upon a couch in one of the luxurious parlors sat a young lady who seemed utterly out of place in such a scene. Honesty, sincerity, and virtue could be seen in her beautiful face, and the furtive glances of doubt and dismay with which she viewed the frivolity and dissipation around her, showed that she was utterly out of sympathy with her surroundings.

Miss Sincere, as this young lady was named, had been induced to attend the entertainment in ignorance of its character, at the request of Mr. Hypocrite and his wife. To her, Mr. Hypocrite seemed a model of all that was upright and good, and his remark that "none but the very select of the city would be there" had induced her to set aside her fears as to the character of the entertainment and consent to accompany him and his wife. Her feelings now were those of regret at her complaisance and of wonder that she could have been so deceived.

"See to it that everybody thinks well of you, and under this cover make the most money and have the best time you can," was Mr. Hypocrite's motto, and it was one likely to prove dangerous to so artless a soul as that of Miss Sincere.

It was she in whose aid the Guardian Angel had come to Earth, and certainly her presence was necessary to combat the wiles of the plausible agent Satan had employed.

Mr. Hypocrite was not one to argue with an opponent. His policy was to agree with all he met in a spirit of affability, reaching his aims by covert means while outwardly friendly.

"A man who flatters a woman hopes either to find her a fool, or to make her one," but on the evening in question the platitudes of Mr. Hypocrite seemed to have no effect upon his fair companion. The company comprised society notables, and the diversions of the evening were in no way different from those of the "Smart Set," but in her soul Miss Sincere heard a voice of condemnation, which, though she did not realize it at the time, was a whisper from the Guardian Angel, who, perceived by none, was arousing a sense of wrong-doing in her thoughts.

"Why was it, Miss Sincere, that you seemed so out of sympathy with the company this evening?" said Mr. Hypocrite as they were on their way to the young lady's home. "If you go into society you must learn to excuse certain things to which one is unaccustomed in a quieter life. There was much hilarity this evening, I admit, and no doubt more wine-drinking than you are accustomed to, but these things are done in the best society, and we must put up with them."

"I do not agree with you," said Miss Sincere with great earnestness. "They may be social customs, but they are not Christian customs. I do not see how one can excuse such acts before the tribunal of conscience."

"That seems very true, Miss Sincere," replied Mr. Hypocrite, "but most of those present to-night are members of the leading churches of the city. You should not be so severe on what is really innocent pleasure. No harm was intended; and the relaxation afforded by the evening's entertainment will the better prepare us for larger responsibilities. You will think better of it all, I am convinced, in the morning."

So they parted. Mr. Hypocrite knew that Miss Sincere was right in her condemnation of the night's events, and was also aware that his own words had been chosen for the purpose of covering their evil tendency. He found much pleasure in the society of Miss Sincere, and with the aid of his wife hoped to "liberalize" her ideas as to the pleasures of the world.

The hours until morning seemed endless to the sleepless eyes of Miss Sincere, for the Good Angel, close by her side, was revealing to her the full meaning of the wrong-doing she had witnessed. "If sinners entice thee, consent thou not," she whispered. "Why trouble yourself about a little evening of social enjoyment?" suggested Satan; and so between the two, the one seeking to save and the other to ruin, the soul of Miss Sincere was torn and distracted.

In absolute dejection, caused by the shame of having even unwittingly participated in the events of the evening, she arose. and, as the bright glory of the rising sun shone through the latticed window of her apartment and kissed her tear-stained face, she knelt in prayer with the gentle hand of the Guardian Angel resting upon her head.

"God give to this, my charge, the victory. Suffer not the Antagonist through the soft words of his dupes to win Thy child from the heavenly way," was the prayer of the ministering one, and it was heard at the Throne, for

"If we confess our sins, He is faithful and just to forgive us our sins, and to cleanse us from all unrighteousness."

In a moment Miss Sincere arose and walked to the window, and, looking out upon the scene which was being quickened everywhere by the energies of a new day, found in her heart a peace like the glory of the calm which rests upon the face of Nature after a tempest has passed. The Grace of the Lord in whom she trusted pervaded her soul. With folded hands and eyes raised to Heaven, she repeated to herself, "I could not live in peace if I put the shadow of a wilful sin between myself and God."

The Guardian Angel smiled as she marked this conquest of a soul from sin, and beheld the holy light of reconciliation on the face of the one she had come to guard and save.

CHAPTER II

The Cross on the Lonely Hill

"In those holy fields
Over whose acres walk'd those blessed feet,
Which, fourteen hundred years ago, were nail'd,
For our advantage, on the bitter cross."
—*Shakespeare, "Henry IV."*

IN my vision it was morning. I drank deeply of the healthful air, and steeped myself in the glorious beauties of a new day. Then I knelt upon the sward in token of deep reverence, and prayed that to me might fall the highest sense of the unalterable existence beyond Earth's rim. I prayed for an enlarged vision; for a deeper insight and a broader hope; and as I prayed I seemed to live in a realm of holy trust and exaltation.

As I rose I heard voices; and then muffled sounds, as when men beat and tear the bosom of old Earth, came on the wandering wind which bent the grass-blades and the leaves, and filled my mind with wonder. I turned toward the place whence they issued, and walked through the soft, warm air till I could look along the valley where the sky seemed upheld by two walls of green.

Through the long vista the eye could discern, though far in the distance, a bare and lonely hill, which my soul told me was the hill called Calvary, where once upon the cross hung the Crucified One; and again I prayed, asking that there might be given to me the meaning of what I was now to see and hear.

THE PATH TO THE CROSS

From where I stood, a path led down to the floor of the valley, and when near its level I paused, for I could see an army of laborers, digging up and destroying the well-worn road which led toward the Cross on the lonely hill, transforming it, and the beauteous plain on either hand, into a quagmire—a veritable morass.

Seated where his eye could sweep the scene, I saw Satan, the arch-enemy of man, in human guise, and as I looked he rose to greet one who approached him. To my surprise I recognized the newcomer as Mr. Hypocrite, whom I had recently seen in so different a place. The two met with the familiarity of old friends.

"You seem to have changed your line of work," said Hypocrite, pointing to the torn and scarred valley.

"Not at all," responded Satan; "I have done this work before, and with a large measure of success. One Bunyan, a writer whom I would like to repay for the mischief he has done, has told of my former exploits in his pestilent book, 'The Pilgrim's Progress.'"

"I have read it," rejoined Hypocrite. "He told of the 'Slough of Despond,' the mire into which Christian and Pliable fell."

"Just so," replied Satan. " 'Here, therefore, they wallowed

for a time, being grievously bedaubed with the dirt: and Christian, because of the burden that was on his back, began to sink in the mire.' I gave him no small trouble, though, if he did finally escape me.

SATAN TURNS THE PLAIN INTO A BOG

"I am working here with the same end in view," he went on. "These workmen of mine have transformed the plain into a bog, and the path by which multitudes were accustomed to reach Calvary, I have caused to be destroyed. That place of the cross stands in my way. I cannot destroy it, but I hope to render it more difficult of approach.

"The work and name of that man are the weightiest matters with which I am concerned. The people of this vast world look with steady hope toward the cross on yon lonely hill. I seek to put a stop to their pilgrimages, as I did in the days when Christian fell into the mire, and Pliable turned back to the City of Destruction."

As they talked the work ended. Satan smiled as he saw the well-beaten path by which the pilgrims were wont to reach Calvary wholly obliterated at this point. One detail of his plan remained, and that was quickly executed. A thick mist was cast over the plain to hide the hill-top where Jesus died, and so form an additional barrier to those who sought to pass through the valley.

"Withdraw!" he cried to those who had wrought for him during the night. "Your work is complete. Withdraw!" The host of workmen vanished from view as if they had been things of vapor.

MR. HYPOCRITE AND DETERMINATION MEET

And now I saw that a great company of pilgrims were coming, and that Hypocrite hurried on to meet them.

"How far is it to the Cross on the lonely hill?" inquired one whose name was Determination. He seemed the leader of the company.

"About a mile on a direct line through the valley," responded Hypocrite with a covert smile. It was a shadow of that on Satan's dark face which peered in dim outline over Hypocrite's shoulder.

"A great mist conceals the path and the way is new to many of us," said Determination. "But we must reach the hill of Calvary whatever betide. The Lord of Mercy be with us and aid us."

At this moment the vast company burst forth in song, and the great volume of their voices could be heard far away.

> "In the cross of Christ I glory,
> Towering o'er the wrecks of time;
> All the light of sacred story
> Gathers round its head sublime."

THE PILGRIMS SINK IN THE MIRE

On came the pilgrim company half lost in the mist, but soon a cry of despair arose from those in advance. They began to sink in the mire of the bog, and the mist was so dense that it was with much difficulty their companions could reach them to offer the hand of rescue. Loud were their cries of distress, and as dismal as had been those of Christian and Pliable when they were in like trouble.

But as Determination was endeavoring to peer into the mist, hoping that perchance he might see the Cross, the hopeful words "Hail Pilgrim!" came to his ears, and, clad in white apparel, her face beaming with confidence, he saw the Guardian Angel approaching through the mist.

THE WAY TO THE CROSS CANNOT BE CLOSED

"Despair not," she said, "for no foe can long close the way which leads to the Cross. This is but an old trick of the Antagonist. Venture not into the mist for peril lies that way. Take this." So saying she placed in his hands a glass of a form I had never seen.

"This is the Glass of Faith," she said, "point it yonder," and as she spoke she indicated the direction with her finger. "Look through it with trust in thy heart, and thou shalt behold what thou seekest."

Determination did as he was told and a glad smile lighted up his face.

"Wonderful! wonderful!" he cried. "I see the Cross through the heart of the mist. Yonder it stands upon the Hill. Holy One, wilt thou not come with us and guide us to the sacred place we seek?"

"Nay," replied the Angel. "My errand is now done and I must be gone. Thou needest only to turn thy glass to the right and all will be well."

Again Determination hastened to do as he was bidden.

"There thou wilt find a highway of the King," the Angel continued. "No hand of man or demon hath power to destroy it. Lead thither thy company and thou shalt find the Cross. Stand thou strong. Be not afraid. Blessed are they that trust in the Lord."

"The way grows clear," said Determination. "But I would fain know, Blessed One, who thou art."

"I am one sent to prepare the way before the face of pilgrims," said the Angel, and with this she vanished.

THE SUN OF RIGHTEOUSNESS DISSOLVES THE MIST

As the throng took up its march again, the sun of righteousness broke through the clouds and dissolved the mist which had heretofore concealed the King's Highway. Led by Determination, the pilgrims turned to the right, where the highway was clearly visible, and headed for the Cross on the Hill, now plainly in view; and as they journeyed they joyfully sang:

> "Every day is a fresh beginning,
>   Every morn is a world made new;
> You who are weary of sorrow and sinning,
>   Here is a beautiful hope for you,
>   A hope for me and a hope for you.

> "Every day is a fresh beginning,
> Listen, my soul, to the glad refrain,
> And, spite of old sorrow and older sinning,
> And puzzles forecasted, and possible pain
> Take heart with the day and begin again."

Satan, who had led the foremost ranks into the bog, now appeared again, full of anger at the failure of his plans. Hypocrite would have accosted him, but with frowning brow he vanished from sight.

But despite all I had seemed to see in my dream, I well knew that Hypocrite had not, in person, conversed with the Prince of Darkness, but that he was present in spirit only. What I had beheld was an allegory in which the nature of the time server stood revealed, for I knew it was not Satan's way to make his wiles evident to his human agents and dupes, but to lead them to destruction while they seemed to obey the impulses of their own souls.

UP-TO-DATE RELIGIOUS LITERATURE

Even as I gazed upon the rising mist and heard the echoes of the pilgrims' song, I seemed transported to the city of my last night's vision, there to behold Hypocrite doing Satan's work as a blind and willing agent. Still intent on converting Miss Sincere to his "liberal" views, he obeyed a secret suggestion from the Tempter of Souls.

"If you would weaken that woman's puritan strictness, try her with some up-to-date religious literature."

Hypocrite accepted the seeming thought with a hopeful smile.

Selecting a volume from his library he sought her home, wondering a little how her untutored soul would meet the insidious views of this artfully written work.

The book had been written by one whose mind Satan had biased, and as Hypocrite turned the leaves, he was himself half convinced, for it laid claims to recent "discoveries" of potent meaning and spoke learnedly of new found "myths," while declaring many of the precious tenets held by Christians to be ungrounded and not worthy of credence.

"This," he said, as he presented the volume to Miss Sincere, "is a book which I know you will find readable and interesting. It is exceedingly popular and is said to solve many of the vexed religious questions of the day. I must say that it has served to broaden my ideas upon certain matters of religion on which I fear I have been narrow and illiberal."

I had watched the destruction of the path to the cross, and Satan's discomfiture at the miscarriage of his plans, with intense interest. It was now high noon, and the words of the prayer I had breathed in the splendors of the rosy dawn came again to me, and I thanked the All-father for what I was learning this day.

THE CREED OF THE PIT

A new scene now appeared before my eyes. I could see Miss Sincere reading the book which she had received from her false adviser, and that its arguments seemed to deeply move her.

"Can this be so?" she asked aloud. "If this presentation be true, then the faith of my childhood and even that of my later years, are but dead leaves of thought and superstition. They were simple and reverent and my soul still draws warmly to them, but——"

She read on, and the teachings of the alluring pages became poison in her veins. She saw the sacrifice for sin upon Calvary distorted by new ideas. She read that a belief in philosophical principles instead of in the Sacred Person was the higher view; that religious faith was, after all, only a result of the educational processes and childish beliefs of centuries past.

THE GUARDIAN ANGEL APPEARS

Doubt, the sequence of a disturbed faith, clouded the vision of her soul; and the tenderness and strength of her old time trust, for the moment seemed to lose their power.

Fortunately, there was one nearby who saw the struggle into which this pure soul had been cruelly cast. This was the Angel whose mission it was to guide and deliver.

"Why are these marks of sadness upon thy face?" asked the Angel.

"The cares and idle thoughts of the day have left their traces upon me," replied the innocent girl.

"Ah, 'tis more than that: thou art filled with an inward unrest. Tell me thy trouble. Tell it all. Has the vision from the Hilltop been dimmed this day?"

Miss Sincere sighed, and her eyes fell upon the book in her hand.

THE ANGEL EXPOSES MR. HYPOCRITE

"What book hast thou there?" asked the Angel, seeking to open the door of her heart.

Miss Sincere wept as she told how Hypocrite had placed in her hands a book which had disturbed the quietude of her faith.

"Then its words are not safe for thee to read, dear child. The Evil One hath poisoned the mind of him who wrote that specious work, and he has caused it to be given to thee by one who is not worthy of such friendship as thine."

Miss Sincere brushed back a tear, as she looked into the clear calm eyes of the Angel of Deliverance.

"I cannot think Mr. Hypocrite would seek to place harm in the way of my soul," she replied. "He is a seeker after truth himself, and is far too kindly a man to wish to do evil to any one."

"Be not so sure of this, my child. Trust my insight rather than thine own. 'Let him who thinketh he standeth take heed lest he fall,'" said the Angel voice. "It is the policy of the Antagonist to employ agents whom the soul least suspects. In my missions to earth I have seen much of his evil methods. The unheeding and the innocent are always in peril from his ruses."

"But tell me of the book," she went on. "What is its character and what are its teachings?"

FALSE CHRISTS SHALL ARISE

Then Miss Sincere told the Angel the story of her inward trials during that day, trials which not only disturbed, but robbed her soul of its peace.

THE CROSS ON THE LONELY HILL 51

"And this unholy book was the cause," said the Angel. "Put it away and hear from my lips the inspired counsel of the Master.

"'If any man shall say unto you, lo, here is Christ, or there; believe it not. For there shall arise false Christs and false prophets, and shall show great signs and wonders, insomuch that if it were possible, they should deceive the very elect. Behold I have told you before.'"

"Did the Master speak those words?" asked the troubled girl.

"Yes, the Master spake them just as He went to the Hill of Calvary to die for you and for all who seek salvation," replied the Angel.

Having thus spoken, the Angel knelt with the trembling girl, and prayed that the sweet vision of the Cross might be restored to this drifting Christian, and that the Antagonist of Souls should no longer disturb her faith.

THE GOLDEN SUNSHINE COMES

Thrusting the book aside with contempt, Miss Sincere, deeply moved by the words of the angelic visitor, took up her Bible and opened it at hazard. Her eyes fell upon these consoling words:

"Thou wilt keep him in perfect peace whose mind is stayed on Thee; because he trusteth in Thee."

"This is the guide book for Christians," said the Angel. "Spurn all others that would, in any way, uproot thy faith in its hallowed and trusted truths."

Gazing deeply into the eyes of the girl, until the pure soul within lay fully revealed, the Angel ministrant saw that her inward vision was now clear; and then, with all the rest of the scene that had held me spell-bound, she vanished from my sight.

Twice that day had I seen Satan's cherished plans defeated, and while I mused upon these matters, I was taken in my vision to a vast and gloomy hall in his castle where the King of Evil sat surrounded by those to whom he entrusted the carrying out of his unholy schemes against those who looked for life eternal through the Redeemer of Mankind.

SATAN SITS IN COUNCIL

He had now thrown off the guise of man and sat in all his demon majesty,—the dark and terrible compeller of sin and foe of virtue.

Those around him were of low and impish aspect, and looked with awe and reverence upon their gloom-surrounded sovereign. There was grandeur in his words, but the language of Pandemonium is not for earthly ears, yet I will translate it as best I can in words of our common speech.

"All has gone amiss this day," said Satan from his throne. "Strongly have we wrought, but the powers above have baffled us at every point."

"Our toil, I fear, has been for naught," responded one high in Satan's favor. "We obeyed thy command and instigated Hypocrite, that foolish wise-man who unknowingly does thy work, to buy freely of alluring but unsettling books, and place them in the hands of certain young people who are yet in the mist of doubt, but that pestilent book, the Bible, has undone all our work."

"An imposing edifice in the midst of a handsome park"

THE CROSS ON THE LONELY HILL

"I advised Hypocrite to place a certain volume in the hands of Miss Sincere," rejoined Satan. "He did so, but that meddling messenger from above, who seems sent to keep her in charge, swept the effect of its teachings from her mind. Not only that, but she sought to make her distrust my useful agent and friend, Hypocrite."

"I am sorely vexed," he went on, "by the evangelistic work that is now so active in the churches. It robs us of many whom we might have employed in the work of unsettling the minds of men. But," he added thoughtfully, "the Angel who guided the pen of old John Bunyan in Bedford jail, did me more harm than a multitude of modern dispensers of Gospel truth."

THE DEVIL WILL NEVER FORGIVE LUTHER

"The Angel at the Diet of Augsburg, many years ago," said one of the chief demons of the Pit, "the one who went around with Martin Luther, that man of mischief, was responsible for the vast damage which was then done our cause."

"I know it too well," answered Satan. "It was she who gave Luther the power to open the pages of the Bible to the common people,—a bit of meddling which has robbed my kingdom of multitudes of souls."

"'Justification by faith,' was a mighty bomb-shell thrown into our camp," rejoined the other. "With the Cross held on high before the eyes of men, Christians are multiplying far and wide."

"The conflict before us is to be a long and hard one," answered His Satanic Majesty. "We need to be more watchfu and aggressive than ever. Above all, we must seek to modify those doctrines of the Cross, and for this purpose, we shall have to do much diplomatic work among the ministers. Let that be part of your future labor, for in that direction lies our hopes of success."

MR. HYPOCRITE IS MADE AN OFFICER OF THE CHURCH

In a moment more my dream brought me from Satan's hall of council to the city again, but the Prince of Evil was before me, and I saw him standing beside Mr. Hypocrite, with face and form as though one of this world. Hypocrite was much elated in manner, and after a brief greeting to Satan, who seemed to him one of his cherished friends, he said in a tone of triumph:

"Congratulate me! I have just left a trustee of our church who informed me I had been elected one of its officers."

"Treasurer, I hope," said Satan with a mocking leer.

"You are right. I have been elected its treasurer."

"I should like to have such a position myself," rejoined Satan. "There ought to be good pickings there for a smart fellow like you," he added reflectively. "Judas, if I remember rightly, was the first church treasurer."

"Come now, don't play off your stale jokes on me," exclaimed Hypocrite. "By the way, do you remember that little saint, Miss Sincere, to whom you introduced me? I have been trying to wean her from her narrow ways and to put a stop to this madness of evangelism, but I confess that I have not been able to stem the tide. The activity of the church grows in spite of all I can say or do.''

''Wesley, Whitefield, Moody, and all of their followers in more recent years, have been active agents in that work,'' said the seeming agent of heresy, ''but I trust to the powers aiding us to defeat them yet.'' So saying, he walked away with a wicked smile upon his face.

Not dreaming to whom he had been speaking, Hypocrite kept on his way to the prayer meeting, where he stood beside Miss Sincere and, smiling to himself in disdain, joined in the magnificent song of victory to be achieved by the Church Militant.

> "Onward Christian soldiers,
> Marching as to war,
> With the cross of Jesus
> Going on before."

CHAPTER III

The Broken Down Altars

"More things are wrought by prayer
Than this world dreams of. Wherefore, let thy voice
Rise like a fountain for me night and day.
For what are men better than sheep or goats
That nourish a blind life within the brain,
If, knowing God, they lift not hands of prayer
Both for themselves and those who call them friend?
For so the whole round earth is every way
Bound by gold chains about the feet of God."

—*Tennyson, "Idyls of the King."*

MORNING had broken, though I knew it not, when I arose from the cushions of the tent in which I found myself and upon which I had slept the sleep of peace and comfort. I thrust aside the curtained door and stepped out into the light of a perfect day.

The sun burned in the sky. The yellowing wheat, fringed with scarlet poppies, was full of a luxurious sense of growth; near by was heard the tinkle of falling water, and the morning song of a happy bird.

Rapt in the fullness of the moment, I prayed with an expansion of mind, and felt my thought widen to receive something beyond the previous revelations of my vision.

EVANGELIST COMES FROM THE EASTERN HILLS

Looking out toward the Eastern Hills, I saw the approach of a stranger. The land appeared a friendly one, and so, with no sense of fear, I went forth to meet him.

As he drew near I saw a man of kindly demeanor and patriarchal appearance. Gray hair in abundance covered his head and rested upon his shoulders, while a beard of snowy whiteness fell upon his breast. His face was that of a saint.

"The Lord be with thee," he said, bowing in salutation.

"And with thee," I replied.

Then there came to me these words of inspiration: "Be not forgetful to entertain strangers: for thereby some have entertained angels unawares," and I said:

"Thou seemest to have come a long way. Wilt thou not rest in my tent and partake of such fare as I can offer thee?"

"I thank thee, child of God," he replied, "I shall be glad to break bread with thee;" so saying, he entered the tent and seated himself.

As we sat at the meal I set forth for him, I inquired the object of his visit.

"Art thou a stranger here?" was his reply to my question.

"Yes," I rejoined. "To-day mine eyes have for the first time rested upon the scene before us; but tell me who thou art and for what purpose thou hast come."

The old man leaned back upon the cushions and looked with eyes of deep observation into my face. A moment of silence followed; then he spoke.

EVANGELIST DECLARES HIMSELF

"I am known as Evangelist, and am come hither to guide God's children toward the Homeland. Hast thou not heard of my work hitherto?"

"I do not recall thy work or thy name," I replied.

"Surely thou rememberest the journey of Christian, of whom John Bunyan discourses so eloquently?"

"Can it be that thou art the one who pointed out to him the way to the 'Wicket Gate'? Well I remember that wondrous tale," I answered.

"I am the same," continued Evangelist, "and the message I carry has been a simple one through all these years. The plain words of Jesus—those promises and comforts indispensable—have been the oil and wine which I have long dispensed for the wounds of humanity."

"Thine is a blessed office, friend Evangelist," I said, "but what has brought thee hither, and what work wilt thou do in this land?"

"Listen, and I will tell thee the burden of my heart," the old man replied. "I am deeply grieved at the broken-down altars in the homes of Christians. The children of God have grown careless regarding prayer, and Satan is pleased. The old-time altar in the home has been battered down by the materialism of the age, and well you should know that the Master's rule cannot be thus set aside without sorrow and loss of peace."

With these words, he opened a book which he carried, and, laying his finger upon a page, spoke as follows:

"Thine eyes are better than mine; read."

I took the book and read aloud these words:

"'When thou prayest, enter into thy closet, and when thou hast shut thy door, pray to thy Father which is in secret; and thy Father which seeth in secret shall reward thee openly.'"

"Such prayer," said Evangelist, "was the secret of power with the Saviour, and with the sages of this world. If a man lack wisdom let him ask it of God. One whose life has been spent in winning souls for the Master has well said, that 'men are growing so prosperous that they are drifting away from God. The very atmosphere we breathe is against Christ. Very many preachers to-day are not preaching the warm-hearted spirit of the Word of God.'

"So far as a mortal can," he continued, "I am come to aid the Angel whom thou didst behold at the bridge. Hidden in the shades, I there saw thee, and knew that a vision of the Lord was upon thee. We shall meet again, my son, but now, refreshed by thy hospitality, I go to minister to one upon whom sickness has laid a heavy hand. The Lord bless thee and keep thee."

IN SATAN'S COUNCIL-CHAMBER

As Evangelist spoke and then went on his way, the scene vanished, and, as though borne on mighty wings I was carried to where the Archfiend sat in council.

Familiar as I had grown with his appearance, I could see that the Enemy of Mankind was sore at heart. His first words revealed the cause.

"We have work before us. There has lately come into these parts one who has long been among my most persistent enemies."

"Is it not an old man of striking aspect, who has several times been seen in the valley between Calvary and the Hill of Faith?" asked one of his trusted attendants.

SATAN FEARS THE GOOD GRAY PROPHET

"That is the man. His name is Evangelist, and a troublesome fellow we are likely to find him. He is noted for his power to guide men past the pitfalls of sin and to reach their hearts with his searching words."

"What work is he here to do, O King and Master? Teach us how to combat this new enemy."

"He is going from house to house rebuilding the altars we caused to be thrown down," replied Satan. "Since he came here many prayers are ascending to the Throne above. It is this we must combat. Our work just now, is to discourage faith in prayer and to bring about carelessness concerning it. This we must accomplish if we would defeat Evangelist.

"Suggest to Christians that they do not need to give so much time to prayer as did their fathers. Whisper covertly in their ears that it is folly to take time from their business, to pray, and that it is far wiser for those who have toiled through the day to

"The three laughed aloud and hurried on."

spend their evenings in rest and recreation, than to weary themselves with church work and prayers. Be vigilant and cunning, and many souls shall be ours. Away to your work!"

SATAN VISITS MR. HYPOCRITE

Like a flight of ill-omened birds the fiendish host sped swiftly to sow the seeds of evil counsel with the hope of reaping a harvest of sin-laden souls. Satan quickly followed, his goal being the home of Hypocrite, whom he had found so able and willing an agent. As before, he bore the form and figure of Mr. Agnostic, one of Hypocrite's most cherished friends. Entering, he found him reading, with a perplexed countenance, a printed tract.

"What have you there, friend Hypocrite?" asked the disguised fiend. "There is something sanctimonious in the look of that paper."

"There is a troublesome old fanatic here named Evangelist," was the reply, "who is making trouble in our church. This is one of the nonsensical tracts which he is sowing broadcast. It is full of played-out ideas regarding private and family prayer which would rob us of our spare time. The man is making mischief, and a number of souls, heretofore good enough, are already growing stupidly sanctimonious."

"One would think that people of sense would not so easily be led into this folly," suggested Satan.

"I don't know that the fellow is a genuine patriarch, but his views are those of the old time saints. He is swaying the minds of hundreds of our people; some of them of high social standing."

"You speak to the point," said Satan. "I have had my eye on the old fanatic and have been watching his work. The rascal has a glib and insinuating tongue. It is only a few days since that I heard him talking to our fair friend, Miss Faithful. As I came near, she begged him not to detain her, as sickness at home needed her attention. Their conversation was as follows:

"'Upon which of thy loved ones has sickness fallen?' asked Evangelist.

"'Upon my dear father,' replied the girl.

"'Hast thou prayed for his recovery?'

"Miss Faithful bent her head and said slowly, 'I fear that prayer has been neglected in our home.'

"'Dost thou not remember the words of Holy Writ?' asked Evangelist, and then opening a book he read:

"'Is any sick among you? Let him call for the elders of the church and let them pray over him, anointing him with oil in the name of the Lord; and the prayer of faith shall save the sick, and the Lord shall raise him up.'"

PRAYER HEALS THE SICK

"Aha! that explains it," said Hypocrite. "Miss Faithful declared in prayer meeting last night, that her father had been cured by prayer. The altar in her family has been rebuilt. Evangelist has made one convert it seems."

"I told Miss Sincere," he continued, "that as an officer of the church I was opposed to all such outside influences."

"'What are you going to do about it?' she asked. 'You cannot stop it and I am surprised and pained that you should wish to. If this is the work of God, as Evangelist says it is, your protests are of no avail and they are a direct aid to Satan's work.'"

"'I fear you are taking too much for granted, Miss Sincere,' I replied. 'Far be it from me to oppose for a moment, anything which I am convinced is God's work. But I have not seen any evidence of impiety in our congregation, and until I do so, I do not think we need to be stirred up by fanatics like Evangelist. We are fully capable of attending to the work of our own salvation.' Do you not think I was right?"

"Yes, right enough, but a trifle too positive," said Satan with a cunning leer. "You cannot drive that young lady; you must lead her. Take my advice and deal with her by insinuation, not by argument or logical reasoning."

With these words, Satan took his leave, trusting they would bear fruit in the mind of his friend.

Hypocrite resented the spirit in which Miss Sincere had addressed him, for it was plainly to be seen that she regarded him with distrust. His long prayers and exhortations were features in the church, and it hurt him when his sincerity was questioned.

EVANGELIST AND THE FAITHFUL FEW

Despite all that Satan and his friends could do, the work of Evangelist prospered. With Miss Sincere and Miss Faithful as his ardent helpers, he preached from house to house his doctrine of the displeasure of the Lord at the overthrow of His altars, and the personal loss in the soul's life that would surely follow this sin. The Guardian Angel, who was never long absent from their councils, aided them in their mission with timely advice and encouragement. The custom of personal and family prayer which had been allowed to lapse, was widely restored, and once more God's word became a subject of daily study.

"If God be for us, who can be against us, my children?" said Evangelist to his little band of faithful workers at one of their frequent meetings.

GOD SHALL CROWN THY WORK AT LAST

"It is the Lord's work we are doing, and He will quicken it in the hearts of His people," rejoined Mis Faithful.

" 'Be not weary in well doing,' continued Evangelist, 'for in due season ye shall reap if ye faint not.' I have been doing the business of the King for many years, and His power has never yet failed, nor has the fulfillment of His promise been wanting."

The little company knelt ere they parted, and the face of Evangelist was uplifted to Heaven. All joined in devout prayer, and as their voices rose in unison, I was constrained to add mine. Together our voices ascended to the Throne of Divine Grace, asking God's aid in combating the wicked work of the Adversary of Souls.

SATAN SPEEDS AN ARROW OF DOUBT

Even as I knelt to join these faithful souls in prayer, I saw the dark and scowling face of Satan looking through the open window of the room. As I looked, he shot an arrow of doubt into their midst, hoping to overcome the effect of their devotions, but it struck upon the breastplate of Faith which Evangelist wore beneath his robe, and the venomed point was blunted and made useless.

The patriarch prayed on, not knowing what had passed.

Miss Sincere had seen what seemed a dark shadow blot out the sunlight at the window for a moment, but it passed away and the heavens smiled again.

"The Master has led us in beautiful paths this day," she said in grateful tones.

"He ever goeth before those who are ready to do His will," replied Evangelist.

MISS SINCERE DOES A GOOD ACTION

"I have heard to-day a story of good Christian work," said Miss Faithful. "It is a poor widow whose house was about to be taken from her by a harsh creditor to whom she owed a small sum of money. She had part of the money, but he would not take less than the whole sum which was secured to him by a mortgage. The poor woman is a pious soul and a faithful worker in the church. She is amply deserving and it hurt me sorely that I could not aid her in her need."

"She is in want no longer. Her home is saved," said Miss Sincere. "A friend aided her with the money and her creditor was foiled in his efforts to get her home at half its value."

"Blessed be the charitable one who came to the aid of the afflicted in their hour of need," said Evangelist, fixing his eyes on the face of Miss Sincere with a look that made her turn away.

She had not told the whole, for it was to her that the widow owed her home; but the old man had been quick to discern the truth.

Had she known all, it would have taught her to avoid a false friend, for Mr. Hypocrite was the one who had sought to rob the widow, and who had been foiled in his purpose by her generosity.

As he counted the money in his desk that day, with a scowling face, Hypocrite failed to see the eyes of Satan looking in upon him, but he was to learn that Satan is rarely far away when deeds like this are done.

"I would give something to know who helped that woman out," he growled. "Whoever it was has done me out of a good thousand dollars, for I could have made that profit on the house to-morrow. If I knew who it was, I would do the meddler an ill turn."

"You are trying to do so now," said Satan to himself, "in your efforts to lead Miss Sincere into my flock. If you knew that she had paid the money, and if she knew that you had received it, I fear your friendship would quickly end."

SATAN CALLS ANOTHER COUNCIL

With a grin of delight, the Archfiend sped away, and unseen I followed him into the great council hall of his castle.

Once more he called his demon host around him, and soon they were engaged in deep consultation over the labors of the day.

"Well," said Satan, "what success?"

"Those Christians certainly are determined to rebuild their altars," said one. "Almost every one has done so."

"Yes," added another, "we toiled all night. We used up our arrows of doubt, but with no effect. A certain shield called Faith, with which they are provided, causes each doubt to rebound; they seem invulnerable to our methods of warfare."

"That man, Evangelist, has been teaching them that by looking toward the Cross, they shall be able in every instance to prevail," said another.

SATAN IS NOT HOPELESS

"That man must be gotten rid of," answered Satan. "He is filling the minds of the people with the teaching of Jesus, and when they become enthused, there is no telling where the movement will end."

"We've never had any success when this man has contended with us," said the first speaker.

"That is so," replied Satan. "It is best to acknowledge it, for our records show that he has defeated our plans again and again."

"The work of Evangelist is hard to overcome," Satan went on, with a frowning brow, "but I am not hopeless yet. I have a plan which may accomplish his defeat."

"Let us have it," cried one who stood near him.

PRAYER MUST BE MADE DIFFICULT

"He has taught church people to rear their family altars again," the Archfiend continued, "and the sound of prayer can everywhere be heard, for the entire valley is pervaded by it. It remains for us to hinder their devotions. This is what I would have you to do. You must make prayer just as difficult to them as possible, and in the end they will gradually grow discouraged and give it up."

"Cannot Hypocrite help us in this?" asked one of Satan's most trusted workers.

"I have talked with him about it," replied Satan, "and he is greatly concerned over the matter, which does not accord with his views of religious duty. He says that Evangelist has been so actively at work in their church, that, although he is an officer, he is entirely powerless to suppress the enthusiasm for this rebuilding of the family altars of prayer."

"The matter may wear itself out if left alone. Agitation is often ill advised in such matters," said the other.

"Agitation is not my method," rejoined Satan. "We must strive to hinder worship rather than oppose it. I have my views, but I wish you all to devise new plans. Away!"

THE WORLD GROWS BETTER

"Every age has its problems, and civilizing processes have not rendered my work less arduous," mused Satan. "I can keep things moving for my ends on the surface of this age, but underneath is more of devotion to truth and reverence for duty than most Christians suppose. I am determined, however, to keep up the old antagonism, and the family altar shall come down, if I have the power to accomplish it."

"An army of laborers destroying the way to the cross."

THE BROKEN-DOWN ALTARS

While I had seen all this in my vision, I seemed not to have left my tent during all of that day. As night fell, Evangelist returned to me. Marks of his soul's toil were upon him, and a long busy day of consecrated efforts lay back of the sun which had now set, but a gleam of satisfaction, such as God gives to the trusted and faithful, rested upon his saintly face.

EVANGELIST'S DAY OF VICTORY

One of his duties had been to call upon Hypocrite and accuse him in the words of Jesus, because he had suffered the altar of prayer in his home to be broken down.

"Great is thy shame! Thou art a stumbling block to many in Zion!" Evangelist had said to him.

Under the scathing words of the prophet, Hypocrite's conscience became uneasy, and he promised to restore the altar in his home, but in his heart he had no intention of fulfilling his promise.

THE CROWN OF SIMPLE PATIENCE IS THE BEST

"This has been a day of victory," said Evangelist to me. "The Lord of Souls has crowned the efforts of His children with success. Around the restored places of prayer, I have seen entire families gather in song and devotion. I have seen them look again to the Divine Father for His blessing."

"They that sow in tears shall reap in joy," I answered.

"Yes, 'tis true, 'tis true," he assented. "Through the centuries in which the dire work of Satan has been so persistent, I have learned the truth—no power on earth or in Hell can stay the influence of Jesus upon the human heart."

" 'And if I be lifted up, I will draw all men unto me.' These were the Master's words," said I.

"Yes," replied Evangelist, "to so exalt Christ that the plain people say, 'behold His beauty,' rightly applies to our present life and needs. In this, man's salvation lies." Then after some moments of devout silence, he added, " 'The seventy yet return with joy.' "

MATERIAL RICHES MAKE DEAF EARS

No one, unless it were Evangelist, had been more active than Determination in proclaiming the word of the Lord, and now I saw him seated in the study of Minister Good. Then it seemed that the gray prophet and I were taken up gently, and after a moment set down where the fearless young preacher and God's older servant were deep in conversation.

"A great host of neglected altars," said Determination, "are again lighted with the incense of prayer; but the land is yet filled with many who in their mad haste for material gains, turn a deaf ear to our entreaties. They seem to enjoy nothing but the creature comforts of this mortal life."

"Thus it was when our Lord was here," answered the prophet.

"Though he entreated with tears, many would not heed his message. We shall have to learn the secret of His patience, and abide the realization of our labors and prayers," said Minister Good.

"Yes, we shall have to abide the day, for the time draweth

near when beside the golden altars of devotion, the prayers of the saints shall everywhere rise before the throne," added Evangelist.

WHAT IS THE CHIEF END OF MAN?

"One of the great thinkers of an earlier generation," said the minister, "a man often irritable, often intolerant, but always sincere, once said:

" 'The older I grow,—and I now stand on the brink of eternity —the more comes back to me that sentence in the catechism which I learned when a child, and the fuller and deeper its meaning becomes, What is the chief end of man? To glorify God and enjoy Him forever.'

WE HAVE SPASMS OF REVERENCE

"It is not very hard—at times, at least," he went on, "for men to glorify God; some of us have spasms of reverence which we give Him and there is a sort of abstract love which we say we have for Him. We think this is quite creditable, and enjoy our mood until another takes its place."

"That is very true," said Evangelist, "but there are many who try to glorify God in other ways, and are on fairly good terms with themselves because they really do sacrifice somewhat of ease and comfort and purse, and because they really do homage to Him."

"Then there are others whose lives are good and wholesome and clean," the minister resumed. "They try to glorify God every day of their lives, and they come very much nearer doing it than those of us whose homage is perfunctory."

"It is helpful to know those brothers and sisters," said Determination, who had sat in silence for some time.

OUR OWN PERSONALITY MUST BE KEPT BACK

"But to 'enjoy Him forever?' That is harder," said Evangelist, following out the minister's thought. "But of one thing we may be sure. The more of self we have given up, the more we have kept back our own personality that our brother might have his chance—the more we have done of this, the more we have enlarged our capacity for enjoying God."

"How the 'great and glorious company of the Apostles' must have enjoyed Him," said Minister Good. "It must have been their delight, as it was their business and their daily task, to learn divine truth from the lips of Jesus and then impart it to others. That is how we can enjoy God. We can learn of Him and then give our knowledge to others.

MAN'S PICTORIAL CONCEPTION OF GOD

"Did you ever think," he went on, "that the highest pictorial conception of God that man has produced shows him as a man? Venerable, majestic, awful, perhaps, but still a man."

"I had never thought of that," said Determination, "but I do know that it is laid upon me to tell men that we have a God that is absolutely satisfying, one that they can enjoy. Oh, the length and breadth of the knowledge that God is good. How welcome this is to those who feel the way long and the burden of doubts and struggles heavy."

"Someone has said," responded the minister, "'Heaven help us on our working days, the level stretches white with dust.' Every day is a working day to those who do not love and worship God, and the hopeless level stretches meet the sky line day after day, with no promise of even the 'shadow of a great rock.'"

WE ARE OUR BROTHERS' KEEPERS

"Determination is right," said the old prophet. "In a sense that should never let go of us, we are our brothers' keeper. If we have a clear and satisfying knowledge of what God is, and how to enjoy Him, we must tell it to our brother."

"Yes," said Minister Good, "If we have found peace in the beauty and simplicity of the Gospel, why not help our brother to find it?"

CHAPTER IV

Hypocrite in the Pew

"Neither man nor angel can discern
Hypocrisy, the only evil that walks
Invisible, except to God alone,
By his permissive will, through heaven and earth."
—*Milton, "Paradise Lost."*

"He was a man
Who stole the livery of the court of heaven,
To serve the devil in."
—*Pollok.*

FAINTLY, as from a distance, words of deep meaning came to me in my dream. I still seemed to be in the tent set up in the Valley of the Cross, and awake, yet sleeping, arose to find the beauty and charm of a new day pulsing about me. Dreaming still, I seemed intensely alive to the scene before me, the brilliancy of the great sun as it climbed the eastern sky, the deep blue of the heavens, and the rich verdure of the earth.

I prayed for a mind to grasp and use the lessons of the day; and as I prayed the sun grew dim, the blue in the sky melted into gray; dark clouds arose with thunder in their midst; and in the gathering blackness I was taken to the great castle which is Satan's home. Unseen, in his great hall of Pandemonium, I listened while he and his hosts set snares for the souls of men.

SATAN SETS NEW SNARES FOR HUMAN SOULS

The King of Evil sat in his seat of power, and about him were gathered his chief advisers. A foul crew they were, the sight of whom made me for a moment close my eyes in fear. When I opened them again, Satan had descended from his throne and was conversing familiarly with his imps of evil.

"I have just come from the City of Worldliness," he said with a look of demoniac glee. "I find that our work there has not been fruitless. There is trouble in the Church of the Disciples, in which we have of late taken such an interest."

"What is going on there?" asked one of the evil crew. "Has Evangelist been stirring up affairs?"

HYPOCRITE'S EXCELLENT WORK FOR THE DEVIL

"No," responded Satan, "Evangelist is not in these parts now. The minister has started out to make it uncomfortable for Hypocrite. I think he has found him out, and I am sorry."

"Our good friend Hypocrite has been doing excellent work for our cause," continued Satan. "He is not alone, but has a fine following, some of his supporters being officers in the church. This is fortunate for us, as Mr. Good-Enough, the minister of the church, has for some time had doubts of the intentions of Hypocrite, and so is working to overcome his influence."

"I would not care to be in the minister's place then," said one who stood near Satan, listening intently to his words. "Hypocrite is up to all the tricks of his trade."

"The secret of our success in these parts has been in our activity among the churches," said Satan. "When we find such men as friend Hypocrite on our side, it is not difficult to drop poisoned thoughts into their pews."

"Especially when they hold official positions," added another.

"Hypocrite has been making the business meetings of the church somewhat interesting," replied Satan. "His control of the purse of the congregation is of great advantage to him."

"Can we not manage to elect several more of his type? If we could do so, the Church of the Disciples might become one of our best distributing centres," suggested another.

"The idea is certainly a good one," replied Satan. "In my experience, nothing will so quickly demoralize a church as dissension among its members."

MODERN CHURCH MANAGEMENT

"Church affairs are not managed now as they were in the days of Pentecost," said a demon retrospectively. "Then the church was a strong fort, now, there are breaches in its walls."

"The Early Church was invulnerable," replied Satan, "but our continued efforts have not been in vain, and after eighteen centuries, signs of weakness are abundant. Let it be our task to get more men like Hypocrite into the churches. In that way we shall solve one of our hardest problems."

"With such men," continued Satan, "Membership in a church is not only a matter of policy, but has become a necessity. It is impossible to weed them out, for their plausible address and insinuating tongues make friends easily, and so give them a certain standing in the administration of church affairs."

"That corresponds exactly with what I have seen," said one, who, apparently of all present, stood highest in Satan's regard. "I have attended many church services and business meetings and it is wonderful how such men get themselves elected to prominent positions."

"That blind fool, Hypocrite, does not dream that he is one of our chief agents," continued the speaker. "It was a shrewd scheme of yours to work him into a position in that church in which, like Peter of old, he now holds the keys."

"The minister is a strong man," replied Satan, "but I feel sure that with the co-operation of Hypocrite, we can hold our own in that congregation."

With these words, the demoniac conference ended, and its members departed on their various missions of evil. As they went their several ways, their place of meeting also vanished and I was set down in the great City of Worldliness.

MINISTER GOOD AND HIS BURDENS

Before my eyes lay open the parsonage of the Church of the Disciples. In it sat Minister Good, he of whom Satan had sneeringly spoken as Mr. Good-Enough.

"My burden is becoming too heavy for me to bear," he was saying to his faithful wife.

"You will be sustained," she replied. "The Lord knoweth our troubles and this condition of affairs cannot continue endlessly."

"I trust so," he replied, "but for five long years I have faced this base chicanery, seeking for the sake of peace to hide my knowledge of its existence. I have seen the cause of Christ suffer sadly because of wolves parading in sheeps' clothing."

"The tares and the wheat will grow together until the time of harvest," suggested his wife.

"I know they will, yet when an opportunity comes to pluck out tares without injuring the wheat, it seems to me that we are not only justified, but obligated to uproot them," replied the minister.

"That may be true," rejoined his wife, "yet you can never estimate beforehand, the trouble that personal interference is likely to cause, even though you act from most conscientious motives."

"The experience of others seems to show that you are right," the minister continued, "but it is hard to see what I see, daily, and keep quiet."

MR. HYPOCRITE IS A STUMBLING BLOCK

"Each church has its Judas," she replied.

"That is no reason why we should help to cover up his sins by our silence; Jesus uncovered the falseness of the Pharisees, and I deem it my duty to lay bare the double life of Mr. Hypocrite, whatever may come of it. He is a stumbling block in our church. Here, my dear, I have another of those detestable letters which have given me so much annoyance. These false and nameless communications make my heart sick. The man who is guilty of shooting such arrows in the dark is a base coward. This is the fifth of these lying epistles I have already received."

"Yes, dear," she replied, "none but the small of soul could do such work. I know how hard it is to bear; but the Saviour had the same kind of people to deal with, and our burdens are light indeed compared with His. We must be prepared even to be crucified with Him, if God so wills."

"It is hard, but it is true," replied the much troubled minister. " 'Except a corn of wheat fall into the ground and die, it abideth alone, but if it die, it bringeth forth much fruit.' So it is spoken, and no worse thing can happen to a man than to be forced to abide alone."

EVANGELIST VISITS MINISTER GOOD

"Good morning, brother," said a voice interrupting this conference, as the door of the study opened and a venerable visitor walked in.

"What a surprise and pleasure this is," said the minister as he grasped the new comer by the hand, and gave him a most cordial welcome.

"How fares it with thee?" asked the visitor, who was no other than Evangelist.

"None too well," answered Minister Good. "The work might be more encouraging."

"I am sorry to learn this," replied Evangelist. "What is the source of your concern? I think it may be something in which I can be of aid."

AN EVIL INFLUENCE IN THE AIR

"I'm so glad of your coming," said Mrs. Good. "My husband has been greatly dejected of late, and in fact, we both have carried a heavy burden. We have sought to work well and faithfully, but our labor seems to be unprofitable."

"It fills my heart with sorrow to hear this," said the good Evangelist. "Has the Foe of Souls been hindering your work?"

"Perhaps he has," replied the minister. "Certainly some evil influence seems abroad in the air."

"Tell me thy trouble," said the other as he drew his chair nearer, and laid his hand upon that of his discouraged brother. "Tell it all: perchance I may be able to offer thee help in this matter."

Taking up a packet of letters, the minister selected one, which bore the signature of Hypocrite. This he handed to Evangelist. "Read that," he said.

EVANGELIST CONSOLES THE MINISTER

Evangelist leaned back and read aloud the caustic words of this ungenerous and unchristian letter. When he had finished, he returned it, saying in cheerful tones: "Brother Good, I have had much to do with men of this kind. Their work always has its day. The Lord will not long tolerate such a person in His sanctuary. Have you taken any action in this matter?"

"None, so far as Hypocrite is concerned. I have sought to do my duty and have endeavored not to notice his attacks."

"Grind, grind, grind at the 'Mill of Fortune.'"

"What say thy friends to his conduct?"

"They are with me to a soul; but they do not see their way clear to take open action in the matter."

"Why?" queried Evangelist.

"Because Hypocrite has entrenched himself, by rendering them indebted to him in business matters, and he has gone so far as to threaten some of them with financial ruin unless they submit to his leadership."

MAN CANNOT HINDER THE CAUSE OF CHRIST

"Oh, is that his plan?" said Evangelist. "So he proposes to stay the progress of the cause of Christ by his worldly will! This method has been tried many times before, and I predict his utter discomfiture. Be not discouraged, brother," he continued. "The Lord will open the way to thee. Maintain a spirit of patience. Thy faithful work is recorded, and the Lord will yet crown thy hopes and prayer with the blessing of true achievement. Keep up your heart and trust me to give you what aid I can." With these words, Evangelist bade them adieu and went forth on his daily errands of good.

The minister and his wife stepped to the window and watched the venerable patriarch as he walked away.

"He's a dear, good old man," said the minister. "One of the Lord's chosen, who lift the burden from the tired hearts of his workmen."

"And he wears the life he lives in his face. He is one of those anointed of God to minister comfort," answered his wife.

THE MINISTER DECIDES WHAT TO DO

"Wife, I have gotten to this point," said Minister Good, as he gathered the letter of Hypocrite and those of anonymous origin, and, crushing them in his hand, flung them into the open grate. "I do not believe that there is a man, or set of men, who can long stay the progress of God's work. I mean to let the Lord deal with Hypocrite."

"That's the best disposition of this matter you can make," replied his wife.

The scene upon which I had been gazing now faded away, and instead, I was in the residence of Mr. Hypocrite and beheld that fomenter of mischief seated in his library with a number of friends whom he had invited to a conference.

HYPOCRITE AND HIS FELLOW-PLOTTERS MEET

"I am sorry to say, gentlemen," said Hypocrite, "that this matter has gone somewhat further than I anticipated."

"Yes," rejoined one of the company. "It has grown to almost unmanageable proportions."

"Do you think it as bad as that?" asked Hypocrite.

"It seems so to me. Minister Good has not replied to a single communication, and seems apparently unconcerned in the matter upon which we have brought pressure," was the reply.

"He must go," said one of the company. "That is the best solution of the question. He has taken a defiant attitude and we had best get rid of him. How will it do to squeeze him on the salary question? You certainly control that side of the situation, Mr. Hypocrite."

"I have thought of that," replied Hypocrite, "and have been trying it. It is a means by which many ministers are put on the rack. It certainly seems to me that we, the representatives and financial backers of the church, should control its policy."

This last remark appealed to the pride of those present, and each seemed to expand with a new sense of importance. Hypocrite chuckled inwardly, for he well knew that he could manipulate them at his pleasure.

"We must put an end to his method of personal preaching," he went on, "and to that singling out as sins the amusements which are popular among society people. Mr. Good does not know how to adjust himself to prevailing conditions." he added; "for, if he did, his nest could be well feathered."

"That's right," interjected one who was anxious to curry favor with Hypocrite, and who had been put into office by him, though he was totally unqualified for a position in God's house. "The church is intended to be only a sort of religious club, anyway, and it is very uncomfortable to be always hearing of the need of 'special baptisms'; and those endless appeals for a 'higher life' grow tiresome."

"What we choose to do," said another, "is none of his business, anyway. The man may mean well, but he is not infallible, and he is rather too fanatical to please my taste."

"I see nothing for us to do but to get rid of him in some way, and then call an up-to-date minister, who appreciates the conditions of these times and the necessities which are a law of the world," replied Hypocrite. "Our church will go to pieces if this man continues with us much longer."

"Those are our sentiments, too," said several of those present.

Satan, who just then passed by in his walking to and fro upon the earth, peered in at the window upon the assembled company.

"That's good enough to be left alone," he said to himself. "Hypocrite is certainly sentencing that preacher to-night. As I was with him in his pew last Sunday in the person of Agnostic, I am somewhat familiar with his plans. He can be safely trusted with this job if he keeps wise and discreet. I shall certainly aid him with my counsel."

The meeting ended in a lunch to which Mrs. Hypocrite now invited the gentlemen, and, after imbibing several bottles of Hypocrite's choice wines, the company broke up.

MISS SINCERE APPEALS TO THE ANGEL

My vision now led me into another part of the city, and there I saw the Guardian Angel whom I had first beheld at the Bridge of Sighs. She was now in the chamber of Miss Sincere.

"I am so concerned about poor Mr. Good," she said to her visitor. "He seems to be greatly troubled. I was at his house this morning, but I am such a poor body to comfort any one. Both he and his wife seemed to be worried, and I felt that it had something to do with money matters. I gave them a little remembrance and they seemed much pleased."

"Mr. Good has his cross to bear," said the Angel. "A minister's lot is not a sinecure, as a rule, and especially in this particular instance. I am in sympathy with Mr. Good and his work, and I have learned that there are wolves in sheeps' clothing in his church.''

"Who can she mean?" Miss Sincere asked of herself.

The Angel sat down by her side, and the glory of the moon, newly risen, fell in a flood of light through the window and upon them, giving its silver glory to their faces.

THE MINISTER SHOULD HAVE SYMPATHY AND PRAYERS

"My daughter," said the Angel, "the lot of God's servant is often a trying one. Few of those to whom he ministers understand or appreciate the burdens which weigh upon his soul. He is an ambassador sent by God, and the sense of responsibility which rests upon him concerning his work, is a matter which none but he can know. Those who serve in this office are entitled to the sympathy and prayers of God's people, and every servant of Christ should have the loyal co-operation of his entire congregation."

"No machine can run smoothly if but one cog of the smallest wheel be broken," she went on. "Chimes cannot bathe the air with perfect melody if a single bell be out of tune. Neither can a minister be truly successful in his work, if there be in his congregation one dissenting or indifferent soul. Unless the heart of the minister be supported and encouraged by a united people, he will be unfitted fully to deliver the message which God would have him tell. A hypocrite in the pew can limit the power of a saint's message."

Miss Sincere looked into the eyes of the Angel, and said: "There are many in our church who seem indifferent to the message from the pulpit. I wonder if we have any who are false to the name of Christian?"

"Perhaps there are some in the pews," replied the Good Angel.

A JUDAS AMONG THE DISCIPLES

Sweet were the visions that came to the pure soul of Miss Sincere that night. Her communion with the angelic visitor had filled her with holy thoughts. As she looked from her window the next morning, she saw the two men who were most in her thoughts—her much loved minister and her trusted friend. They met beneath her window and she listened with pleasure to their words.

"Good morning, Mr. Good," said Mr. Hypocrite, extending his hand with all the apparent warmth of real friendship. "Let me congratulate you upon your sermon last Sunday," said he.

"Thank you," replied the minister, in a polite, but cool tone. After a few words they parted, each pursuing his course.

"Fair without, but foul within," said the minister to himself as he walked away. "Now I am commencing to realize what it was for Jesus to have Judas among His disciples." Had these words been spoken aloud they might have thrown new light into Miss Sincere's mind.

EVANGELIST SCORES HYPOCRITE

When Hypocrite entered his office he was surprised to find Evangelist there. The old man who had awaited him for some time, received his salutations with slight response, and with little ceremony explained to him the purpose of his errand.

"Mr. Hypocrite," he said in severe accents. "I have seen the finger of the Lord, and it pointed at thee. The words of thy condemnation are already written on the wall. Thou art false to thy vows, and holdest a pew in yonder church under the guise of a Christian, when thy heart is filled with sin."

Hypocrite was bewildered. He was speechless for the moment; a frown of anger gathering on his brow. Before he could speak the hot words that came to his lips, Evangelist went on.

"It is mine to speak!" he said in commanding tones. "I am come in peace, trusting, perchance, wise counsel may cause thee to turn from thy evil ways. Thou art a hindrance to the Church of Christ, and being without conscience art heaping burdens upon the heart of a worthy man of God. But a day is coming when thy prestige acquired by shrewdness and gold will be worthless; a day when the light of God's searchings shall reveal the rottenness of thy soul."

NOTHING IS HID FROM HIM

"Thy secret intrigues with Satan, the barter of that which is religious for the base returns he offers, are known by Him who watches over all who dwell in the valley between the Cross and the Hill-lands of Faith."

Hypocrite, whose first impulse was to eject the old man from the office, heard the last words with an agitation he could not control. His anger vanished and terror took its place. Had he indeed held actual conference with Satan? It seemed to him that the old man had divined the truth; for at the moment he felt that the foul fiend was his intimate friend.

"I know not of what you speak," he faltered, with whitening lips. "You are wronging me! You have been listening to my enemies."

"Not so, Mr. Hypocrite. I speak that whereof I know. Your soul tells you that it is the truth, and you will learn that the way of the transgressor is hard. The words of the very servant of God whom thou art seeking to depose by dishonorable methods, shall in the end become thorns in thy unenviable crown."

"You are doing me a great injustice," protested Hypocrite. "I am the friend of Minister Good. My church is the object of my pride and devotion."

GOD'S MESSAGE TO HYPOCRITE

"Seek not to hide behind lies," rejoined Evangelist. "Mine eyes have seen and mine ears have heard. Hear me further. This is the message of the Lord to thee:

" 'Can the rush grow up without mire? Can the flag grow without water? Whilst it is yet in its greenness, and not cut down, it withereth before any other herb. So are the paths of all that forget God; and the hypocrite's hope shall perish; whose hopes shall be cut off, and whose trust shall be a spider's web. He shall lean upon his house, but it shall not stand; he shall hold it fast, but it shall not endure.'

"This is the message of the Most High to thee," and with these words of warning, Evangelist passed from the room and disappeared from sight.

The false-hearted merchant dared not stop him, for the message of Evangelist had come to him as a warning from the Most High.

SATAN FOILED BY EVANGELIST

As he sat there lost in deep thought, Satan peered in upon him and saw with dismay that his chief earthly agent of mischief was in sore trouble. He could not quite divine the cause, but he had seen Evangelist leave the door and knew that he was connected with Hypocrite's distress.

With all his power he sought to infuse the old irreligious spirit into Hypocrite's thoughts, but the arrows of Evangelist's words had struck too deeply, and for the time, the foul fiend was powerless.

Was he indeed in danger of eternal woe from the course he had lately pursued, and especially for his hypocrisy? Such was the dread that filled the merchant's mind, and it inspired him with terror which all Satan's artillery could not overcome.

SATAN'S PHILOSOPHY

Doubts, sneers against the ultra pious, specious arguments against the teachings of the church, the whole quiver full of arrows of the atheist and the impious, were hurled at him by Satan in vain, and the Evil One went his way in wrath at this seeming relapse of his clever agent and hoped-for prey, but a cunning leer came upon his face as he thought:

"This is but for a day. Hypocrite is too deeply dyed in sin, and far too weak in righteousness for this mood to last. Tomorrow I look to find my own again. Sudden conversions rarely sink deep."

For the rest of that day, Hypocrite remained the slave of the terror which Evangelist had awakened in his soul. He attempted to redeem some of the evil he had done by sending the minister a check for his over-due salary, which he had illegally kept back; and went so far as to send a small sum to the Widow Faith, whom he had sought to despoil of her home. But that night, some of his old frame of mind returned. "Had he become a pious weakling?" he asked himself, and then shook off much of the fear which had moved him so deeply.

THE ANGEL COMFORTS MINISTER GOOD

Minister Good sat in his study on the morning of the day on which Hypocrite had been so deeply moved. The day's experience had added new courage to the pious pastor. Evangelist had called again, and so had Miss Sincere, and both had pledged him their sympathy, and bade him be of good cheer. And the unexpected check received from the Church Treasurer had relieved him of trouble of a material kind. As he thought over his work for the morrow, the Good Angel entered the study and stood by his side, unseen by him, though he felt the presence and seemed to hear the voice of a divine agent.

"Thou hast thy troubles, dear pastor," came the soothing words in his ear, "but the Master had His, and thou art but a servant traveling in His steps. Let not thy heart be troubled concerning these problems of thy parish. The Angel of the Lord goeth before thee to prepare the way. Thine enemies shall not prevail. This is the message of God, which is to be thy message in times of trouble and care.

"'Yet I have left me seven thousand in Israel, all the knees which have not bowed to Baal and every mouth which hath not kissed him.'"

As the Angel withdrew, the minister said to his wife: "There is yet a bow upon the cloud, even though there is a hypocrite in the pew."

"We are touching days of greater blessing," the minister resumed, "for while I am unable to grasp the Angel's vision, I believe that what she hath foreseen is true, and we must push forward with trustful hearts.

IN THE MINISTER'S STUDY

I was inexpressibly stirred as I heard these earnest and faithful souls comfort one another with words from the Book of Books, and I strove to fix in my mind both the words and the scene before me. I heard the sweet-faced woman add:

"What could we do without the Bible?"

"Nothing, nothing," answered the minister. "Its thought and teachings have been the foundation of all enduring literature, and its spirit the inspiration of that immortal heroism which everywhere throughout Christendom, for centuries, has subdued the kingdom of darkness, and hate and sin, and ushered in the rule and reign of the Cross."

"It is God's answer to all human hearts," rejoined his wife.

THROUGH ALL THE UNQUIET YEARS

"Yes," assented the minister, "the truths from this sacred book have removed thorns from dying pillows through the ages; and spoken peace and courage to the soul in the agonies of its Golgothas.

"This book has been the one window in the world's dark night through which the stars of promise shone through the early hours, until the sun of righteousness foretold by prophets and sages crossed the peaks of time to flood the hills and valleys of earth forevermore with the light from the life of the Son of God."

"He is the light," said Mrs. Good, "who lights the path down to the river where souls set sail for the eternal shores; who points the way across billow and storm into harbors celestial."

A STRONG TESTIMONY

" 'Tis a blessed book," said the minister, "and has appealed to the greatest minds the world has ever known.

"Milton found no songs to be compared with the songs of Zion; no orations equal to those of the prophets. In twenty-four of Bacon's Essays he has more than seventy allusions to the Bible.

"The 'Divine Commedia' of Dante; the works of Shakespeare,

the greatest literary genius the world has ever seen; the masterpieces of hundreds of writers of eminence are witnesses to the wonderful influences of this wonderful book.

"The works of the leading poets and prose writers of the nineteenth century bear the distinct impress of biblical thought and expression," he went on, "and hosts of others testify to the supremacy of the Bible over all other literature. What can be stronger than the testimony of Ruskin, the leading art critic of the world?

" 'All that I taught of Art, everything that I have written, whatever greatness has been in any thought of mine has simply been due to the fact that, while I was a child, my mother daily read with me a part of the Bible, and daily made me learn a part of it by heart.' "

OUR PERSONAL LESSONS

"Yes," rejoined Mrs. Good, "and every time we study its pages there is a personal lesson to be learned, for in its histories, its commands, its promises, we find that we must be in harmony with God."

"Indeed you are right," said the minister. "Just as the children of Israel could look back on monumental acts of badness, rebellion, impious beliefs, degrading sensualities, just so there is something to answer to these in the lives of all of us. Every life has its own story, but there are experiences common to all."

"I have felt this too," replied his wife, "but you remember God said to the children of Israel, 'Thou shalt remember the day when thou camest forth out of the Land of Egypt all the days of thy life.' It should require no effort for us to remember the day when we came out of our Egypt, for, it stands out boldly against the dreary background of weaknesses and imperfections to which we were accustomed. It was the day we began to get away from sins that had an evil eminence, from the giving away to hatred and anger, from profane and sensual influences."

WHAT GOD REQUIRES

While she was speaking, her husband had been turning the leaves of the Bible, and now he said:

"The study of this book reveals many things. That we must have charity in our judgment of others is one of them, and then we find that, we must be humble before God for such knowledge of truth as we have, and for our determination to know more of it, to live it, and to teach it to others. And now," he added, turning the book before him, "hear what the prophet Micah says:

" 'He hath showed thee, O man, what is good; and what doth the Lord require of thee, but to do justly, and to love mercy, and to walk humbly with thy God.' "

CHAPTER V

THE MODERN THIRST FOR GOLD

"Commerce has set the mark of selfishness,
  The signet of its all enslaving power,
  Upon a shining ore, and called it gold;
  Before whose image bow the vulgar great,
  The vainly rich, the miserable proud,
  The mob of peasants, nobles, priests and kings,
  And with blind feelings reverence the power
  That grinds them to the dust of misery,
  But in the temple of their hireling hearts
  Gold is a living god, and rules in scorn
  Al' earthly things but virtue."
                                            —*Shelley.*

IN my dream I overlooked the Great City of Worldliness in all its vast extent. By its side, past a thousand great warehouses, a broad river raced to the ocean. Deep-laden ships lay at the wharves, or glided out into the mist, and floated away with the stream.

The noise of traffic reached me,—the clatter and din of a thousand footsteps, a thousand hoofs, a thousand wheels. Streams of human life flowed in straight and devious ways, yielding, pushing, driving, in a stress of feverish excitement.

I saw men there absorbed and rapt in eager self-seeking, crossing each other's course in every direction, and women as well—men and women of all conditions—and I asked myself, Where will these be in a hundred years, and what will be the sum and outcome of this labor?

Then I was borne down into the very vortex of the city, that wild whirlpool of wealth and woe in which men and women are driven by the thirst for gold and pleasure, past the market-place, the banks and exchanges—a thousand places in which the war for wealth goes on day by day, the victors exulting, the vanquished mourning, the field strewn with the wrecks of human souls.

But the gold-fever was not in every heart in that city. Thousands were there whose souls were clean and pure; to whom honor and righteousness were worth tenfold all the wealth of the world. Here and there I saw temples with their spires pointing to heaven as if in warning to the fevered throng, and their doors were open invitingly to all to whom prayer and devotion had a living meaning.

At length I found myself in the unpretentious dwelling of Minister Good, and saw him seated in his study. Beside him was one of radiant face. A queenly woman of earthly mould she seemed, but my eyes saw in her lineaments those of the Guardian Angel of the bridge. Their talk was of the greed for wealth by which so many in the great city were swayed.

"How hardly shall they that have riches enter into the Kingdom of Heaven! It is easier for a camel to go through the eye of a needle than for a rich man to enter Christ's fold," said the

"'What can he do?' replied Mrs. Hypocrite."

Angel. "Temptation surounds him, and strong indeed is the soul that can resist."

THE THIRST FOR RICHES A DISEASE OF THE TIMES

"The *love* of money works half the evil in the world," replied the thoughtful minister. "If the busy world would only learn to 'render unto Cæsar the things that are Cæsar's, and unto God, the things which are God's,' far better would it be for all mankind."

"This thirst for riches is a disease of the times," said the Angel. "It has always existed, but is growing intense in these latter days. The hot haste to be rich in the world's goods has kept many a one from reaching a better life. Those words of the Master, 'What shall it profit a man if he gain the whole world and lose his own soul,' seem to have lost much of their significance in these times. To be rich! to be rich! ah, that's the sole ambition of hosts of those about us."

THE DAILY TOIL AT THE MILL OF FORTUNE

"Too true," answered Minister Good with a sigh. "There are thousands in this city alone, who look no higher than the roof which covers them. It is grind, grind, grind, from Monday until Saturday, at the Mill of Fortune, and the controlling thought is, how to turn every transaction into gold, no matter who may suffer or fall in the strife."

"There is no easier way for Satan to win a wavering soul than to point him to a hoard of imaginary gold," said the Angel.

"That is an old trick of his," replied the minister. "He resorted to it on the mount when he tempted the Master with his 'All this will I give thee if thou wilt fall down and worship me.'"

"Alas, many Christian people seem to lack the moral stamina to rise up in the face of his designs and say: 'Get thee behind me Satan,'" continued the Angel.

THE LESSONS AND OBLIGATIONS OF WEALTH

At this point in the conversation, Miss Sincere entered the room. Wealth was hers, but it had come by inheritance and had been won by the honest endeavors of a pious father, to whom honor outweighed gain. It was her habit to use it freely in doing good.

"We have been speaking of the great thirst for gold, which is so widely prevalent in these times," said the minister.

"All power to obtain wealth comes from the Lord," she replied. "Wealth, to my way of thinking, is a curse to its possessor unless it has been gained by honorable labor and unless it be consecrated to the giver. Some one has truly said: 'A man's true wealth is the good he does in the world.'"

THE LACK OF CONSECRATED WEALTH

"It gladdens me to see that you are making a wise use of your possessions," said the Angel. "A tender heart and a charitable soul are the best inheritance that have come down to you."

"Do not praise me, I pray you," protested the modest caller. "Who could have done less than I to stem the tide of misery?"

"The covetousness of God's children is a source of deep sadness to me," replied the Angel. "Even the Church suffers from lack of consecrated wealth. Christians give so little, compared with their earnings. I fear that with many of them, piety is not strong enough to untie the purse strings."

"Yes, the treasurer's book of most churches would condemn a large number of those whose names are on the membership roll," assented Minister Good.

"No doubt it is as you say, and that those who are most blessed and prosperous often give the least," observed Miss Sincere.

"The parable of Jesus, wherein He pictures the grasping spirit of His time in the foolish rich man, who enlarged his barns and crowded them with his gathered grains, yet applies to our day," said the minister, his face growing grave and severe.

GOD LOVES A CHEERFUL GIVER

"Certainly the poor often surpass the rich in openness of heart," rejoined Miss Sincere. "No one gives more to the cause of Christ in our church, in proportion to their income, than Widow Faith. She has four little children for whom to care, and her means are very small, yet I am told she contributes fifty cents each week. Such a sum is more to her than as many dollars to many of our members, for it must represent self-denial."

"She is laying up treasures in Heaven," said the minister.

100   THE MODERN THIRST FOR GOLD

"The Lord will not suffer her to want, because she giveth generously and in answer to a quickened conscience."

"They that sow sparingly shall reap also sparingly, and they that sow bountifully, shall also reap bountifully," said the Angel.

THE SINK OF POLITICAL CORRUPTION

After their conversation had continued for some time longer, Minister Good remarked, with a face of grave concern:

"Much as we condemn the greed and dishonor in the business world, it is by no means the sorest spot in our city's affairs. There is a field in which dishonor broadens into unblushing dishonesty and greed expands into barely concealed theft."

"I do not comprehend. What field is that?" asked Miss Sincere with a look of concern.

"The field of politics," answered the minister. "The management of public affairs is a mire far deeper and fouler than that into which Christian sank when he set out for the straight gate and narrow way."

"Politics is something we women know little of. It is outside the ordinary sphere of our duties and of our churches."

"Oh, no, not outside the churches," protested the minister. "Vice, here, wears often the mask of respectability, and you will find some of those deepest in the business of defrauding the public, posing as good church members. It is sad, but true."

"I have heard the name of Mr. Man-of-the-World spoken of as the 'boss of city politics,' 'the head of the ring,'" said Miss

Sincere, "but I must confess I know but little of what those words signify."

"That man is a sad reflection upon the fair fame of our city," answered the minister. "For two years past, he and the political combination of which he is the leader, have been in full power in the public offices. They decide who the people shall vote for; they give out all contracts; and they fill their pockets out of the spoils of office.

"Man-of-the-World began his political career with scarce a penny. To-day he is rich. He began with a reputation for honor; to-day his name is spoken with a sneer all over the land. He has sold his soul to Satan as really as did Faust of old."

"It is sad, sad indeed," mused Miss Sincere. "You have opened to my eyes a new form of iniquity which I hardly knew existed."

"You will learn more of it in the days now coming," said Minister Good, significantly. "It is widely felt that the powerful political ring is laying new plans which will surpass in shrewdness those of the past. And the people slumber on, and vote blindly as they are told. Oh! that Christ would come to this city and wake the public conscience, which I fear is in a trance."

I heard no more. A thin mist, deepening momently, spread over the humble parsonage, shutting it from view. The last I saw of the group was the glorified face of the Guardian Angel. Soon that vanished too.

When the mist rose again, a widely different scene met my view. I had last looked upon the radiant features and sparkling eyes of the Angel of Deliverance. I now found myself gazing upon eyes through which the fires of hell seemed glowing, and a face that appeared as the dark emblem of sin. It was Satan who rose before me on a sombre and gloomy heath, upon which every trace of green seemed blasted by his presence. With him were a number of his demon horde whom he had summoned to his side.

GOOD NEWS COMES TO SATAN'S CREW

It was with a look of malign triumph that Satan met his crew, and the expression of exultation upon his face bore in it the concentrated evil of the Pit.

"I bring you glorious news," he said, "tidings of great moment. You know how diligently I have worked upon the double-dealing spirit of Man-of-the-world, the leader of the political ring in the City of Worldliness. The fellow had grown afraid of the public and dreaded to go further in his schemes, but I have been at his ear and put new courage in his heart. The people of the city will hear of something *not* to their advantage before many days."

"What is it?" asked his eager crew. "Can we help in it?"

"Don't be too eager. You will soon learn. Curiosity is a sin you know," said Satan with a cunning leer. "I promise that you will be kept busy."

"We should know the secret now, so that we can prepare to do our work faithfully," said a prominent demon.

"Ha! Ha! are you there, old devil of curiosity?" laughed Satan. "Very well, you shall learn. Listen, and I will tell you of an interesting talk I happened to overhear in my daily visit to the City of Worldliness."

The demons gathered round with gleaming eyes, while Satan seated himself on a low mound as on a throne.

"You know that I am much in the habit of calling on my useful friend, Hypocrite," began Satan. "I was in his office to-day, unseen by him, unless he chanced to notice a big beetle that sat on the bust of Mephistopheles in one corner of the room."

A demoniac burst of laughter greeted these words.

"He had a visitor," continued Satan, "no other than Mr. Man-of-the-World. I knew at a glance that my plans were ripening, for this meeting was one that I had been seeking to bring about. They were alone, the door was locked, and their conversation went on in low tones. I was in time to hear the gist of it, and this is how it ran:

" 'You are the man I want, and the only one,' said Man-of-the-World. 'You know the value of cash as well as the best of us, and are not squeamish as to how you get it. I promise you this will be a mint.'

" 'But I fear defeat,' said Hypocrite. 'I am not in the best of odor in the city, as you know. There are hosts who will vote against me, and I do not care to be turned down; a man's pride enters into a thing of this sort.'

" 'Leave it to me and the boys to manage all that,' replied Man-of-the-World. "The entire machine of the city is back of you. We have the cash to push your candidacy, and it is money and organization which obtain results in these days. You must agree to let your name stand, for it is a safe thing, and I can tell you it's no small matter to be mayor of a city of this size.

" 'Aside from the salary,' he went on, 'the rake-offs are not to be despised, and besides this, in dealing with corporations, there are many emoluments worth considering. Come now, friend Hypocrite, this matter must be settled to-night and you are the man we want. Give us your answer by six o'clock, and see that it is favorable.' With these words and one of his knowing looks, Man-of-the-World left the place."

"As Hypocrite sat musing, I whispered in his ear," continued Satan, "it is an office worth having; and it has come to you unsought. It will pay you richly, and, aside from that, you will have new facilities for broadening out your business. What goes on back of the political screen never comes to the public ear. As for winning, you can count on 'the machine' for that.

"I could see that my suggestions impressed him favorably, and I kept on whispering what he fancied were his own thoughts. It is lucky I was there, or I fear he would have been afraid to take the nomination. As it was, I won him over, and he wrote his acceptance before I left the place."

SATAN PROMISES PROFITABLE WORK

"Good! good," cried the demon crew, with a shout of approval. "With Hypocrite at the head of affairs there will be profitable work for all of us to do. The man is a coward and will need bolstering up, but that, you can attend to. We shall have enough to keep us busy among the rank and file of the gang."

"I fancy you will," said Satan with a meaning look. "Many of them will need your aid, for they will have to defy all the honor and decency of the city for years."

MR. HYPOCRITE AT HOME

Again my dream changed, and I found myself in the home of Mr. Hypocrite, the candidate for Mayor. He had just entered, and with hat still in hand was in eager conversation with his wife.

"I have taken a step to-day, which I think you will approve," he said. "There are some matters of immense importance to the city coming up next year. Large public works are on the programme which will mean the handling of millions. I propose to have my share of them. You know we have talked of the possibility of my receiving the nomination for Mayor. It has been offered to me and I have accepted it."

"I am glad of that," she replied. "We live only once, and I believe in getting all we can, and you are not required to take your conscience into politics," she added with a laugh.

"You are right there," rejoined Hypocrite. "As for being elected, I fancy that will go through, for Mr. Man-of-the-World controls the situation; but I must say this, I'd feel a great deal easier about the affair if it were not for that interview with old Evangelist. He always leads me to feel, when I am in his presence, as though the Almighty were not far away, and then I become a sheer coward. It's a species of sorcery, I am sure; but the weirdness of it makes shivers come over me when I think of it. Those eyes of his look right through you and seem to pierce your very soul."

SLEEP HATH ITS OWN WORLD

That night Hypocrite had a dream in which he saw a great vault containing a large quantity of gold, and there came to him a voice saying: "Enter and help thyself, 'tis for thee, but beware of the door." He saw his friends outside and heard their congratulatory words, but as he entered the vault and took up a bag of gold, the door suddenly closed and he was alone with the treasure. He cried for aid, but his friends seemed to have forsaken him. The gold by which he was surrounded and which he had sought, seemed as worthless as sand, in the terror that now seized him.

AND CURDLES A LONG LIFE INTO ONE HOUR

For hours he remained there in utter despair. At length he saw the approach of one like to Evangelist, who, with a key which was called "Salvation," unlocked the door, and provided a way of escape.

The significant dream troubled Hypocrite all through the next day, but he told no one of it.

"It is strange what fancies invade our brain," he said. "Dreams are but the fabrications of a wearied mind, but this one surely has a strange meaning." With all his efforts to banish it by engrossing himself with other matters, it was days before he could throw off its full effect.

Without taking note of intervening time, I saw the election scenes, and was aware that Hypocrite, with the aid of the political ring, was elected Mayor by a large majority. Encouraged by this, he did not hesitate to run the office for the benefit of himself and his political friends, setting at defiance the honest element of the city.

EVANGELIST AND THE MINISTER DISCUSS THE SITUATION

"It is a long road which does not have a turn," said Evangelist to Minister Good, upon whom he had called.

"Yes, it is a long road; so long that it does not look as though we would ever come even in sight of a turn," was the reply.

"It must come though," continued Evangelist. "Hypocrite represents the great number of those who are thirsting for riches, and who, for the sake of gain, smother their consciences, and stoop to the world's standard. This mercenary greed obliterates their finer sense of honor, and everywhere, dishonesty is running rampant, having been given its legal freedom under the guise of the 'laws of trade.'"

ALL BOW BEFORE KING GOLD

"It is hard to preach the Gospel to such people," Minister Good observed. "Men have no time now-a-days to do any religious thinking. Gold is king, and both the large man and the small man bow adoringly before him."

"Think ye it is worse now than when He was here?" questioned Evangelist.

"When who was here?" asked the minister.

"When Jesus, the Christ, was here, and preached the word of the kingdom in Jerusalem and in Capernaum," answered Evangelist.

Minister Good pondered for a moment, and catching the significance of the question, replied: "It ought to be better now than in those times, better, rather than worse."

HONESTY AND WORTH SHALL INCREASE

"It is better now, though the old greed is still here," said Evangelist. "Twenty centuries of divine ministry have, at least, put leaven in the meal."

"So long as God's ambassadors keep the Cross on the Hill before the mind of this mercenary age," he went on, "the softening influence of His teachings will break up the hard cold surface of the world's life, and the seeds of honesty and truth, in the mutual relations of life, will take root and grow."

The voice of the good prophet fell to a whisper as the scene melted into shadow. Then another took its place.

HYPOCRITE IS "TAKEN CARE OF"

I saw Hypocrite and Man-of-the-World seated in their political club, intently occupied with a scheme which was to be presented to the city councils the next day.

"The home of the Adversary crowned the summit of a ragged cliff."

"If we can get the matter properly brought forward," said the political autocrat, "and have the proper committee appointed, the measure will be safe to pass. I have a big sum invested, and am sure that it will net me largely if I can get the contract."

"No doubt of that," said Hypocrite.

"And I mean to take good care of you if our plan succeeds," said Man-of-the-World.

"You can trust me. I am here for what is in it, and I promise you that the bill shall have my signature when it reaches me," said Hypocrite.

"That's settled then," said Man-of-the-World with a grin of satisfaction. "You shall be in it 'on the ground floor.' Trust me to see to that."

"We understand each other," said Hypocrite.

Man-of-the-World knew well how to do his work, and when to "see," in the phrase of the "machine." A storm of protest broke out in the city against the villanous project, but in spite of all opposition the bill was passed and signed.

"It hurts my conscience to do jobs like this," said Mayor Hypocrite to himself, "but there is a clear million in it, and no conscience can stand against a price like that."

WE MUST KEEP PACE WITH SOCIETY

Since the day of Hypocrite's marriage, he had made a confidant of his wife, and to all his efforts to amass a fortune, she had given her earnest encouragement.

"If your plans succeed," she said, "we shall summer at the

centre of fashion next year. We must keep up with the advance of society, but to do that, takes means."

"Our desires in this direction shall be gratified beyond a doubt," he replied. He had trained her to his way of thinking, and her shrewdness, in many instances, aided him in covering up his sins.

Nearly all the newspapers in the city were unsparing in their denunciation of the acts of the Mayor, and boldly stated his connection with the schemes of Mr. Man-of-the-World to rob the city treasury. But the subsidized papers protested vigorously against these statements of fraud, and lauded Mr. Hypocrite as an honest man, appealing to his record as a business man and a church member.

HYPOCRITE IS IN THE HANDS OF HIS FRIENDS

"Mr. Hypocrite is sadly worried about these newspaper lies concerning him," said his wife to Miss Sincere, who had called upon her. "It's just awful how these jealous men are seeking to slander his good name. His church record is even attacked."

"It's too bad," said Miss Sincere, whose faith in her old friend was not entirely shaken. "But a lie, like a false act, never fulfills its intentions. Why does Mr. Hypocrite submit to these statements, since they are doubtless untrue?" she asked.

"What can he do?" replied Mrs. Hypocrite. "He is simply in the hands of his friends. He said last night that probably his best course would be to keep silent until the matter blew over. All

THE MODERN THIRST FOR GOLD

he can say will not convince these people who are ignorant of his motives in the matter."

"Well," said Miss Sincere, "the Good Angel has taught me to do my best, and then leave all in the hands of the Higher Power. Mr. Hypocrite as a consistent Christian should do the same."

"Yes, yes," answered Mrs. Hypocrite, "but that is different. Matters of this kind are purely secular, and in the business and political world, while the tide is rising, affairs move with such force and swiftness that men do not get much time even to think about praying."

"It is a sad condition, if such is the case," said Miss Sincere. "'Cast all your care upon Him,' is the command. This thirst for gold is the curse of the age, and if our representative leaders set such a pace, what can we expect of the rising generation?"

"Perhaps I said too much," said Miss Sincere to herself, after she had taken her leave. "That woman does not think of anything beyond apparel and the latest whim of fashionable society. She is determined to shine in the select circle of the 'four hundred,' if money can accomplish it, and even Christian counsel, I fear, is too weak to combat the strong desire of her worldly mind."

MR. MAN-OF-THE-WORLD WRITES A LETTER

One day Minister Good was surprised to receive in his mail a letter from Mr. Man-of-the-World.

"Listen to this, wife," he said as he glanced at the signature.

"Here is a missive from a new correspondent. What can he want?"

He read:

"*Rev. Mr. Good:*
"*Dear Sir:*
"*You are no doubt much interested in the work of our honored mayor, who is a loyal member of your communion, and have read with sorrow, the scurrilous attacks of certain newspapers upon his motives and character as a public officer.*

"*Unknown to him, I have taken the liberty of requesting that you write a line endorsing him as a man, and stating therein, in shortest terms, the confidence you place in his religious integrity.*

"*Such a line from you at this time, will be of great comfort and help to Mr. Hypocrite.*

"*Thanking you in advance, I remain*
"*Very truly yours,*
"*Man-of-the-World.*"

"I wonder what that political reprobate thinks of me?" said Minister Good indignantly. "Does he imagine that I am blind to what is going on? I shall never endorse Mayor Hypocrite. He is beginning to reap some of the harvests for which he has been sowing these many years. I don't propose to 'whitewash' him. To leave him in the mire may be the best way of showing him the error of his ways. I fear, though, that his case is hopeless."

The next scene in my dream showed me the moving power behind this letter. As I suspected, it was a scheme of the Adversary. His voice came plainly to my ears.

SATAN PLOTS AGAINST THE MINISTER

"They are certainly giving the Mayor a 'roast,'" he said to one of his attendants. "He can stand it though, for he is getting well paid. The last contract he secured, netted him at least half a million."

"It's the old story," said the other, "'Uneasy lies the head that wears a crown.' But there is no need to worry about Hypocrite, he will wear the crown all right, if the returns are satisfactory."

"I think that perhaps I can get the minister into this game also," said Satan, and then he told how he had proposed to Man-of-the-World to have the minister endorse Hypocrite and his administration. "If he writes the letter, it will mean his utter failure in his church," he added with considerable satisfaction.

"If he only does it," said the other, "and that, I greatly doubt."

THE GUARDIAN ANGEL TELLS EVANGELIST OF THE PLOT

The Good Angel knew of the trouble, and, seeking Evangelist, revealed to him the plan of Man-of-the-World to identify Minister Good with the political complications of Mr. Hypocrite.

"This must not be," said Evangelist, and, with these brief words, he hurried away to counsel the minister.

"Come in, you are welcome, my dear Evangelist," said Minister Good as he admitted him.

"Stay thy heart and hand from any interference in this matter," said Evangelist, after he had announced the purpose of his visit. "Thou art sent to preach the Gospel. Back of this matter is a design to impair thy influence. Seek guidance of the Lord."

"Thanks for your advice and counsel," said the minister. "I know well that the love of gold lies at the base of all Hypocrite's proceedings, and I had no thought of being drawn into writing any such letter. His associations only whip his spirit into greater haste to be rich."

MAYOR HYPOCRITE'S ADMINISTRATION

As time went on, Man-of-the-World and Hypocrite—having Satan always at their elbows, pursued their evil ways even more boldly, eagerly staining their hands with gold that had upon it the curse of dishonesty and corruption.

They levied a systematic black-mail upon every form of evil doing, and "protected" the Devil's agents who shared with them their ill-gotten gains, from any terrors the law might have for them. Soul-destruction was licensed; bribes were unblushingly accepted; and even the judicial ermine was stained by decisions dictated by those who controlled the administrative affairs of the city.

Saloons, gambling dens, and brothels did a thriving business because a goodly proportion of their gains went into the coffers of the "machine," and made possible the elections which re-tained in office the friends and tools of the real political manipulators.

Satan's gilded traps to ensnare the youth of the city were left unmolested, and the Archfiend smiled approvingly upon the administration of Mayor Hypocrite.

THE MAYOR POCKETS TAINTED MONEY

"The thirst for gold is the cause of all these damnable temptations," said Evangelist to Determination, as with the Angel they walked through the City of Worldliness.

His words were scarcely spoken when I beheld the three standing over against the mayor's office, where they could see Hypocrite sitting at his desk.

Looking up, his eyes fell upon Evangelist and Determination only, for the Angel was invisible to him. Quickly he dropped his eyes upon the desk, as though he had not seen them, while a paper he was holding fell from his hand, as for a moment he felt the sting of an accusing conscience.

"You are responsible for the vice that is rampant in this city! The Lord shall require at thy hands, the souls of those who perish because of it." So spoke a voice in the soul of Hypocrite. It was the voice of the Angel, but he knew it not.

PRICE OF MANY A CRIME UNTOLD

A handful of gold lay before him. It was a bribe, which his wily henchmen had accepted from a dive-keeper whose license was about to expire. The paper to which his signature was about to be affixed, was in his hand when the Angel addressed his soul.

"I am responsible for the condition of the city, and souls that perish shall be required at my hands?" asked Hypocrite of himself as he nervously toyed with the gold. "No, indeed. I'm only a figurehead. I'm only a small part of the machine."

So saying, he gathered up the gold, and as it jingled into his pocket, I heard him say: "This is but my share in the deal anyway." Then having trampled upon conscience, he took his pen, affixed his signature to the document and passed it on to a clerk.

"There! That is done," said he as he arose.

"Yes," replied the Angel once more, "Yes, 'tis done; but thou hast sinned against the voice of conscience—thou hast sinned!"

Hypocrite frowned as he heard the condemning words, but saying to himself, "these things are done every day," he passed from the office.

A MOTHER'S INDIGNANT CURSE

That night he had a strange dream. He thought himself a king enthroned in gorgeous splendor within a marble palace, while on every hand innumerable attendants obeyed his every command. He saw his coffers filled with gold and treasure, and his soul was supremely happy until an angel appeared as he stood at eventide in the palace doorway of his dream. With a motion of her hand she caused a light to fall upon the darkness, a light which dissolved intervening barriers and showed a mother bending over her two sons who were steeped in debauchery. Turn-

"Thou art weighed in the balances, and art found wanting."

ing toward him, with eyes of piercing indignation, the mother pointed to her boys; and then at him, as she said:

"Accursed be thy kingdom and thy gold, for thou art guilty of the damnation of these, my sons."

Hypocrite awoke from the dream with great beads of perspiration standing upon his brow. Sitting upright, he gazed in consternation in the direction of the vision, but it had gone with his awaking.

"It is some wild nightmare," he said.

WHY PRIZE SO MUCH THE WORLD'S APPLAUSE?

Then came the voice again;

"In thy mad thirst for power and riches, thou art opening paths of perdition to the youths of the city. Wealth gained at such cost is poverty; power thus won, is impotence. Men are worth not what they have, but what they are."

The dream would not fade from his memory. Seated in his office on the following day, I heard him say:

"Two dreams! I wonder what they portend?"

Just then Man-of-the-World came in and said in jocular vein, as he handed his friend a check. "Here's your share of another 'rake-off.'"

Hypocrite took the check with a mere "yes?"

"I'm afraid that license matter yesterday was all wrong, Man-of-the-World," he ventured by way of changing the conversation.

"Wrong! Nothing is considered wrong in this game. There

is no such word in our lexicon. Brace up! That was all right. Did you not get the fee?"

"Yes, but it 's blood money," replied Hypocrite.

"Don't be chicken-hearted," replied Man-of-the-World. "Has Evangelist been after you again?" and with this he laughed heartily.

Throughout the day, the memory of his dream came and went, and as often, the accusing finger of the mother made Hypocrite miserable; while the words: "Thou art guilty," alternated with the message of the Angel.

HOARDED, BARTERED, BOUGHT AND SOLD

Unseen, the Good Angel had followed Hypocrite that day, and when, that evening, in the home of Miss Sincere, she communicated the fact of his troubled soul to Evangelist and Determination, I heard the good prophet say:

"Hypocrite hath power and is possessed of great riches, but the time shall come when he shall say, 'I have no pleasure in them.' "

As these words fell upon my ears, I felt an invisible hand lead me from the spot. Easily we traversed the space between the City of Worldliness and the valley in which my tent was pitched, and as I threw myself upon the cushions where Evangelist had sat, I heard a voice which I recognized as that of the Angel say:

"Rest now, Child of the Vision, for on the morrow, thou art to see strange things."

CHAPTER VI

The House of Selfishness

"Sin of self-love possesseth all mine eye
    And all my soul and all my every part;
And for this sin there is no remedy,
    It is so grounded inward in my heart.

"Methinks no face so gracious is as mine,
    No shape so true, no truth of such account;
And for myself mine own worth do define,
    As I all other in all worths surmount.

"But when my glass shows me myself indeed,
    Beated and chopp'd with tann'd antiquity,
Mine own self-love quite contrary I read;
    Self so self-loving were iniquity."
        —*Shakespeare, "Songs and Sonnets."*

IT was a dewy morning world upon which I looked. The keen breath of the woods came sweetly to me; a band of puzzled bees droned nearby in the grass. The young day was very fair, and as I drank in its beauty I seemed borne away upon the perfumed air.

On I floated, as in a vague warm dream, and soon the words of the Angel came back to me and I remembered that I was to see strange things that day. As I mused upon what these might be, all sense of limitation fell away, and I thanked God for a mind that could receive and hold all that should be shown to me.

WHOLE-SOUL AND DETERMINATION SEEK THE HILLS

When my feet touched the ground, I was beside the King's Highway where it left a grove of shapely rounded elms. Just beyond, the massive trunk of a venerable oak marked the spot where a road led away to the hills. Passing along this road, although some distance from me, I could discern the figures of Whole-Soul and Determination.

Soon I was able to overtake them, and, although they knew it not, I was their companion as they breasted the ascent and stood at last upon a sort of table land or plateau, gazing upon an imposing edifice in the midst of a handsome park, upon which much skill and labor had been expended.

From where we stood we could see men and women, with singular countenances and staid demeanor, moving about the grounds or passing in and out the edifice, with apparently no thought for anyone save themselves.

Although the sun was high in the heavens, the air was chill, and nowhere was there to be heard the song of a bird. The very water, as it ran over the rocks of an artificial stream, had a hollow sound.

The barren hills which formed a background for the scene, lay in silence under a mass of sombre clouds, and everything was wrapped in an uncanny atmosphere. Still, with all these weird conditions, those dwelling here appeared satisfied with themselves and their environment.

"This place has a strange look," said Whole-Soul as he pointed to the scene before him.

"It is indeed singular that such an isolated spot should be so well kept, and be attended by so large a concourse of people," Determination replied.

"I wonder what place this is," Whole-Soul rejoined, as they walked along a little further, stopping at a pleasant way leading into the park.

"This is indeed wonderful," said Determination as he looked up the path toward the building.

"It has the appearance of an ancient castle," Whole-Soul observed.

THE CHARMED PATH SEDUCES THEM

"Yes," Determination assented. "It certainly has upon it the marks of age, and in spite of the ungracious atmosphere there is a peculiar fascination about the place."

"I feel it too," replied Whole-Soul, and, as though led by a power they could not resist, both he and Determination would have entered the path, had it not been for the Angel who now appeared.

"Stay thy steps!" she cried. "Venture not upon the Charmed Path, for it is fraught with great danger!"

THE ANGEL BREAKS THE SPELL

By her words the charm was broken, and, as men aroused from stupor, they looked into the face of the Angel.

"Fear not," she continued. "I have come to save thee from the subtle influence of this path," and so saying, she led them forth a little way.

"What place is this?" asked Determination.

"This is the hill upon which the Christ was once tempted; and yonder edifice is known as the House of Selfishness," the Angel answered.

"The Hill upon which He was tempted!" said Whole-Soul, soliloquizing.

"Yes, the mount of a far-reaching temptation," replied the Angel. "And those who inhabit this place were tempted of Satan to set forth upon the Charmed Path."

"It is then of the Archfiend's planning," ventured Determination as he strained his eyes to see far into the place.

"It is his plan to thwart Christians by deadening their sense of love for mankind, and recentering life upon self," said the Angel.

SELF-LOVE APPEARS

"But look ye yonder!" she continued, as she pointed to the Charmed Way, where there appeared an old man who stood with extended arms close by the house, while in the path were a number of persons bearing peculiar looking parcels. Impelled by the will of this old man they rushed forward and were soon lost within the place.

"Who are these?" asked Whole-Soul.

"These are they, who, susceptible to greed and self-satisfaction, have yielded to the magnetism and charm of the keeper of the place," answered the Angel.

"And who is the keeper of the place?" Determination asked.

"One whose name is Self-Love, a man of many years, and a warm friend, although a dupe, of the Archfiend," the Angel replied.

"Then he hath served long in this place," rejoined Determination.

"Yes," she responded, "since the place was first instituted; then it was that the Archfiend gave him charge of it. He hath been a trusted servant."

IN SELFISH BONDS

"When was this establishment begun?" asked Whole-Soul.

"Since the day when the first parents disobeyed the will of God to please self," the Angel sadly replied.

"Is it then an imprisonment to reside here?" asked Determination.

"Those who live here, do not so regard it; but none are so surely incarcerated as those who have suffered the finer sensibilities of the soul to be bound by the treacherous hands of Self-Love," she answered.

"And are there many who are imprisoned?"

"Thousands live and end their days here," replied the Angel with a tone of regret.

Thus I learned the nature of the place and understood the plan by which Satan fastened his curse upon the souls whom he thus ensnared. Every comfort calculated to gratify the individual, characterized the appointments of the edifice, where scores of servants moved about anticipating the whims and foibles of those who resided here.

DECEPTION COMES ON THE SCENE

Then I beheld one hurry by and pass up the Charmed Way, and noted that his manner betokened familiarity with the place. Self-Love, the keeper, came forth to meet him, and extended his hand cordially in his greeting.

"What success?" he inquired of the new comer.

"Only fair," was the reply.

"Hast thou had a long journey?" Self-Love again inquired.

"Quite a way. I have just now come from the castle, whither I went for further instruction," he replied.

It occurred to me that I had seen this one before, but I was confused in mind as to where it had been, and what might be his name.

Then I heard the Angel say:

"Self-Love and Deception are men of bold action and have enticed thousands up yonder path and lodged them in the House of Selfishness."

Then I knew that the stranger was none other than Deception, the colleague of Satan, whom I had seen aforetime.

"'Fifty thousand dollars for one vote!' exclaimed Minister Good."

THE HOUSE OF SELFISHNESS

Within the House of Selfishness which had been furnished by the Archfiend, I saw two men seated comfortably by a window, and noticed how thoroughly absorbed they were with self as they looked out upon an expanse of country called the Park of Ease.

MAN-OF-THE-WORLD AND HYPOCRITE AT THEIR EASE

Looking again, I saw that the two were Man-of-the-World and Hypocrite.

Falling in with Deception some days before, he had led them into the Charmed Path and introduced them to Self-Love, who, by reason of their standing in the city, paid special attention to their comfort.

"This is indeed a remarkable spot," said Man-of-the-World. "The atmosphere frees you of all relation to others. One has time to give thought and attention to self."

"There is nothing like doing as you please, and the sense of independence which prevails here is certainly delicious," answered Hypocrite.

"Every one for himself, is our motto here," said Self-Love to the two. "Eat, drink and be merry. Let the world run on. We have solved the secret of getting rid of all anxiety concerning others."

"It is indeed refreshing," they both replied.

As Determination and Whole-Soul turned to go toward the city where they intended to meet Evangelist, the Angel said to them: "Now thou dost know that, he that saveth his life shall lose it."

Again I saw the dark clouds touch the rim of the barren hills, as the Angel parted from the two; and then I heard her say as she passed on toward the Valley of the Cross:

"Would I might rescue those who tarry within yonder dwelling, ere their souls become insensible to the needs of mankind."

THE COUNCIL AT THE PARSONAGE

Whole-Soul and Determination found Evangelist at the home of Minister Good, and after relating the experiences of the morning, began to question him regarding the House of Selfishness. In reply, the prophet, who had long known of its existence, told them many things, which I, still their unseen companion, could hear as well.

"The House of Selfishness," said Evangelist, "was created by Satan at the time his Castle of All Evil was built. To Self-Love, the keeper, whom you saw, was committed the task of its construction, and when the house was completed, the management of it was entrusted to him. So well has he attended to his duties that a great host are yearly ensnared by the subtleties of its comforts, and seldom are able to quit this abode. The House of Selfishness hath been the source of great harm to the race; and some day the forces of the Christian Church must be massed against it."

"The place is certainly a great evil to mankind, and yet, it stands not a great ways distant from the Cross," replied Determination.

"All of Satan's strongest conceptions are worked within this vicinity; for he recognizes the Cross as the point from which the power of the Church proceeds," explained the prophet.

"We understand," answered Whole-Soul. "Dwelleth any other soul in this section?"

THE STORY OF MISER

"Yes, one by the name of Miser, who was educated by Self-Love centuries ago. He established himself on the hillside beyond the park in which it stands, that he might have ever in sight the House of Selfishness. He is gray, being of great age and hath accumulated much wealth," answered Evangelist.

"To what purpose does he live?" asked Determination.

"To none save himself and his gold. He despiseth the cry of the poor and those in distress, and seldom departs from the seclusion of his chosen resort."

"And is he a friend of Self-Love, who keeps the House of Selfishness?" queried Whole-Soul.

"Yes," answered the prophet. "The two have been close friends for centuries, and through them, the Archfiend hath done much to retard the progress of Christ's Kingdom, for they have discipled all nations with their false philosophy."

With these words, his form and that of the other faithful servants of the Most High, melted away into shadows and then were lost entirely.

THE ANGEL INSTRUCTS DETERMINATION

Once more that day, I saw Determination, and the Angel was

with him; for they had met beyond the city in the Valley of the Cross. It was night, and in the distance, the House of Selfishness could be plainly seen by reason of the blaze of light which streamed from its many windows.

"Son of man," the Angel said, "it is for thee to defeat the projects of Satan in yonder place. The Lord hath directed me to guide thee in the undertaking."

"I shall follow thy instructions," Determination replied, and so saying, the two passed along the King's Highway till they came to a knoll where they sat down to confer.

Then I saw the Archfiend stealing noiselessly along in the shadow to learn the secret of their conference.

"Begone, thou Enemy of Souls! Begone!" cried the Angel whose keen sense had detected the satanic presence; and then as her finger steadily pointed at him, the heart of Satan failed him and he hastened into the darkness, and the two were left alone.

THE HOUSE OF SELFISHNESS IS DOOMED

"Thou hast before thee a task demanding much wisdom and patience," said the Angel to Determination, "but the Lord will supply thy need according to His riches of grace in Christ Jesus. Fear not, for thou shalt succeed as thou hast hitherto done."

"With thy help, I shall not hesitate to undertake the annihilation of the House of Selfishness," answered Determination.

Then the Angel began to instruct him concerning the place, first revealing the Archfiend's purpose in locating the edifice at that spot.

THE HOUSE OF SELFISHNESS

"Thou hast seen the bare hills which lie between the house and the Cross?" she asked.

"I have seen them and the dense clouds which rest upon their barren crests," replied Determination.

THE HILLS OF DELUSION HIDE THE CROSS

"These are known as the Hills of Delusion," she continued, "and serve as a wall by which to hide the Cross from the eyes of those who dwell under the care of Self-Love. Satan, in locating the house, planned that these barren hills should serve this purpose."

"Many of those who dwell there, have seen the Cross and heard the message concerning it," said Determination.

"Yes," replied the Angel. "This is true, but the spirit of the house can alone be taught to those from whose soul the vision of the Cross is concealed."

"To thee it is given to destroy the work of Satan which hath long been operative in this place. The Lord shall aid thee. Seek wisdom of Him," and thus assuring him, the Angel departed and Determination was alone.

"What canst thou do?" said a voice out of the night, and with the words, Determination heard a mocking laughter from the darkness.

"It is the Enemy. Fear him not," whispered a voice within his soul.

DETERMINATION DEFIES THE DEVIL

"Get thee behind me, Satan!" said Determination with a voice of resolve which caused a tremor of fear within the Archfiend.

THE HOUSE OF SELFISHNESS

"This desert shall yet bloom; and the glory of the Cross shall yet bathe the fields in which the insidious poisons of thy vile heart have been sown. The Lord Almighty hath named an end to thy liberties, and I am he upon whom the task of redemption hath fallen. I defy thee and all thy demoniac band!"

"We must go and warn Self-Love against this man. All must be on guard at the House of Selfishness, for this fellow hath worsted our plans heretofore," said Deception, "for it was he who had mocked the fearless servant of God."

"It is the only thing to do," replied Satan, who accompanied Deception.

"O God, give to me Thy strength, and lead me in Thy ways, that I may bring the influence of Thy love unto the souls of those who abide in the House of Selfishness."

With these words, Determination voiced his desire to the Lord of Hosts, as for a time he tarried upon the knoll in the darkness.

"Go thou forward, I shall be with thee," came the words of assurance to his soul.

DETERMINATION DELIVERS HIS MESSAGE

On the morrow, Determination stood within the grounds around the House of Selfishness. The keeper, Self-Love, was much confused by his presence; for many began to gather about Determination as he stood in the Park of Ease preaching in plain words against the witchery of the place, and with great earnestness describing the glory of the Cross which lay beyond the Hills of Delusion.

Many doubted the message and sank back into ease, while others believed his words and expressed a desire to journey thither.

"We make a pilgrimage on the morrow," said Determination. "We shall stand upon yonder barren hills and behold the beautiful land of the Cross in which dwell the children of the King of Kings; the land in which all is love; and where no evil thing can offend."

"We shall go with thee, that our eyes may behold the glorious land of which thou hast spoken," said quite a number.

"And have ye never journeyed to the summit of yonder hills to behold what lies beyond?" asked Determination.

"It is against the rule of the place; and Self-Love forbids those who live here to journey further than the Park of Ease," they explained.

SELF-LOVE AND DECEPTION ARE SCARED

Then I beheld that the old keeper was in great confusion of mind; and that soon he and Deception were closeted together seeking to devise means to defeat the work of Determination.

At length it was agreed that Deception should address the people, and soon they gathered in a large auditorium, each wearing upon the face the marks of selfishness which had its severest expression in the hard and cruel lineaments of Self-Love, who occupied a prominent seat.

In well chosen words, Deception sought to lull the hearts of such as had heard the message of Determination, into complete satisfaction with themselves and their surroundings.

"Trouble begins for all when their eyes have once seen beyond the hills," he announced. "To keep the heart placid and undisturbed by considerations other than those for your own comfort and peace, this place, into which good Self-Love hath led you, hath been provided."

The old keeper, with a grin upon his wrinkled face, nodded his head in confirmation of Deception's words.

THERE IS A GRANDER LIFE

Suddenly the door opened, and there stood Determination, whom many had come to know by name. Both disgust and chagrin showed themselves upon the faces of Self-Love and Deception.

"Let the young man speak!" cried many voices. "Let him state his mission!"

Amid words of protest from Self-Love and his plausible colleague, Determination said:

"The story of the heart is recorded upon the face; and I behold lines of disappointment drawn upon the countenances of those here gathered.

"There is a grander life than that which is here taught. The Christ whose shining Cross yet stands beyond the hills which cloud this valley, lived to bear the wealth of love's blessing to all mankind. He went about doing good. He taught, and experi-

"The procession arrived at the 'Pavilion of Pleasure.'"

ence hath proved the truth of His words, that those who keep life but for themselves shall lose its joys. There can no harm come in beholding the Cross except to disturb the hurtful complacency of this life. To-morrow at day-break, we shall cross the Hills of Delusion and behold the splendid vision of the Cross," so saying, Determination left the place.

These words of the stranger broke up the repose of spirit into which many of this house had drifted; and the desire upon the part of them to look beyond the hills, put at naught the persuasions of Self-Love and Deception which quickly followed the announcement of Determination.

EVANGELIST LEADS A PILGRIMAGE

Evangelist, who had learned through the Angel, of Determination's labors, gathered a number of faithful men, among whom was Whole-Soul, and started with the desire of facilitating the efforts of this servant of God. "We shall seek the summit of the hills, and there we shall meet Determination and those whom God gives him, to behold the Cross."

In my vision I saw the prophet and his company traverse the Valley of the Cross, and beheld them toiling up the barren hills. The first streaks of dawn welcomed them as they stood upon the crest, and saw the Hill of Calvary emblazoned with the glories of a new day which held the promise of great victory for God, over hearts long chained by the enslavement of Self-Love and his servants.

"Let us pray while we await their coming," said Evangelist,

and there under the mist clouds which were being kissed away by the sun, the company knelt and sought divine leading for the work of the day.

THE WAY IS MADE EASY

By direction of the Angel, Determination, as he led forth his party from the House of Self-Love, came upon the path which Evangelist and his company had made, and marvelled within his soul that the way to the mountain should have been thus prepared for their ascent.

Enthusiasm everywhere abounded and the spirit of Determination possessed the mind of all who followed him.

"Here they come!" shouted Whole-Soul as he cast his expectant eyes toward the House of Selfishness. "Here they come, and in the lead is Determination!" Then across the barren crest of the hills rang out a chorus of jubilant voices, which put new heart into all who had made the toilsome ascent.

Then came the great moment when the two companies met. The eyes of all from the fold of Self-Love rested upon the gray prophet, who welcomed Determination and gave to each of the company an earnest word of salutation, in the name of his God.

THE CROSS IS IN SIGHT

"Yonder lies the object of thy quest," said he, as with his staff the prophet pointed to the Cross which stood as a work of pure gold under the marvelous touch of the morning sunlight

The company stood in silence as they beheld the scene, and in turn Evangelist and Determination interpreted to them the story of love written for all mankind by Him who once hung upon it.

"He calleth thee to leave the abode of ease and comfort of which the keeper is Self-Love. He calleth thee, to follow with us, in His path; for after all, no way is so charmed with blessings as the way He took to heal the hearts of the sinful and lowly," pleaded Evangelist.

"We have sinned; we have been ensnared by the cruel philosophy of Self-Love; we shall follow Jesus," replied the company.

" 'Tis the way of Sacrifice; 'tis the way of the Cross; but the path is rich with blessings; for His angels yet walk with such as have His mind," added the prophet.

Then as the glories of the light from beyond pencilled the hills with a glory such as they had never seen, the company burst forth in a song which Whole-Soul taught them, and I listened with rapture to the words by which those of the House of Selfishness consecrated their lives to the mission of the Cross. The barren hills echoed and re-echoed the sound of their voices and carried the song nigh to their former home hard by the Park of Ease.

"It is our duty, in the name of the Christ, to destroy the influence of the House of Selfishness, and rescue those who are daily led into its retreat," explained Determination to those who had followed him.

THE SEED CALLED HEART'S DESIRE

A member of the company then revealed to Determination one

of the secrets of Self-Love by which many, passing along the King's Highway, were tempted to enter the House of Selfishness.

"Close to the Charmed Path," said he, "lies a field in which Deception and Self-Love have planted a seed called Heart's Desire, and this, when matured, exhales a fragrance which stupefies the nobler purposes of those of weak resolve who pass by. Close to this field, thousands have halted, only to find the warm hand of Self-Love clasping theirs. Then he entices them into the Charmed Path and soon he has them in the House of Selfishness. Thus we came to it; and had it not been for thee, the vision from beyond the barren hills had never been seen by us."

"It is of Satan's sowing, this field of Heart's Desire," said Evangelist who had listened intently. "Herein lies the danger to pilgrims' feet. Temptations in these days come with fragrant breath."

Then I beheld the Angel take Determination aside and whisper to him a message of instruction, and as he returned, his face was bright with the light of a new resolve, which took shape later. Gathering his company to him they stole out in the hours of the night and mowed down the growth of the field; and as morning dawned, Self-Love looked forth to behold it withering upon the ground.

OTHERS SEEK THE BARREN HILLS

From his house by the hillside, Miser marked the change in the atmosphere, and many who had dwelt with ease and nonchalance within the home of Self-Love began to grow restless and discontented. Longings for departure came into their hearts, and not many days after, the old keeper stood in despair at the entrance of the Charmed Path entreating passing pilgrims to enter. His power was gone.

Daily, those of his household took the path Determination had made, and each morning the barren hills witnessed the presence of those who longed to look beyond. Evangelist was there to instruct them in the meaning of the life of which the Cross spoke; and such as made the pilgrimage returned not, but followed Determination into the path of a life of loving devotion to truth, and service among men.

BUT SEE HIM ON THE EDGE OF LIFE

Deception lost heart as he saw the waning prestige of the House of Selfishness; and a wail of lament went forth from the soul of Self-Love as he acknowledged the hopeless plight into which, after the labors of long years, he had fallen.

Miser sought to comfort him in his despair, but lo, his soul, as well, was in the hold of helpless confusion, and the wrath of Satan but added to the indescribable misery of the pair.

"Thy house is left deserted; thy choice field is waste, and thy mountain of defense hath become the battlements from which pilgrims behold the Cross and learn the message of the Saviour's love," said Evangelist as he met the miserable old man. "Come thou with us. Deny thyself and follow the Christ."

Self-Love looked wonderingly into the face of the prophet; but much as his desire struggled, the chains of the past bound him, and in my vision I beheld him standing alone under a starless sky, with the day of his once fair hopes fading beyond his reach.

SATAN CURSES HIS TOOLS

His house was empty. A strange sense of abject loneliness hung as a depressing vapor upon the place; and in the hush of night, the hooting of the owls alone broke the silence, as they flitted to and fro along the eaves of the empty edifice. The sobs of Self-Love were pitiable; for sleep was now a stranger to his eyes; and by his bed were none to comfort; for the Archfiend in derision stood there heaping upon his crushed and disappointed spirit, volleys of wrath and displeasure.

"Again hath the Almighty torn asunder my plans! Again hath these puppets of His thwarted me! The trusted servants in whom I placed the utmost confidence are impotent to serve me!" muttered Satan as he passed into the night; only to hear a song of triumph from the company of Determination encamped upon the hills between him and the Cross.

"Child of the Vision," said a voice beside me, as alone in my tent I meditated long and deeply. "Did I not tell thee thou shouldst see strange things? Take thy rest now, for on the morrow, much more shall be revealed to thee. God has thee in His holy keeping."

Then kind sleep wrapped me in its arms and I knew no more.

CHAPTER VII

THE PATH OF THE PRIMROSE

> "You must begin your education with the distinct resolution to know what is true, and make choice of the straight and rough road to such knowledge. This choice is offered to every youth and maid at some moment of their life;—choice between the easy downward road, so broad that we can dance down it in companies, and the steep and narrow way which we must enter alone."
> —*Browning, "Mornings in Florence."*

I WAS awakened by the touch of the Angel's hand, and together we left the tent in the valley. "This day thou shalt stand upon the Hill of Prospect," she said in answer to the question in my eyes.

The way was long and steep and the summit was only reached after much arduous climbing, but the clear atmosphere at that height gave to my eyes a far-reaching sight.

Then the Angel handed me a glass of curious form and bade me look through it in the direction she indicated. "Thou shalt see spiritual things," she said; and at her words my soul was strangely stirred, for as I looked I beheld the Bridge of Sighs, and passing over it was the great company of the redeemed from all the nations of the earth.

"Look to the far land beyond the bridge," she said, and I obeyed; and then, for the first time, I saw with rapture the "city which hath foundations, whose builder and maker is God." To this holy and glorious city the vast multitude were hastening with gladdened steps. Willingly would I have gazed upon it for hours and days, but my guide soon bade me turn away from the joyous vision, and before the glass arose the world in which I had my sojourn.

A GREAT LIGHT FALLS UPON THE CITY

Before my eyes rose the City of Worldliness, and as I beheld that home of greed and corruption, a great search-light fell upon it. The doings of its people soon became plainly visible. The light pierced the walls of the houses, and I saw those who lived within the great city, the pious and the sinful alike, the pure of heart and the corrupt.

"Now thou dost see as God sees," said the Angel, "for there is nothing hidden from His view."

I placed my hands to my eyes, seeking to hide the soul-disturbing vision, but the Angel said:

UNDER THE LIGHT OF REVELATION

"Let not thy heart fail thee. I have brought thee here to behold the secret depths of the city under the search-light of revelation, for the Lord has appointed thee to behold its sin and hideous hypocrisy and to reveal them to the world."

I looked again. Still the light grew more piercing. Before me lay the false and foul conditions of modern society, and I saw, afar, the Primrose Path by which Satan leads his blinded victims into the Pit of Destruction. The city's walls and roofs grew thin as delicate draperies, and became transparent as the strange light touched them. From mansion to hovel, the loathsome tragedies of sin were being enacted before my eyes.

THE LIGHT FALLS UPON THE CROSS

"Where is the hope of salvation amid such sinful scenes as these?" I asked.

"Be not of doubtful mind," replied the Angel; and as she spoke the light was turned aside and its searching gleam fell upon the Cross whereupon had hung the world's Redeemer.

"Here is the hope you crave," she said, "for it is written, 'And I, if I be lifted up from the earth, will draw all men unto me.'"

With these words she vanished, and sadly I retraced my steps. At the foot of the hill I met a venerable form, which I recognized as that of Evangelist.

"Whence hast thou come?" he inquired.

Then I told him of the vision which it had been mine to behold, and of the terrible array of sin which had been revealed to me within the great city.

"Ah, thou hast seen it from a distance," said he. "I have come from its midst and have witnessed it in all its noisomeness."

"And what has been thy mission there?" I ventured to inquire.

"To bear the name of the Christ to the downtrodden," he answered.

Far as the city was, I quickly reached it in my dream, Evangelist still beside me. As we passed through the streets, he showed me many of the things he had learned.

THE PLEASING BEGINNINGS OF SIN

He brought me to a large mansion, where feasting, music, and dancing were in progress, and the effect of the wine-cup was visible in the faces of many of those present.

"Have I not seen this place before?" I asked.

"Very likely. It is the home of Mr. Hypocrite, the mayor of the city—the man who grants unbridled license to sins which undermine the morality of its citizens."

Men and women, many of them pillars in the churches, were there, sharing in the pleasures of worldly dissipation, forgetful of the vows which they had taken.

"These are the beginnings of sin," said Evangelist. "While the sweet is yet unmixed with the bitter, it is hard to turn men from the paths of error."

"From the Hill of Prospect I saw the end to which such beginnings lead," I said. "Will the Lord spare the city?"

"The Lord is very long-suffering. It is not His desire that any should perish," he answered.

"But many of these who are walking in the ways of sin have wilfully broken away from the influences of religion, and wantonly chosen a life of dissipation and pleasure; will He not punish such?"

"The time of all such shall come. Sorrow, like wormwood, shall in time be mingled with their wine, and wails of anguish shall supplant their songs of merriment and feasting," gravely said the patriarch.

THE ANGEL PLEADS FOR THE CITY

Passing onward, and witnessing scene after scene of sinfulness, we came at length to the city's confines, and here, in a moment, I found myself alone. I turned my eyes backward and again looked upon the city, which lay in its iniquity under the cover of darkness, for night had fallen as we pursued our mission. Suddenly I saw above, in the air, the form of the Angel with hands outstretched and head uplifted, facing the Cross.

"O God, spare this city! Spare it, Almighty Father! and save Thy erring people!" she cried in thrilling accents. "Spare it for the sake of Him who was crucified for the sake of the whole world upon yonder Cross."

Then I heard a voice from out the great depth of Heaven in answer to the prayer of the Angel.

"Thy intercession hath reached mine ear, and in the name and by the power of Him who sitteth on my right hand, thy prayer in behalf of the city shall be answered."

DETERMINATION PROPOSES TO REFORM THE CITY

Then, her face beaming with joy, the form of the Angel faded and the light died away. The wonderful scene which I had been suffered to behold vanished and I was amid earthly things again.

Near me stood one with familiar face. A second look showed me it was Determination, who had led the company to the Cross and who also had, at the instance of the Angel, mastered the intrigues of Satan in the Valley of the Mist.

I had last seen him planning to cut down the growth of Heart's Desire in the pleasant field by the Charmed Path, and now upon his face was the stern look of resolution which he had then borne. There were with him a number of earnest souls, and listening to their words, I found they were conversant with the perilous condition of the city, and also heard them with intense enthusiasm pledge themselves to seek to reform it.

"You then have traversed and studied it?" I asked of Determination. "You are familiar with its evil ways?"

"I have been here many times with Evangelist, in his work of mercy," he replied.

SATAN TEACHES A FALSE PHILOSOPHY

He went on to give me a vivid description of the corruption which he found to prevail, adding: "And Satan has an army of quiet workers in this city, who, by teaching false philosophy concerning life, are corrupting the very elect.

"Not a day passes but what the wives and daughters of prominent men play games for the sake of paltry prizes; and so steeped are they in this empty frivolity, that they are ready to sacrifice their home, time, health, and the few offices of mercy to which hitherto their most gracious hours and earnest prayers were given."

"Thousands spent their time on the 'Boardwalk.'"

"What can be done to remedy these conditions?" I asked.

"For this very work we have come," said Determination. "By the power of the Cross, we propose to inaugurate a movement which shall reform and cleanse the city."

"Thy discernment of the city's sin is too true, and the need of a thorough cleansing is everywhere apparent, but think you that thy methods are the wisest?" I asked.

"I have planned to prove them so," he replied.

Then he left me, and in a moment more the Guardian Angel stood by my side.

THE SILENT WORK OF THE ANGEL

"Whence camest thou?" I inquired

"From prayer and silent work among those who this past night have strayed from their higher and truer convictions," replied the Angel.

"Hast thou met with Determination, who, with others like himself, is seeking to reform the city?" I asked.

"Yes," replied the Angel, "and I sought to dissuade him from pursuing his purpose along the lines he has in mind. The slumbering conscience, first of all, needs awakening, and perhaps the harvest of sin must be gathered, before the bitterness of the pleasures which now engage men is fully realized."

SATAN ORDERS SIN MADE MORE POPULAR

Then the Angel once more took me by the hand, and unseen we

traversed many streets. Halting before one of the most fashionable drinking-places in the city, she pushed back the door and we passed in. Beyond were quiet rooms, and in one of these we saw Satan and a band of his most skilful fiends.

"I hear the city is to be reformed," he was saying. "I wonder if these fanatics think I can be deposed from the rulership of this great human hive?

"Fill the city with new pleasures and delights, and see to it that they are made as attractive and enticing as possible. Seek to introduce each sin by making it popular among the aristocracy. Mr. Hypocrite and Mr. Man-of-the-World will be successful leaders if you can interest them. This is an age of pleasure-seeking, and if you can allure the young, you have solved the problem."

"We shall execute your orders," said they, and sallied forth.

"Now," said the Angel, as once more I felt her hand touch mine, "another scene awaits you," and we departed as we had entered, unseen by mortal eyes.

MISS SINCERE'S LOVING WORK

"'The poor always ye have with you,'" the Angel had once said to Miss Sincere, and from that time the earnest worker for the Master had mingled with them daily, teaching the lessons of Jesus' love and life.

She had become especially solicitous that the children of those among whom she lovingly wrought should be kept from sinful paths as they grew to manhood and womanhood, and as a result a mission school had been begun to which she devoted much of her time and means. It was to this mission that the Angel was now leading me.

"Thou hast this night seen Satan plotting to ensnare the souls of men," she said to me. "Thou shalt now see God's child thwarting his plans." So saying, she opened the door upon which were the words GOSPEL MISSION and we passed in.

Miss-Sincere was alone in the room kneeling by her chair, and we could hear the words that fell from her lips:

>"Teach me, dear Lord, what Thou wouldst have me know;
> Guide me, dear Lord, where Thou wouldst have me go;
> Help me, dear Lord, Thy precious seed to sow;
> Bless Thou the seed that it may surely grow;
> Thus guided, helped, and taught, and blessed, I know
> That from my life a stream of love shall flow
> To brighten other lives where'er I go.
> In my heart, dear Lord, Thy blest abode now take,
> And grant my prayer, dear Lord, for Jesus' sake."

"Her work for the day is over," said the Angel, as we regained the street. "She is asking guidance for the morrow. Her work is pleasing to the Lord."

With these words, the Angel left me, and as I stood watching her retreating figure I was swiftly caught up and borne along until I was set down at the door of the tent which I had come to look upon as my earthly home.

The sun was high in the heavens when I awakened, and soon I

was on my way back to the City of Worldliness where I hoped to find the Angel.

THE PATH OF THE PRIMROSE

Before reaching the city, however, I met Evangelist, who had just left it on an errand of mercy to a home in the valley. While we were conversing, quite a company of young men and women came out of the city, and the prophet accosted them.

"Whence journey ye?" he asked.

"To the Pavilion of Pleasure," replied one whose name was Light Heart.

"This is not a safe path for inexperienced feet like thine," rejoined Evangelist.

"Pay no attention to him, he is some old fanatic," said Light Heart to his companions, at which they all raised a shout of laughter.

With Light Heart were two others, who, with himself, seemed to be leaders of the company. Their names were Presumption and Incredulous. As the three loitered somewhat behind their companions, who had gone forward merrily, Evangelist entered into conversation with them.

"Knowest thou the name of this highway?" he asked.

"It is called the Path of the Primrose," was the reply.

"So it is," said Evangelist. "It takes its name from the flowers which border it, but knowest thou the dangers which lurk nigh to it?"

"There are no dangers," hastily replied Presumption.

"You cannot frighten us," said Light Heart.

"Far be it from me to fill thy souls with false fears, or to limit thee in any legitimate pleasure; but this is one of the ways of death which Satan maintains for the peril of immortal souls, such as those of your merry company," said Evangelist.

"Ha! Ha!" laughed Incredulous, "you cannot turn us back with such chaff; thousands of others have taken this way and have come to no harm."

"Little dost thou know, my young friend, of what has happened along this road. These primroses are placed here by design. The peril is hidden by the flowers."

At this the three laughed loudly, and hurried on to join their friends.

Bidding adieu to the good prophet, I kept on my way to the city, and entering it moved slowly along its busy streets meditating upon Evangelist's warning to those who danced so merrily along the Primrose Path.

Seeming to care not where I went, I allowed myself to be carried along by the human current that ebbed and flowed along the thoroughfares, and, although I saw much that day, I made no record of what befell me until night had fallen upon the fevered city. Then I felt once more the touch of the Angel's hand, and under her guidance saw many strange things.

SATAN'S MIDNIGHT MARAUDERS

Passing along the quiet streets, I saw Satan meet a band of his demons whose errand was to entrap the young. The leader of the company saluted the Archfiend and then said:

"Old Evangelist and the Angel intend to reveal the truth concerning the Primrose Path. I fear that the young people of the city will detect the danger ere we can entrap them."

"That's news to me," rejoined Satan. "Are these two at work again in the city? See to it that the path is well kept, and suffer not these untiring enemies of ours to destroy our work."

"Who can hinder them if they begin to show the dangers of the Primrose Path?" asked one who remembered some past experience.

"Stir up trouble everywhere, and so take their attention from the Pavilion of Pleasure," was Satan's reply.

"That man, Determination, is working in the city and has wrought much damage already," said Satan to himself, "but nothing that cannot be repaired," he added. "He is too hasty. Evangelist and the Angel are our most formidable antagonists."

THE PIT OF DEATH

During the night Evangelist prayed, and in answer the Lord caused a great death-dew to fall upon the flowers along the Primrose Path, and in the morning their beauty was consumed and the borders of the Pit of Death, which they had concealed, were plainly to be seen.

"See! See! the danger of this path," said Evangelist to those who had come forth from the city to behold the unusual sight. "Yonder pavilion at which the young people of the city congregate is but a snare of the Devil, and these flowers were intended to conceal the death-trap into which a great number have already fallen.

"Come near," he entreated, as Determination and his company raked back the dead flowers. "Gaze upon this," as he pointed to the ravine where lay the bones of hundreds of young men and women who had fallen over the brink and there found an untimely death. As they looked upon the scene, all shrank back and many fainted.

"Look ye all!" cried Evangelist. "There lies the harvest of the city's recklessness and sin. The Lord will not hold those in authority innocent of this work."

Once more the multitude looked down upon the dry bones of those slain by the lust of pleasure, as they lay there in the light of the morning sun.

EVANGELIST SOUNDS A NOTE OF WARNING

Satan stood not far from Evangelist as he denounced the sins of the city, and dared not utter one word in defense of the calamity he had secretly wrought.

As the Angel sought to direct attention to him, he fled, while the gathering multitude lingered near the valley of dead bones, to hear from the lips of the prophet the words of warning to such as were lovers of pleasure rather than lovers of God.

" 'Turn ye even to me with all your heart, and with fasting, and with weeping, and with mourning: and rend your heart, and not your garments, and turn unto the Lord your God: for he is gracious and merciful, slow to anger, and of great kindness, and repenteth him of the evil.'" With these words did Evangelist address the multitude as they gazed into the ravine below, where lay those whom the very sins they tolerated and encouraged had slain.

Hypocrite stood amid the crowd, and as he looked up into the face of Evangelist, he saw that the keen gaze of the patriarch's eyes was upon him; and he remembered the message of this man to him days before. Trembling with fear, he turned his face back toward the city; and the Angel whispered in his soul again: "Thou art weighed in the balances, and art found wanting!"

The Angel, hitherto unseen, now came forth, and, standing by the side of Evangelist, awed the gazing company, for they looked upon her as an apparition.

"Fear not," said she, and, with outstretched hands, she pointed them to the Cross on the Lonely Hill.

"Look! Look!" she continued, "salvation for this city and for each soul lies in the sacrifice for sin which was there made of God in the crucifixion of His only Son."

THE PIT OF DEATH IS CLOSED

The day following the exposure of the dangerous chasm bordering on the Primrose Path, a violent earthquake shook the city to its very foundations; and the great ravine into which the youth of the City of Worldliness had found their death, through the dalliance of the Primrose Way, was closed as by the direct intervention of Providence.

That evening, still in my vision, I saw two men, under shelter of the darkness, walk toward the place where the chasm had been closed by the earthquake. When they reached the spot, the moon broke through the huddled clouds and its beams fell upon the faces of the twain, and I saw they were those of Mayor Hypocrite and Mr. Man-of-the-World.

HYPOCRITE AND MAN-OF-THE-WORLD WALK ABROAD

"It has been levelled as though the work of man did it," said the Mayor.

"It is certainly a clean job. There is not even a trace left of the chasm," added Man-of-the-World.

"This is where I stood yesterday when Evangelist addressed the crowd by the pit's mouth. It was a hideous sight with the Primroses gone," spoke Hypocrite.

"The Angel was also here, was she not?" interrogated Man-of-the-World.

"Yes, she stood with the prophet. It was her hand that singled me out. That is a strange couple."

"They certainly are," replied Man-of-the-World.

THE WRITING ON THE CLOUDS

As the two turned toward their homes, suddenly a bank of clouds overhead was brilliantly illuminated. As they stopped to gaze upon it, a hand appeared, and in the hand was a stylus with which it wrote, in dark letters upon the clouds, the words: *Mene, Mene, Tekel, Upharsin.*

Then by their side the Angel appeared, and pointing to the words upon the clouds, she said:

"This is the interpretation: 'Mene; God hath numbered thy kingdom, and finished it. Tekel; Thou art weighed in the balances, and art found wanting,'" and ere they could speak she vanished.

"This is a strange phenomenon," said Man-of-the-World.

"I have heard these words before, and I like not their sound," replied Hypocrite. He also recalled his dream, and the hand of the indignant mother pointing at him.

Then the two passed on in silence; for both were perplexed in heart as to the meaning of what they had seen.

The day following, Hypocrite, as mayor of the city, received a letter from Minister Good in which he strongly appealed for a more righteous government. In stirring words he pointed to the mighty workings of the hand of God in the closing of the chasm, and then he added:

"I beg of thee, in the name of God, by the power which is entrusted to thee, to destroy the works of the Devil. I pray thee be not wanting in courage in the hour when the strike for purity and righteousness may be given by the power resident in thee. That gold is dearly earned which is gathered at the sacrifice of conscience and enduring principle." So ran the words of the letter which the Mayor read over several times.

MAYOR HYPOCRITE IS TROUBLED

"Be not wanting!" These words sank into his troubled mind; for he had seen them upon the cloud.

"It is not an easy matter to govern a city," he was saying to himself, when the door of his office opened and in walked Man-of-the-World.

"Read that," said Hypocrite, as he handed him the letter of the minister.

Man-of-the-World read the communication carefully and then returned it. "Men in our positions," he said in reply, "get hundreds of this kind of letters. There should be a big pigeonhole for such communications. File it away. It's never wise to say much about such letters."

CHAPTER VIII

Judas in Twentieth-Century Clothes

"Avarice breaks all the commandments. Often has it put the weapon in the hand of the murderer; in most countries of the world it has in every age made the ordinary business of the market-places a warfare of falsehood. Why does the sale of the bodies of men and the hearts of women flourish from age to age, and practices utterly indefensible continue with the overwhelming sanction of society? It it because there is money in them. Avarice is possessed of demoniac strength; but it may help us to keep it out of our hearts to remember that it was the sin of Judas."

—*Stalker.*

"FIFTY thousand dollars for one vote in the Legislature! What do you think of that!" exclaimed Minister Good.

"It is enough to supply the needs of ten missionaries for five years," said his wife. "What is it all about?" she added.

Minister Good laid aside the paper he was reading and explained how Mr. Man-of-the-World had secretly offered this amount for the vote of a senator in behalf of a bill which he had presented.

"Did he accept the bribe?" she asked.

"Yes, it was a case of every man having his price, and the temptation was too great, I presume."

"It is too bad that such corruption obtains among those that are chosen to represent our interests at the Capitol. What is the world coming to?"

FEAR THE WORKS OF THE DEVIL

"It is hard to tell," he replied. "The Devil seems to have his own way in legislative halls. It is no longer what will conserve the highest interests of the people, but what will best fill the hoppers of the syndicates and trusts. These corporations have the money, and send out their keenest agents to search for itching palms. In the home, in the church, and in the state, there are those who are ever ready, for the sake of gold, to incarnate the Judas spirit and betray their trust."

"What is the price of manhood and integrity anyway, nowadays?" asked the wife.

"Among those who make their living as politicians, in many instances the largest bribe offered is the price," he answered.

"Satan may no longer go about as a roaring lion seeking whom he may devour, but he is here all the same, and clothed in modern dress; it is very difficult for the inexperienced eye to detect his presence," she rejoined.

"Luther saw him with horns, and tail, and cloven feet, when he flung the inkstand at him," said the minister.

"Yes, but Satan has learned to disguise himself cleverly in these times. He conceals his deceit and subterfuge under the guise of a friend. That is the way in which he operates in the world to-day," he continued, "and the eye of the experienced cannot always discover his approach."

Several times in my vision I had been taken to the home of this God-fearing couple, and upon each occasion had brought away with me something more of a desire to do the Master's will than I had ever known before. Their conversation taught me much, and as I meditated upon what I had heard this day, the room grew dim and the figures of the minister and his wife vanished into thin shadows.

Soon I felt myself borne gently along until I was set down where a cool wind blew upon my face. My eyes had seemed to be closed, but now I opened them and saw before me a castle-like structure which I knew could be no other than the abode of Satan.

Forbidding of aspect and hoary with age, this home of the Adversary crowned the summit of a rugged cliff. Dense shadows reached nearly to its highest tower and enveloped it in gloom. Its only means of access was a devious foot-path, dark and dangerous, and unfrequented, save for those who sought instructions within its walls. Upon the front of the building I could discern the words:—

SCHOOL OF MODERN METHODS

As I marvelled at the scene, I saw Mr. Hypocrite and several of his friends—all citizens of the City of Worldliness, approach and gain admittance to the castle. As they entered, something of the significance of the words above the frowning portal dawned upon me; and, turning to see if others followed them, I beheld the Guardian Angel by my side.

"How long has this school been in existence?" I inquired.

"From the year of Satan's expulsion from Heaven," replied the Angel.

"Doth the Lord know of it and its design?" I asked in my surprise.

"Yes, He knows."

"Why then doth He not shake it down by some gigantic earthquake?" I asked.

"The Lord does not so deal with this enemy. He shall hammer it down with the weapons of truth, and the day is coming when not one stone of this strong castle shall be left upon another," the Angel replied.

TALL MEN WHO LIVE ABOVE THE FOG

"Might not the soldiers of Jesus reduce this fortress of iniquity?" I inquired in my eagerness.

"If the Lord of all the earth shall give them the power to do so," the Angel answered.

"Hath it ever been attempted?" I ventured to ask.

"Yes, many impetuous and presumptuous followers of His, have, during the ages, sought to batter down the place; and once a company of devoted ones besought of the Lord that He would rain lightning upon the place and consume it," she said.

"And did He grant the request?"

"Nay," she answered.

"But why was the petition denied?"

"For reasons known alone to His eternal wisdom, He rebuked those who asked it of Him, saying, 'Ye know not what manner of spirits ye are of, for the Son of Man is not come to destroy men's lives, but to save them.'"

With these words the Angel took my hand as though to lead me toward the castle, but for fear of what might befall, I shrank back until she bid me "follow and fear not."

"Whither art thou bound?" I asked.

"To enter the castle," she replied, "that I may show thee the seductions of the Evil One, and explain to thee the arts by which he instructs his pupils."

"Is it safe?" I inquired.

"It is safe for thee in my company," the Angel made answer, and so we went forward and entered the building.

THE DARKENED WINDOWS

"Why are the windows on the East closed and darkened?" I asked the Angel, for the thing seemed strange to me. The way to the tower was also closed, and none were permitted to ascend.

"I will tell thee the reason," replied the Angel. "Years ago the Church of Christ began the work of clearing away the timber lands and leveling the mountain on this side, so that the Hill of the Cross might be visible from these heights, and immediately the windows that faced the East were darkened. None who reside here can endure the vision of the Cross."

"The Archfiend stepped into 'The Home of Lies.'"

"Why did the Church desist from the work, if it had such an influence upon Satan?" I asked.

SATAN IS LEFT ALONE

"For the reason that the Lord did not care to convert the Devil, but to save men; and so he caused the warfare upon Satan to cease, and turned the efforts of his followers upon saving a lost world," the Angel replied.

"Then the Lord does not fear Satan?" I asked.

"Not at all. His work has been outlined in the eternal ages, and what is to be, will be manifest in the years to come. There is no power in earth or hell which can hinder the purpose of His will," was the reply.

"Is not Satan a real foe to mankind, and do not his works call for the most sagacious wisdom upon the part of man?" I asked.

"Most surely," replied the Angel, "but Satan was doomed from the beginning."

THE WHOLE ARMOR OF GOD

"How should we be equipped to meet him upon the battlefield of life?" I inquired.

" 'By taking unto you the whole armor of God, that ye may be able to withstand in the evil day, and having done all to stand,' " was the reply.

"What is the armor?"

"Even the same which Jesus brought for the equipment of His followers, and left with them, upon His ascension to Bethany," the Angel replied.

162 JUDAS IN TWENTIETH-CENTURY CLOTHES

"And of what does this equipment consist?" I persisted.

"Truth, righteousness, peace, faith, salvation and the word of God; and prayer and diligent watching as well," replied my guide.

IN SATAN'S SCHOOL ROOMS

We had now come to the part of the building which contained the School of Modern Methods.

Unseen, we entered the class-rooms where teachers provided by His Satanic Majesty were busy instructing their pupils.

"Seest thou how carefully the work is done?" inquired the Angel.

"Yes," said I, "and each pupil seems anxious to catch every word of the instructor."

There were classes in deceit, in gambling, lying, thieving, murder, money-getting by up-to-date methods, and other diabolical arts; and I learned that each student was expected not only to benefit himself, but to disseminate what he learned in so subtle a manner as to seduce those of the world among whom he mingled.

There was one class much larger than any of the others, at which I wondered. The teacher was engaged in his work as we entered the room, and we heard his words.

"You are to be shrewd and plausible. Hold back for no consideration, except that of losing the prize for which you aim. The end always justifies the means. Tell the lie boldly, and in all misrepresentations look men in the face with calm eyes, lest

JUDAS IN TWENTIETH-CENTURY CLOTHES

they detect your motives. Do as the world does, and never waste any time in debating whether a thing is right or wrong. You are in it to win, and win you will, if you modernize your methods of approaching men."

"What class is this?" I asked.

"This is Satan's class of modern business methods, and the students here are from various representative professions. They are eager 'to get rich quick,' by the latest methods of the Devil," was the reply.

"Do not regard any one as a brother," the instructor continued. "Disguise your motives and strike home. What though you do cause another to lose; his loss will be your gain, and if a lie can win you the best of the bargain, use it and you will be considered the most up-to-date man on the street, and no one will be the wiser as to the secret of your success. Don't be conscientious in your dealings, for thereby many have remained poor, and crept along at the slow pace of self-denial all their lives. Live for this world."

These words were eagerly taken down in note-books with which each pupil was provided, and as we left the room, the students were in the act of applauding one of the striking sentences of this diabolic address.

JUDAS AFFECTS MODERN DRESS

"Do men of this world follow such teachings?" I inquired as we left the castle grounds.

"Yes, thousands of them, many of whom are in the higher walks of life. Men and women disregard absolutely the law of

Christ, by reason of its imposed conditions, and choose the methods of Satan because of the material gains they offer."

"Then they disguise false and low motives under the beautiful name of Christian?" I said.

"So they do," said the Angel. "There are some, who, like Judas, carry the bag, and by reason of avarice, associate with the friends of Satan, while walking in name with the followers of the Nazarene."

"Do you mean to say," I inquired, "that Judas still lives and mingles with men, dressed in twentieth-century clothes?"

"That is one way of stating the lamentable fact," she continued.

"And shall such continue to live on under the guise of this falseness, and daily deceive those with whom they move?" I asked.

"I fear it shall be so until the children of God look upon all the dealings of life in the Christ spirit," said the Angel.

EVANGELIST DISCOURSES ON THE KINGDOM

"If men were only honest and single in their lives," said Evangelist, who now joined us. "If those of this age lived in the open, with cleanness and honorable motives, what a different world this would be!"

"Ah yes," said I, "but this cannot be until the Kingdom comes."

"The Kingdom is here," he answered.

"Where?" I asked.

"In the hearts of the good and the true," was the reply.

SATAN EMPLOYS SHREWD TEACHERS

I then related to Evangelist what I had seen at the School of Modern Methods, and told him also of the activity with which it was conducted, and the number of those who were there as pupils.

"Yes," he replied, "that school has been in existence a long while, and much time and money have been spent upon it. Shrewd teachers are employed at lucrative salaries; for Satan stints not at means that shall gain his ends."

"Then it is not a secret?" I asked.

"Nay, 'tis no longer a secret, and the principle upon which he works is well known to all true souls in these regions," replied Evangelist.

"Yet a great number fall into his net," I added.

"It is true," he replied, "but in each instance, there exists in the heart of such a predisposing motive. The conscience is a tower of light for the guidance of all men, and it is only when men extinguish or hide this light, that they can choose evil without compunction."

IN THE BUSTLE OF MAN'S WORK TIME

Then opening a small volume the patriarch said: "Listen to these words, for they sum up the real things to be sought after in life, and they are what we must keep on teaching to men," then he read:

"To live content with small means; to seek elegance rather than luxury, and refinement rather than fashion; to be worthy, respectable and wealthy, not rich; to listen to the stars and birds, babes and sages with open hearts; to study hard; to think quietly, act frankly, talk gently, await occasions, hurry never; in a word, to let the spiritual, unbidden and unconscious grow up through the common,—this is my symphony."

"Such living would eliminate the false from thought and feeling and action, and not only sweeten life; but attract to it the blessings of the mind of the great teacher," said I.

"This is our ideal, and though the world be full of sin, the heart must breathe in daily that breath of optimism which rushes down from the Holy Hill of Calvary," said Evangelist. "The Christ is as old as God Himself; as far-reaching as His goodness; more pleasant than air or sunshine."

THOU SHALT LOVE THY NEIGHBOR

"But tell me," I continued. "Why is it that men differ so in religious beliefs? Moses and Jesus, Isaiah and Paul, Jeremiah and Peter, the Jew and the Chrstian, are to dwell together at last; why not promote a great religious 'Trust' and so hasten the day when men shall say as did Joshua of old, 'as for me and my house, we will serve the Lord.'"

"It is to be regretted," replied the prophet, "that men will not often work together in religious matters unless they agree in doctrinal beliefs. They scatter their fire and waste their money

JUDAS IN TWENTIETH-CENTURY CLOTHES

in denominational rivalries, and so, it seems that the children of the world are wiser than the children of light, for when they wish very much to do a thing, they do it."

WHO IS MY NEIGHBOR?

"The world at large," continued Evangelist, "has not yet learned to love its neighbor as itself, and they are comparatively few who seem to understand the meaning of this divine law. It is time that men should live it, and teach it as well, in a way which shall make people more pitiful of need and sorrow, and more kindly and helpful.

"It is not enough that we say we love our neighbor, we must really understand that in its truest sense, this means that we are our brothers' keepers," the patriarch went on. "It is time that we gave reverent appreciation and enthusiastic obedience to this plain commandment. It is not enough that we obey only when our emotions are stirred and it is a pleasure to do so. It is an every day service we must pay.

MONEY WILL NOT ALWAYS BUY SUCCESS

As Evangelist spoke these words, he and the Angel vanished from my sight, and I was taken, still in my vision, where I could hear the familiar voices of Mr. Hypocrite and his friend and ally, Man-of-the-World.

"The vote of that Senator came high," said Hypocrite to his associate, "but I trust it will be worth the price."

"Came high!" replied Man-of-the-World. "I should say it did. The money was wasted," he added, with an oath.

"Wasted?" cried Hypocrite in an excited voice.

"Yes, wasted," rejoined Man-of-the-World. "That scoundrel sold us out. He took our money and then voted against the bill; and what is more, we have no redress, for it would not be wise to quarrel with him, even if we dared to do so."

"That's too bad," said Hypocrite, as he nervously paced back and forth. "What can we do?" he inquired.

"Do? Charge it to profit and loss. There is nothing else to do," was the reply.

THEIR FEET SHALL SLIDE IN DUE TIME

"'A house divided against itself cannot stand,'" commented Minister Good. "The papers of the city have exposed the duplicity of the Mayor and Man-of-the-World."

"Then those who boldly do crooked work are not companions in honor, it seems," replied his wife.

"The Lord's hand is in it," continued the Minister. "Judas is yet incarnate in men, and even those who wear his clothes, are often deceived in each other."

"The wicked shall not prosper," rejoined his wife.

THE DOWNFALL OF ARTFUL

As they thus conversed, Evangelist entered their dwelling and told them of one Artful, a friend of Hypocrite, and formerly a member of their church. He stood high in the community and many private interests had been committed to him with perfect confidence.

"What! is he dead?" earnestly inquired the minister.

"Nay, not dead, but proven false,—a betrayer of trusts. He has fled, and behind him are left, not only well-to-do investors, but laborers and widows, who entrusted to him their scanty savings for investment," replied the old man.

"He seemed worthy of confidence," said Minister Good, "and for a while took an active part in the affairs of Zion, but he left when Mr. Hypocrite was asked to resign."

"Yes, he was a friend of Hypocrite, who has also suffered loss by this man's wrong doing," said Evangelist.

DISCRETION, LIKE A VAPOR, SINKS

"Artful has been an earnest student in Satan's School of Modern Methods," continued Evangelist, "and by reason of that which he learned there, it seems he has succeeded in causing great sorrow and loss, especially to the trustful poor, but his sins have gone on to judgment, for the accounts are not yet closed."

"His avarice proved his ruin," said the minister.

"Yes," said Evangelist. "The gold he coveted was in the bag, and for the sake of possessing it, he betrayed his friends."

"For twenty pieces of silver, Judas of old delivered his Master into the hands of the enemy; for twenty pieces of silver he perjured his soul," said Minister Good.

While the minister was speaking, it was given me to see Artful, disgraced and covered with the mire of sin, sitting, a sorrowful vagabond, over against the Castle of Satan; with no balm for a conscience awakened to the enormity of its guilt.

THY SIN SHALL FIND THEE OUT

"This, I learned there," he said to himself, as he pointed to the grim castle, "and this is the harvest from the seed which they planted in my soul."

He turned suddenly as though pursued by an avenger, when from the castle a shout of laughter fell upon his ears.

"Laughter but precedes sorrow to such as study in those halls," he said as he sought to hide from an imaginary pursuer under the dense hedge. Then he looked upon the gold he had borne with him and began to loathe it. "It is a burden upon my soul," he cried aloud.

Instinctively his better nature reached forth for sympathy and help, but in the darkness of his retreat, there was none to hear or pity, and as night came on he saw naught but the eye of an offended Saviour, looking into the depths of his very soul.

"Let me die," said he. "What remains for such as I, but a life of prolonged sorrow and retribution."

MORE HEAVILY THE SHADOWS FALL

The wind, as it whistled through the trees, semed to mock at his fears, and the light from the castle windows caused his spirit to shudder.

"Let me die! Let me die!" he cried. "I will end it all!" he cried suddenly, as in great desperation of spirit he arose, and flinging the ill-gotten treasure aside, started forth with the intention of casting himself headlong into the ravine.

For a moment he halted, and, gathering the gold again, buried it beneath some stones, and then hastened wildly on to carry out his determination of self-destruction.

"Stay thy rash deed!"

These were the words that rang in his ears as he struggled to behold from whence the voice came. A cold sweat stood upon his brow and a shiver of fear ran through his body.

"Stay thy rash deed! Add not sin to sin!" and though for the time he knew it not, the Good Angel was standing at his side; and placing her hand upon his, she added:

"Be calm! Thou must not do thyself harm; for though thou hast sinned, thou canst make restitution, and making thyself right with man, thou canst find forgiveness with God."

"The door is closed; the door is closed;" he muttered, as sobs of anguish and remorse shook his frame.

"Look yonder!" she said. "The Christ who died there; died to expiate all sin, if truly repented of."

His eyes were too heavy to look, and all that he could utter was, "the door is closed!"

"The door was opened once for all by those pierced hands," said the Angel, "and even the Archfiend himself who inhabits yonder castle has not the power to close it. Suffer not such hideous doubt to blind thine eyes."

"Ah, had I remained true to my childhood's faith, and maintained with integrity the vows of my religious life!" cried Artful, "but I lived a life of falseness! It is too late."

> "Late, late, so late, and dark the night and chill!
> Late, late, so late; but we can enter still."

Thus spoke the Angel in tender assurance, and bade him look in contrition toward the Cross on the Hill beyond.

While she entreated, God, the soul's Father, gave to the spirit of this erring one the birth-moment of a peace which held the hopes of that real life which had been bartered for the treasures of earth.

And as I gazed in silence, upon the sorrowful sight, the Angel said to me: "Tell it unto the world, that even they upon whom is the stain of Judas may yet touch the compassion of the Christ, if, forsaking sin, they will repent and believe."

CHAPTER IX

In With the Priests

"Strange! to think how the Moth-kings lay up treasures for the moth; and the Rust-kings, who are to their people's strength as rust to armour, lay up treasures for the rust; and the Robber-kings, treasures for the robber; but how few kings have ever laid up treasures that needed no guarding ——."
—*Ruskin, "Sesame and Lilies."*

PARTING from the Angel, after her command to tell the the story of Artful to the world, I sought a retreat which I had discovered on the day she had taken me to Satan's School of Modern Methods.

It was a spot where one might, with little chance of being observed, see whatever passed along the path that led to the Archfiend's Castle of All Evil, and now, from its seclusion, I saw Satan leave his stronghold and hasten down the narrow way. His rage at the escape of Artful was frightful to behold, and as he drew nearer, I heard him say to himself:

"That Guardian Angel and the priests of God will be the ruination of my business. Here's another failure to record, and close by the castle too," and with an oath he stamped his cloven foot upon the ground.

"I'd have had that fellow, Artful," he went on, "had it not been for the Angel. The temptation of that ravine would have been too much for him to overcome and I would have had his soul. Curse her for her interference!"

He walked to the edge of the precipice and looked over the steep ledge of rocks.

"More than one mortal I have caught here," said he with a chuckle of satisfaction, which for the moment replaced his frown.

SATAN IS IN AN UGLY MOOD

A band of fiends came rushing up the path, and as they beheld Satan they halted and waited for him to speak.

"Where were you when Artful was in the grounds?" he demanded of them.

"Guarding the castle," they replied.

"A nice lot of guards you are!" said their master in derision. "Why did you not help Artful to accomplish his purpose of self-destruction?"

"The Angel persuaded him from it before we could reach him," ventured one of the band in reply.

"If we could have gotten hold of him first, the capture of his soul would have been an easy matter," added another.

"You must have been frightened by the Angel," Satan declared. "Why were you afraid of her?"

"There was a strange light around her," one confessed, "and before we could recover from our fright, she had saved him from the deed."

IN WITH THE PRIESTS

"I thought so," said Satan, with increasing rage; "you are a lot of silly cowards."

EVANGELIST GIVES SATAN A SCARE

At that moment the sound of a voice was heard from the other side of the ravine, where a form like unto that of a person could be dimly traced.

"Hark! He speaks!" cried several of the fiends.

"Spirits have not flesh and blood such as he," answered Satan. "Listen! It would address us," he added.

" 'I beheld Satan as lightning fall from heaven. Behold, I give unto you power to tread on serpents and scorpions, and over all the power of the enemy: and nothing shall by any means hurt you. Notwithstanding in this rejoice not, that the spirits are subject unto you; but rather rejoice because your names are written in heaven.' "

"He speaks of thee?" said one of the demons in an awe-struck voice.

At this moment a huge rock was loosened by some means from the hillside and fell with a crash into the ravine; while owls and bats, frightened from their retreats, flew excitedly about the heads of Satan and his company.

"Curse these interferences," said Satan, once more in a rage. "That Angel is planning some scheme again."

The person whom they saw was Evangelist, who, with Determination and other priests of God, met in an unfrequented spot for prayer and praise. To this company Evangelist had addressed the words which Satan and his company had heard.

THE PRIESTS OF GOD ARE THANKFUL

"As the anointed of Christ, ye have all seen the witness of His great power," said Evangelist. Then with face and hands uplifted toward Heaven he said:

"This is the great promise of Jesus to you who are in the midst of the conflict with Satan and sin. 'He that believeth on me, the works that I do shall he do also; and greater works than these shall he do, because I go unto my Father. And whatever ye shall ask in my name, that will I do, that the Father may be glorified in the Son. If ye shall ask anything in my name, I will do it.'"

THE COMMUNION UNDER THE CEDAR

Then Evangelist gathered the priests of God around a rudely built altar under a spreading cedar, and, after offering a prayer passed to each bread and wine, the emblems of the Passover which Jesus, whose Cross was in view on the opposite hill, had bidden such as love Him keep, until He should again appear.

As Satan and his company listened, they heard the echo of their parting hymn and then all was still.

"This sort of performance puts a chill upon everything," said Satan, as he saw Evangelist and his band descend the mountain and pass along the King's Highway toward the city.

"'Halt!' the Angel cried. 'Ye cannot pass!'"

"Back to your posts," he commanded his still frightened attendants. "By great vigilance you may regain my favor."

To himself he said:

"They have planned some new campaign and are going forth to put it in operation. I'll seek the home of Hypocrite and find out what is going on."

As Satan announced this determination, I heard the Angel whisper to me, "Come;" and then, before I could signify my willingness to accompany her, we were in the home of the Mayor of the City of Worldliness.

SATAN MAKES A FRIENDLY CALL

Hypocrite was seated in his library when a knock upon the door startled him.

"Well! Well! What's gone wrong now?" was his salutation to Satan. "More trouble I'll venture, else you'd not be here."

"Trouble enough to turn my hair grey," replied Satan, as he drew up a chair beside Hypocrite, and began to engage him in conversation.

"How are matters progressing down at your church?" he asked.

"What do I know about the church? I've withdrawn from active service," answered Hypocrite.

"You still have some friends on the board of trustees, have n't you?" asked Satan, with a grin.

"Oh yes, a few," replied Hypocrite.

"How are you and the minister getting along, nowadays?" he continued. "Are you on speaking terms?"

"Certainly we are."

SATAN IS SOLICITOUS ABOUT MANY THINGS

"And how is the young woman, Miss ——?" asked Satan.

"Miss Sincere, you mean?"

"Yes, Miss Sincere, the one to whom you were so attentive at the banquet," said His Majesty.

"You have a good memory. That was quite a while ago."

"Yes," replied Satan, "she was one whom I had marked for my own, but that meddling Angel was too much for me there."

"She is still busy with her mission and her work among the poor. She is a great help to Minister Good," said Hypocrite.

"Have you seen the Angel in these parts lately?" asked Satan.

"I am told that she resides at the home of Miss Sincere," replied Hypocrite.

"Between ourselves," said Satan confidentially, "that Angel and Minister Good are my worst foes."

"Foes! They are not your foes. You each work for a principle, and if they outwit you, you are to blame, not they. It is a game of 'best fellow,'" answered Hypocrite.

"Yes, but they bend every effort to defeat my plans."

"Well," added Hypocrite, "that is about the size of your own game, as I understand it."

"Say, Hypocrite," said Satan, as he slapped him familiarly upon your shoulder, "you 're not going back on an old friend, are you? You must not lose your nerve at this stage of the game. I am sorry that you lost in that last deal; but the preachers were against you. You 'll have better luck next time."

"That 's what you always say," answered Hypocrite.

"But," persisted Satan, "are you still with me in this game?"

"You know well enough where I stand without asking," replied Hypocrite.

"There is no need for you to be offended," Satan hastily rejoined.

"Well, I 'm looking on just now," said Hypocrite.

"You 're dreaming, old fellow," said Satan, "That 's what ails you. Wake up! Things will turn your way."

HYPOCRITE DEFINES HIS POSITION

"No, I 'm not dreaming, but I 've had a dream that has come strikingly true in many particulars, and I 'm going to slow up a bit," replied Hypocrite.

"That day I saw that old rascal, Evangelist, in your office, I knew you 'd have trouble of some sort. Better keep clear of him," said Satan.

"He has given you quite a chase several times, has n't he?" inquired Hypocrite in a sardonic tone.

"He 's all bluff," replied Satan.

"He 's stronger and wiser than you and the whole pack of your fiends, when he 's aroused," said Hypocrite, as he watched the chagrin on the Archfiend's face.

"I 'll get him and that Angel in my net yet," said Satan with a positive air.

180   IN WITH THE PRIESTS

"You'll have to be a little quicker than you were with Artful," rejoined Hypocrite.

"I may have to change my tactics," Satan admitted, and soon afterward took his leave. As he did so, I ventured to follow him.

A PAIR OF CONSPIRATORS

Shortly after leaving the home of Hypocrite, Satan fell in with Man-of-the-World, and they strolled together for quite a distance.

"I hope business is booming with you," said Man-of-the-World.

"Well," replied Satan, "I have had some reverses lately, but matters are now looking up."

"I hope so," replied Man-of-the-World.

"Do you know the priests of the city quite well?" inquired Satan.

"I have had dealings with many of them," was the reply.

"Then perhaps you can aid me in a little project I have on hand."

"I shall be glad to aid you in any way I can," said Man-of-the-World.

"Good! that is kind of you," was the pleased reply.

Thus assured, Satan explained to Man-of-the-World his scheme. He feared the efforts of the ministers whom he had seen in communion with God, for Evangelist, their leader, was a constant menace to his plans.

"The priests must in some way be won over," he began. "You

IN WITH THE PRIESTS 181

cannot stop the people from hearing them. My plan is to poison their sermons, especially those to the children," said Satan.

SATAN ATTENDS CHURCH MEETINGS

"If you can get in with the priests, you can control the situation," replied Man-of-the-World.

"They have been rather rough in their denunciation of both of us of late," continued Satan.

"How do you know? You don't attend their churches?" asked Man-of-the-World, jokingly.

"I most certainly do," was the reply, "I have not missed a service, rain or shine, since the Church was inaugurated."

"You've done better in this matter of attendance than many Christians," responded Man-of-the-World.

"I always drop in to see what is going on. It's the only way to keep posted," said Satan.

THE SCHEME TO CAPTURE THE PRIESTS

"I don't know what your plan would be," said Man-of-the-World, "but mine would be to show these preachers a specially good time. Obligate them to you, no matter what it costs. What is money compared with their good will? See that they are indebted to you, and the more you have them in your debt, the greater the success will be. That's the plan I adopt in my political life."

"You're a philosopher; your suggestion is a capital one," answered Satan, with an air of flattery, "but how shall we set to work to capture the priests?"

"Mr. Hypocrite is the one to aid you in this project, for he is up in church matters," resumed Man-of-the-World.

"I had just left him when I met you," replied Satan, "but he was not in a mood to be interviewed; said he did n't know just where he stood."

HYPOCRITE'S HELP MUST BE SECURED

"Never let go of him," replied Man-of-the-World. "He holds the key to the situation. He knows every priest in the city and surrounding country. He is just the man through whom to make your proposition to the preachers."

"I don't know about that," answered Satan. "That old rascal, Evangelist, who is roaming about these parts, has been telling him things which have affrighted him. Then, too, he has had a troublesome dream."

"I 'll fix him all right," said Man-of-the-World. "We have had dealings together for years, and I know his idiosyncrasies. I must leave you now to keep an engagement," he added.

"But what is your plan to get hold of the preachers?" urged Satan.

"Oh, well, take them out to the park. Give them a banquet and a day of pleasure. Offer to pay off their church debts. That will touch the spot. After you have helped them, you have muffled their voices."

"Capital! Capital. That 's a new idea," said Satan exultantly;

and with this he hurried away to arrange the details of the plan, while Man-of-the-World went about his own affairs.

THE SCHEME TAKES SHAPE

"Say, Mr. Hypocrite," said Man-of-the-World, as they met down-town the next day, "I 've a little outside matter—a stroke of policy, in which I want you to help me."

"What is it?" Hypocrite inquired.

Then Man-of-the-World told him of the plan to give the ministers of the city an outing, and suggested the "Pavilion of Pleasure" as a fitting place. "We can give them all a good time; and my plan is to arrange to have it given under the auspices of the League, and so make a big affair of it. We shall include their wives and children in the invitation, and so publish the matter widely."

"That 's quite an idea," replied Hypocrite. "Well," he added thoughtfully, "you will have to work the matter carefully, else it will be a fizzle. You can't catch ministers nowadays with chaff. You will have to have some object for this unusual procedure."

"The business men's interest in the churches will cover it," replied Man-of-the-World.

"Yes, but the League is composed of men whose church affiliations are rather weak," continued Hypocrite with a laugh.

"We can invite other men of business, who are active in church work, and thus make it appear as a general movement," said Man-of-the-World. "They will never suspect."

"That will be the better plan," said Hypocrite.

The day was fixed upon, and the League, with other representative men, extended an invitation to all the ministers of the city for a day of recreation. The plan seemed well conceived, for the majority accepted. Satan had adroitly suggested to the committee on invitation that they include Evangelist, and so the patriarch was invited.

When the day arrived, everything was in readiness for the entertainment, for no expense had been spared. Mr. Man-of-the-World and some of his intimates had a plan which they proposed to carry out during the day, but it was a secret to all save themselves.

Automobiles had been provided to convey the ministers and their families to a central point in the city, and then this procession on wheels, headed by the City Band, proceeded, with great chatter of merry voices, to the Pavilion of Pleasure, where everything for the pleasure and comfort of the guests had been provided. Crowds of people were attracted to the spot and everything gave promise of a notable day.

Innocent games and sports were followed by an elaborate banquet, and all the clergy were in a pleasant frame of mind when they surrounded the bountifully spread tables.

Man-of-the-World presided at the banquet in his most affable manner, and Satan, assuming an invisible form, stood back of him with a grin of satisfaction upon his face, and from time to time stooped to whisper some suggestion in his ear.

"Be sure to keep your eye on Evangelist, and do not let him spoil the occasion," was his special counsel.

IN WITH THE PRIESTS

The programme for the occasion had been so arranged that a number of the most prominent ministers should address the gathering, speaking upon topics which had reference to their work, and Satan saw that a great round of applause was given to each speaker. When a sufficient number of addresses had prepared the mind of those present to receive it, Man-of-the-World made a secret sign to Hypocrite, who sat at the far end of the table, to arise as if for an impromptu speech.

HYPOCRITE'S PLAUSIBLE ADDRESS

The eyes of all present were fastened upon the Mayor, as with well-chosen words, seasoned with a degree of flattery, he extolled the clergy, and boasted of the power and influence of the Church, making personal reference to the various local churches there represented.

His remarks were interrupted, again and again, by generous applause, instigated by Satan, and led by Man-of-the-World.

Evangelist and Miss Sincere, who, as a prominent church worker, had also been invited, sat together, and at a point where the former could look direct into the face of Hypocrite. The aged patriarch's eye now ran down the table, and noted the keen attention given to the speaker by the priests of God there assembled. Then he bowed his head and while none knew it, was in converse with the Good Angel, who stood by his side, unseen.

THE ANGEL ADVISES EVANGELIST

"Denounce this malicious sham when the right moment comes.

This is not an occasion which shall glorify God," whispered the Angel "Satan stands by the side of Man-of-the-World, and Hypocrite is his partner in the scheme to make friends with the clergy."

"I will," replied Evangelist.

"In looking into the condition of the churches of the city," Hypocrite was saying, "we find there is an indebtedness of several hundred thousand dollars. This is a great incumbrance to the successful furtherance of the Lord's work.

"As a compliment, and with sincere appreciation of what the clergy of the city have done for the benefit of society, I am authorized by the Business Men's League of this city to say that they shall esteem it an honor to pass to the credit of these churches an amount necessary to cancel all mortgages and other indebtedness that rest upon them."

As Hypocrite sat down, the applause was deafening for several minutes, the clergy, their wives, and nearly all present joining in with great gusto.

"A capital speech, and the scheme is a success," whispered Satan in the ear of Man-of-the-World.

"I think the game is ours," was the reply.

EVANGELIST EXPOSES THE INIQUITOUS SCHEME

Then it was that Evangelist arose and stood silent and dignified for a moment, yet the fires of indignation could be seen burning in his eyes, and all faces were turned towards him.

IN WITH THE PRIESTS

"Curse him," said Satan under his breath. "He's going to undo all our work."

"Utter the truth fearlessly, and the Lord shall bless thee," whispered the Angel, as Evangelist, with outstretched hand, began to speak.

"'What fellowship hath righteousness with unrighteousness? and what communion hath light with darkness? and what concord hath Christ with Belial? or what part hath he that believeth, with an infidel?'" fell from the lips of the prophet.

"Speak on, in boldness, the words of truth," encouraged the Angel.

Man-of-the-World and his friends began to tremble, and Satan, in a rage, insisted that Evangelist be silenced.

Then, extending his arms toward the ministers of Christ, as though he would protect them from evil, Evangelist continued:

"My brothers in the blessed ministry of Jesus, open thine eyes to see a serpent's shrewdness in this offer. What agreement hath God with idols? for ye are the temple of the living God; for God hath said, 'I dwell in them, and walk in them; and I will be their God, and they shall be my people.'"

SATAN'S SHREWDNESS IS LAID BARE

Turning toward Man-of-the-World, who represented the League as its presiding officer, he rebuked the knavish scheme.

"There is one at the table, who, though unseen by our eyes, is the promoter of this iniquitous scheme," he said. "He is here to further his own ends."

For an instant Satan was startled at the words, for he seemed to feel the eyes of all present upon him.

"The Church of the Living God doth not need the gold of those who have designs upon her," Evangelist went on. "The Lord of Heaven desires consecrated wealth, and better far that the churches of this city stand in debt, than that their burdens should be eased by tainted gold."

Bewilderment fell upon all, and as the company hastily disbanded, the voice of Evangelist, in words of bold denouncement, was heard above the confusion. Looking directly at Man-of-the-World, he said:

"Thy money perish with thee, because thou hast thought that the favor of God's anointed might be purchased with gold."

Then the prophet gathered the priests of the Lord around him, and once more admonished them to beware of the wiles of the wicked one.

"Separate yourselves from among those who do wickedly, and touch not the unclean thing," he exhorted. "Go ye to your homes and with thankfulness be content to work faithfully in the Master's cause, for the Angel of the Lord hath this day delivered us from the snares of the Devil."

As the company went homeward, the Angel, still invisible, lifted her hands as though pronouncing in the name of her God a benediction upon each servant of the Most High.

Evangelist accompanied Miss Sincere, and as they looked out toward the crimson west where the day was dying, she said:

"We have indeed seen strange things this day."

"Yes," replied the patriarch. "The Lord has enabled us to triumph over our enemies."

A MEETING OF CONDOLENCE

Man-of-the-World, Hypocrite, and Satan met later at one of the clubs and condoled with each other.

"You remember, I told you," said Hypocrite to Satan, "Evangelist is stronger and wiser than you and the whole pack of your fiends."

"You made the mistake," replied Satan, "of not working the plan secretly. You might have been certain that Evangelist would oppose it."

"That's just like you, Satan," replied Hypocrite. "You always place the blame for your own failures upon some one else. What a perfect fellow you must be."

"The expense for this banquet will be heavy," he went on, "and a few of us will have to reach into our pockets and bear it. No more experiments of this kind for me! I have had my hands burnt this time, but—"

"Don't let a little thing like this annoy you," said Satan, assuming an air of indifference. "We'll make up for it."

"I should think it was a pretty well defined annoyance," answered Hypocrite.

"Yes, and as far as making it up is concerned, that is always your way out of a thing, Satan," indignantly added Man-of-the-World. "The future for you holds a comfortable solution for everything. Well, as for me, count me out of your scheme."

"Honesty is the best policy," yawned Hypocrite, at which, though incensed, both Satan and Mr. Man-of-the-World laughed; for, coming from him, the words had a very odd sound.

One by one the figures before me melted into shadows and then vanished entirely. I was alone with a new sense of God's omnipotence, and as I thanked Him for it, I closed my eyes and slept.

CHAPTER X

Butterflies in Vacation Time

"In this God's world, with its wild-whirling eddies and mad foam-oceans, where men and nations perish as if without law and judgment. for an unjust thing is sternly delayed, dost thou think that there is therefore no justice? It is what the fool hath said in his heart."
—*Carlyle, "Past and Present."*

IN my dream my eyes rested on a summer land. Living things were leaping in the grass, drifting upon the air. The wind, wandering past me, left a scent of violets and clover, and dusted the white pollen of the grasses upon the ferns and rushes that here and there overhung the edges of a shallow pool. Over all hung a dreamy haze which enameled each quivering leaf and swinging grass blade.

A yellow cloud drifted through the limpid air, hung over the pool, then settled beside it. Drawing nearer I saw that it was a vast aggregation of butterflies. I also saw that the pool was stagnant and that in many places its edge was foul and slimy, and already held in its grasp thousands of the insects in the agonies of death, while others fanned the sun-kissed air with their bright wings in vain attempts to escape. Beings of strange appearance, swift-footed and nimble, darted among them with nets in their hands, and many fell victims to their skill in using them.

THE ANGEL INTERPRETS THE VISION

As I gazed upon the scene, I wondered what lesson the vision held for me, and, as I meditated, the more I was mystified. Then it was that I saw the Guardian Angel approaching, and soon she stood by my side.

"Dost thou understand the meaning of thy vision?" she asked.

"I am unable to interpret it," I answered.

Taking me aside, we sat down under an overspreading oak, and she began to unfold its meaning.

"Thou shalt see this vision fulfilled in actual life during the vacation season," she began. "These butterflies, light and fantastic of wing, typify the gay set, who frequent the famous watering-places in search of pleasure.

"The stagnant pool symbolizes modern society, and the muddy edges upon which many of the butterflies ventured represent the danger-points where many a fair young life has besmirched its character, and sometimes lost its soul. The strange beings who scampered about with nets are modern imps of Satan whom he teaches to ensnare the innocent. Such is the interpretation of the vision, and thou shalt later behold its fulfillment."

"Are not the enjoyments of mountain and seashore during the summer season—the period of relaxation after close application to business, innocent delights?" I asked.

"They are when rightly used," replied the Angel.

"Then a dozen others were on their feet at once."

At Longshore, the first to greet my eyes were Light Heart, Presumption and Incredulous, the foolish trio whom Evangelist had met in the Primrose Path near the City of Worldliness. They were dressed in the latest mode, and with apparently all restraint cast to the winds, were squandering money in a fashion that astonished even the fashionable set in which they moved.

WHERE SATAN SPREADS HIS NET

Meeting on the boardwalk a bevy of girls, whose attire had taxed the resources of the most fashionable modistes, they bent low in affected salutations, and after much senseless talk all sauntered off together. I wondered then if the girls were not the beautiful butterflies I had seen, and the three fops, the strange beings who sought to ensnare them.

Then the explanation of the Angel came to mind. "The stagnant pool symbolizes modern society, and the muddy edge in which the butterflies are imperilled represents the danger-points where many a fair young life is besmirched in character, and where ofttimes the soul is lost."

"Ah, I see," said I again to myself. "The pool typifies the condition of society life, wherein the Archfiend accomplishes his secret and seductive work."

And now for many days I abode in this summer city by the sea, taken hither and thither in my vision. At times I saw the untiring King of Evil plan fresh snares for the souls of men; at others I could hear above the sound of old ocean, prayers of deep supplication or hymns of praise to the Most High.

Many faces did I see—bright and ruddy youth; middle life,

prosperous or scarred by toil or passion, old age, serene and calm or bowed with years and infirmities, passed before me, an endless procession where hope and fear, prodigality and greed, purity and lust, mingled in inextricable confusion.

And this is what I saw and heard.

SATAN ISSUES ORDERS

"Fix up the saloons, the pool-rooms, the ball-rooms, and the dancing-pavilions in the most attractive manner, and do not neglect to install the latest gambling devices," the Archfiend ordered.

"I will attend to it, and see that all are patronized," was the reply of the one to whom Satan entrusted such matters, "for what we lost in the city, last year, we must make up this summer.

"We shall succeed, too," he added, "if the Angel and Evangelist keep away from Longshore."

"No danger of their ever coming here," replied Satan. "They are too busy at the camp-meetings and summer schools."

"Those gatherings are matters we must look after, too," said another fiend, who also seemed to be an active worker.

"You can't do much when a revival is in progress, or where summer schools for college students are being carried on. I've had experience in such things," explained Satan. "However, I have sent out a few trusty workers to see what is going on," he continued. "They can, at least, make trouble, and it is always worth while to do that."

"I saw that enthusiastic fellow here to-day—what's his name?" inquired one of the fiends.

"Who?" anxiously inquired Satan.

"I forget his name, but he led the pilgrims the day we destroyed the Path to the Cross, and hung up the mist," explained his informant.

"You don't mean Determination?"

"Yes, that is the man."

"Curse him!" said the Archfiend in a burst of wrath. "What is he doing here?"

"I don't know, but he was very much in earnest about something, and was engaged in conversation with three others whom I did not recognize," the fiend continued.

"He's planning to give us some kind of trouble," said Satan. "I must look into this."

WHAT SHALL THE HARVEST BE?

Still in my dream I saw a mansion, furnished lavishly throughout. Exquisite tapestries and paintings adorned the rooms where young and old mingled in revelry. Men and women, youth and maidens, abandoned themselves to the pleasure of the wine-cup and the dance, while Satan looked on approvingly.

Peering more closely through the costly windows, I saw that the host and hostess were Mr. Man-of-the-World and his wife, and that, as floods tear away walls and spread their debris on fair gardens, so the glamour of the evening was devastating the finer instincts of many who were for the first time participating in such festivities. My heart was heavy, yet I was powerless to reach forth a saving hand.

As I watched the progress of the night's debauch—the more shameful because of the high standing of the participants—these words came to me like a prophecy:—

> "Sowing the seed of a lingering pain,
> Sowing the seed of a maddened brain,
> Sowing the seed of a tarnished name,
> Sowing the seed of eternal shame,
> What shall the harvest be?
> Ah, what shall the harvest be?"

Sick at heart, I turned away and walked forth under the silent stars.

I heard the sea sounding on the shore, the green sea, white flecked, which great ships tore into tattered foam-laces as they passed by and were lost in the night. Its tirelessness and ceaseless motion rested me, and I thanked God for the glory of it, and for the stars—broad Orion and flashing Sirius and all the lesser hosts—the unknown in space. I prayed that each might give me of their knowledge of the All-father; that they might give me fresh vigor of soul.

SATAN'S GILDED ATTRACTIONS

Thousands of souls daily strolled back and forth on the ocean-front "boardwalk" and crowded the pavilions at the bathing hour to watch the scene; thousands, for lack of anything else to do, spent their time in investigating the attractions Satan had lavishly provided. Children and youth whose minds were yet untarnished were there, and though under the surveillance of parents, or more often of hired attendants, were being touched for the first time by sights and suggestions of evil.

As I wended my way from the beach to the city of Longshore, I came to a wide and well-paved avenue on which stood rows of costly dwellings, separated by lawns to which the florist's art had given an added beauty. One whom I met told me in answer to my question, that this was the fashionable section of the city, and only those resided there who could boast of blue blood which had coursed through an ancestry dating back a century or more.

"Here," said my informant, "dwell for the summer the aristocracy of our larger cities.

"There is n't another place like this in all the world," he added. "They say there is one in Europe that comes pretty near to it, but I don't believe it."

A JOHN THE BAPTIST IS NEEDED

Determination and his band of faithful workers had come to Longshore to bear the message of the Master to the gay and frivolous set who were wandering far from the safe paths of life.

"What can we do in the midst of these conditions to prepare the way of the Lord, and make straight His path before the people?" inquired Whole-soul. "We are His followers."

" 'Whose fan is in his hand and he will purge his floor, and will gather his wheat into the garner, but he will burn up the chaff with unquenchable fire,'" said Determination thoughtfully, in reply.

"It is our duty as His disciples to warn this heedless multitude of their peril," replied Whole-soul.

"It is a tryst between us," answered Determination. "May the Lord baptize us with the Holy Ghost and with fire."

"The Lord grant it," responded Whole-soul, in the spirit of a prayer.

A CHAPEL OF EASE

A beautiful stone edifice stood on one of the principal streets of the residential district of the city, and close by its entrance I noticed a sign on which in letters of gold were inscribed, The Church of the Redeemer.

It was a Sunday morning, and people from the fashionable set met at the church door and passed in to observe during the service every outward form of religious worship. Attendance upon this particular church was fashionable at Longshore, and therefore, its pews were filled with young and old.

The minister, the Rev. Mr. Please-all, conducted the service, and I learned that he was a favorite among the aristocracy, because he was willing to wink at their purpose to serve both God and mammon. They paid him a handsome salary and housed him in splendor; for a man of his habitude and style was difficult to secure.

His sermons were brief, and delivered with the grace of a polished orator. His themes were pleasing and never calculated to disturb a conscience. Music of an operatic character was rendered by a choir of trained voices, specially engaged for the season, and this feature of the service attracted many visitors.

Among those who were notably present this morning were Mr. Man-of-the-World and his wife, and Mr. Hypocrite and his wife, and the rustling garments of the ladies attracted much attention as they passed slowly down the aisle to their pews.

"That was a hollow mockery," said Whole-soul to his friend, as they came forth from the church. "The spirit of worship was not there, and neither the sermon nor the singing was calculated to inspire it."

"It is what these people want, or else they would not support it financially, as they do," replied Determination.

"Think of a church being officered by men of such character as Hypocrite and Man-of-the-World," said Whole-soul.

"So long as conscience is lulled to sleep by this butterfly existence, men will be content with mere religious performance, and Satan will reap his harvest," added Whole-soul.

OLD FRIENDS CONFER

Man-of-the-World and Hypocrite had large investments at Longshore, and many pleasing entertainments to which the fashionable set resorted, were made possible by their financial encouragement.

"The races will net us a big gain from the way the books have shown up thus far," said Man-of-the-World to Hypocrite.

"Yes," replied Hypocrite jokingly, "we shall be able to reimburse ourselves for the banquet given the ministers last year."

"That sounds funnier the further you get away from it," said Man-of-the-World. "That old fellow, Evangelist, is a sharper."

"It was n't quite so funny at the time, though," replied Hypocrite; at which remark they both laughed heartily.

They were seated together in one of the pavilions overlooking the scene, puffing choice cigars with much satisfaction; seemingly at peace with all the world.

ANOTHER FRIEND JOINS THEM

As I gazed intently upon the pair, some one joined them.

"Well! you seem to be taking things easy," the new comer said.

"Well! well! I have n't seen you for an age; where have you been since we parted after the ministers' banquet?" inquired Mr. Hypocrite.

"You look tired," said Mr. Man-of-the-World. "Longshore does n't seem to agree with you."

"I 'm all right," responded Satan, for it was none other. "I 've been in this vicinity for a great many years. I always spend my summers here."

"Profitable?" queried Mr. Hypocrite.

"Yes, things are spinning along all right, down here, this season," added His Majesty with a chuckle.

As they chatted, Man-of-the-World noticed a crowd collecting

BUTTERFLIES IN VACATION TIME 201

on the beach, and the words of a hymn were carried to their ears by the winds of the sea.

"Onward Christian soldiers,
Marching as to war."

Satan quickly turned to the direction from whence the sound issued, and then grew pale.

THE MEETING ON THE BEACH

There stood Determination and Whole-soul; and with them his face uplifted to Heaven, stood Evangelist, and Miss Sincere was with them, also.

"What in the name of ——" ejaculated Satan, and without finishing his remark he hurried away.

"All of that preaching crowd are here," said Hypocrite to Man-of-the-World, "and take my word for it there will be some fun."

Both started to leave the spot, when the voice of the patriarch attracted them, and they bent over the balustrade to catch his words.

TAKING RISKS FOR ETERNITY

"The wives and daughters of the men of this city are vying for positions in 'society' and are controlled entirely by a thirst to get into the so-called 'four hundred.'

"There are scores within the hearing of my voice, among young and old to-day, who, if they can achieve their desire for pleasure, are satisfied to take all risk as to where they shall spend eternity.

" 'Woe! Woe! unto them that say concerning evil it is good, and good evil; that put darkness for light and light for darkness; that put bitter for sweet and sweet for bitter.'

" 'Woe unto them that are wise in their own eyes and perfect in their own sight.'

" 'Woe unto them that are mighty to drink wine, and men of strength to mingle strong drink, which justify the wicked for reward, and take away the righteousness of the righteous from him.'

" 'Therefore, as the tongues of fire devoureth the stubble and the flame consumeth the chaff, so their root shall be as rottenness and their blossom shall go up as the dust; because they have cast away the day of the Lord of hosts, and despised the word of the Holy One of Israel.'

" 'For all His anger is not turned away, but His hand is outstretched still.' "

MAY EVERY HEART CONFESS THY NAME

These were the words which Evangelist hurled against the sins of the city by the sea, that day. With hands outstretched, his voice changed to ineffable tenderness, as he plead with the gay and frivolous to seek the safe path, and with these words entreated them:

" 'Come unto me all ye that are weary and heavy laden and I will give you rest.' "

Then a great silence fell upon the multitude, which was broken only by the low moaning of the sea, until Miss Sincere arose, and with a clear voice sang:

> "Hear the sweet voice of Jesus,
> Full, full of love;
> Calling, tenderly calling, lovingly,
> Come, O sinner come."

Then an earnest prayer from Whole-soul followed, and the living throng scattered and went its way.

Satan had mingled with the crowd and noticed the effect of Evangelist's words.

"The Church of the Redeemer won't hurt our business," said he to one of his fiends who accompanied him, "but I'm afraid of Determination and his band."

"That message of Evangelist has already done harm to our schemes," replied the one addressed.

"The singing was as harmful to us as Evangelist's message," rejoined the Archfiend. "That man and his fellow-workers seem ubiquitous."

LIGHT-HEART LEAVES HIS FOOLISH COMPANIONS

Each of the beach meetings was attended by larger crowds than the one preceding it. The younger set in large numbers were seen daily, and many of the fashionable functions were sparsely attended in consequence.

"That man, Evangelist, is in dead earnest anyway," said Light Heart to his companions.

"Yes," responded Presumption, "but I do not let his words have any effect upon me. People are foolish for listening to him. He's an old fanatic. People don't believe that kind of preaching in these times," replied Incredulous.

"I have more faith in him," continued Light Heart, "since his exposure of the Primrose Path. He did know a thing or two about that. The exposure may have saved us our lives for aught we know."

"You speak as though you were converted," said Incredulous, at which remark both he and Presumption laughed heartily.

"Well, I'm for hearing all he has to say. I think the people hereabouts feel that he speaks the truth. Anyway, things are not quite the same since he came," answered Light Heart.

"Come on fellows," said Satan, as the three were about separating. "Come on, find your ladies, and take in the theatre tonight. It's going to be a great show."

Incredulous and his friend, Presumption, sauntered off with His Majesty; and at Light Heart's refusal to go with them, Satan laughed in ridicule.

The opening sound of the beach meeting just then attracted the attention of Light Heart, and he hurried down, until he stood near the little company. The hymn sung by Miss Sincere served its purpose in getting a great crowd around the speakers. The placid stars looked down upon them and threw their calm light over Evangelist and his band of helpers.

The Angel was there also, and though unseen, mingled with the throng, that she might open the door of the heart to the message of God's anointed ones.

At the same time I saw a little company of people in earnest conversation in the library of Mr. Man-of-the-World, and noted in particular, the presence of Rev. Mr. Please-all and Mr. Hypocrite.

A BURNING QUESTION

"Can we not bring influence upon the authorities to have this business agitated?" asked Please-all of Man-of-the-World.

"It would be pretty difficult to attempt that now; for it would meet with strong opposition on the part of those who seem to be captivated by Evangelist and the singer," replied Man-of-the-World.

"Our church attendance is falling off woefully, and besides, the question of finance is troubling our officers. Of course, we would not admit these facts to outsiders," continued Please-all.

"We shall have to do something to offset this beach-business," replied Man-of-the-World in a half interested and conciliatory tone.

"What can we do?" queried Hypocrite. "Neither the man nor his methods are at fault; neither are his helpers, and the message of Evangelist is nearer the truth than we are perhaps ready to admit."

"That may all be true," continued Please-all, "but the Church of the Redeemer is suffering from this prolonged sanctimoniousness; and there must be relief of some kind. I feel that it is the duty of the authorities of Longshore to insist upon their departure."

A quiet member of the committee, whose name I learned later, was Thoughtful, had not spoken a word during the discussion.

Please-all now turned in his chair, and with considerable deference, appealed to his judgment concerning this important matter.

"What is your idea concerning the disposition of this question?" he asked.

GAMALIEL'S ADVICE IS QUOTED

Thoughtful sat in silence for a moment, and then looking direct into the eyes of the minister said:

"Gamaliel's advice to the council of old, concerning such matters, seems to me to apply to this situation."

"What is that?" asked Man-of-the-World, who seemed aroused to new interest by Thoughtful's words.

"It is this," continued Thoughtful.

" 'Take heed to yourselves what ye intend to do as touching these men. Refrain from them and let them alone, for if this work be of men it will come to naught; but if it be of God, ye cannot overthrow it lest haply ye be found to seem to contend against God.' "

"That may be the true light in which to view this matter," responded Hypocrite, who had a keen remembrance of Evangelist and his pointed words.

"Yes, yes, Mr. Thoughtful," answered Please-all, excitedly, "that is good advice, but you know the church acts by different methods nowadays. Then, too, this case is so apparent. Gamaliel would no doubt adopt our proposed course in dealing with this question, were he here to-day."

"Do not impute such action, even by inference to Gamaliel, Mr. Please-all," said Thoughtful in a firm and decided tone.

NOTHING IS ACHIEVED

"We had better think over the matter and have another conference a little later on," added Man-of-the-World, who saw that the minister was being silenced by the sounder wisdom of Thoughtful.

"Perhaps we had, as it is growing late," answered Mr. Please-all.

NEITHER DO I CONDEMN THEE

Still in my dream, I saw a little room facing the sea, from whence its roaring and beating could be heard; and within the room were three persons in the attitude of prayer.

"Look to the Cross; there alone is hope. Jesus died to save the lost."

I recognized the voice of Evangelist.

"It is true, sister; nestle thyself in His love," came from the lips of Miss Sincere; and then I learned that the hour's communion was for the rescue of a Magdalen who, touched by the message of Evangelist, had brought to him her sin-stained life, that she might find the Christ.

"I have fallen through the temptations of a fashionable life; all which it delights in, I have tasted;" and, with a burst of tears she cried in the language of a broken heart, betwixt her sobs, "I have sinned in the glamour of a life which has left its scars on this very city. There is no hope for my soul! There is no hope!"

Kneeling tenderly by her side, Miss Sincere, with a yearning which the Angel which stood in her midst alone could fathom, brushed away her tears, and pressing her cheek against that of the penitent, whispered:

> "'Once in Jerusalem a woman kneeled at consecrated feet,
> And kissed them, and washed them with her tears.'"

The Magdalen looked up, inquiringly, into the face of Miss Sincere, and asked, "What then?"

"I know that our Lord is pitiful. Lay thy trembling life beneath His smile."

"Oh, will He forgive me?" entreated the sin-tossed soul, as she looked trustingly into the eyes of her friend.

"Yes, 'though your sins be as scarlet, they shall be as white as snow; though they be red like crimson, they shall be as wool.'"

"Listen, daughter," said Evangelist, "to what Jesus said to one like thee," and opening his Bible he read:

"'Neither do I condemn thee. Go and sin no more.'"

In that little room I saw a soul was won to the love of Christ and a pure life; and heard the Angel whisper:

"'Let him know that he which converteth a sinner from the error of his ways shall save a soul from death, and shall hide a multitude of sins.'"

"I thought her captive. Curse that Evangelist. This season has brought nothing but defeat," said Satan to his helpers, when he heard of the work of the prophet and Miss Sincere.

"No hands but his own can mix those death-dealing potions."

"The heads of hundreds are turned and we are losing inch by inch. There is no way I know of to resist it; our plans are, up to this time, failures, even among the 'smart set,' " was the sullen reply.

"Yes, they are compromising everywhere," added Satan, "and that old fanatic, Evangelist, is at the bottom of it all."

DEATH IN LIFE

As Rev. Mr. Please-all stood before his church the day following, much disturbed in mind, his eyes rested upon the gold-lettered sign by the door with its words, The Church of the Redeemer. As he did so, the Angel who stood near, said within his soul where none save he could hear:

" 'Thou hast a name that thou livest, and art dead.' "

The preacher whitened with shame and turned away.

CHAPTER XI

Running Past the Signals

"Four things come not back: the spoken word, the sped arrow, the past life, the neglected opportunity."

"Before you begin a thing, make sure it is the right thing to do: ask Mr. Conscience about it."

—*Spurgeon.*

ONCE more my vision led me into Satan's stronghold. As my eyes became accustomed to the gloom of the corridor along which I seemed to be guided by unseen hands, a door near by was thrown open and Satan stepped out, accompanied by the governor of the castle.

"I have made up my mind," I heard the Archfiend say, "that we must teach men not to pay much attention to the signals that the church hangs out. We must show them that they lose altogether too much time in waiting for the signals of danger to change to those of safety as they speed along the road of life. Besides, we can capture more souls if we cater to man's love of independence. To do this we must display false signals among those they ordinarily meet, and let them choose which they will observe."

"The idea is excellent, Your Majesty; and when you have given your usual careful attention to the details of the plan, there can be no doubt of its success," replied the obsequious fiend.

IN SATAN'S WORKSHOPS

Dismissing his companion, Satan now descended a staircase which led to a tier of rooms hewn out in the solid rock upon which the castle was built. In these shops his ever busy workmen manufactured whatever was needed to carry out the schemes he originated in his own apartments in another part of the castle. Still in my dream, I followed him and heard his orders.

"Place plenty of poison in that ink," said Satan to a grinning demon who was busy stirring the contents of a huge caldron.

"More than the usual supply has been put in to-day," was the reply, accompanied with a fiendish chuckle.

A score of fiends with vile countenances were busy at benches back of the caldron, bottling the fluid, and another set were engaged in pasting on the labels, upon which appeared in bright yellow:

INK FOR PRINTING BAD BOOKS AND PICTURES

"That stuff is doing us great service," said Satan. "See that you keep the mixture up to the standard."

"Is there as great a demand for it as ever?" asked the foreman of the shop.

"Yes, indeed. Thousands of printing-presses are using it.

Spread on the pages of catchy novels it makes captivating reading for young boys, who flock to the news-stands of the cities for it. Such literature is just what we want to accomplish our purpose among the young. If we can only kindle the flame of sensual imagination in boys and girls, we shall dwarf the qualities of character which the teachers of God are seeking to inculcate. Yes," he continued, "books and pictures printed with this ink will pollute their minds, shrivel their understanding, and curse them down to old age. This ink is doing a great work in corrupting character; no other could produce such an effect."

Satan seemed in a confidential mood, for he continued:

"I am personally interested in the output of certain printing-presses in a few of our large cities, but the 'Purity Societies' are very vigilant, and great care has to be used in shipping this ink. Last year *eighty-two tons* of our literature was seized and destroyed by agents of those fanatical societies. This, of course, is but a fraction of the product, but we do not encourage attacks upon this particular line of business, preferring to have it carried on secretly."

Unseen, I followed Satan from the room and watched him pause for a moment beside a door upon which was inscribed—

INSPIRATION BUREAU OF FOUL THOUGHTS

In reply to some signal the door opened, and, still unseen, I entered with the Enemy of Man and heard his greeting to the sole occupant of the room:

"Still busy in our cause, I see."

"Yes, more busy than ever," was the reply.

Since the vision had been upon me I had seen many of Satan's attendant fiends and helpers, but never had I seen one that inspired me with such disgust as he who now arose from a table covered with papers and writing materials, and drew near to confer with his chief.

He was very old, stooped, and shrunken in form. Long, straggling hair, through which he from time to time ran his thin fingers, fell over his wrinkled forehead. His face showed the utter depravity of his mind; its expression was hideous to behold. As he shambled forward, a lecherous fire shone in his evil eyes.

Satan regarded him intently for a moment.

"Upon what have you been working to-day?" he inquired.

"Inventing details for the society scandal you wanted written up for that big newspaper. I've made them as *risque* as the dear public will stand," was the reply.

"Finish the story as quickly as you can," Satan continued, "for I have a new commission for you. I have an order for a novel which must be as filthy as it can be made and yet keep within the law. I can safely leave the plot with you, but I would suggest that the narrative open with the murder of a husband by a faithless wife, and end with a double suicide—that of the woman and her lover."

"I have never failed you at this sort of thing, have I?" inquired the loathsome scrivener. "Leave it to me. I will put more brutality and lust into these pages than have ever before been compassed in one book. The vilest characters in the story shall be members of some church—that will bring religion into disrepute and the plot shall be handled so cleverly that each reader shall peruse the book to the end."

"Make it your masterpiece," remarked Satan, "and your reward shall be doubled. More than that," he added, "when it is at the height of its vogue it shall be dramatized, so that thousands may nightly applaud its carefully veiled lewdness.

"Success to the brain that conceives and the pen that writes the Devil's books and plays!"

Once more in the long corridor, for I still seemed able to accompany Satan unseen by him, we passed several doors only to halt before one which bore the legend:

THE HOME OF LIES

This door Satan unlocked with a key of intricate design and stepped into the room.

A machine of curious construction occupied considerable space in the room, and from it wires connected the place with the entire world, each marked with the name of the country it served.

Operating this machine with a rapidity and ease that told of long practice and a thorough acquaintance with its noiseless mechanism, was a fiend whose crafty eyes lighted up with pleasure as his visitor entered the room. A red lamp suspended from the ceiling cast its rays full upon his weazen face, and in this ruddy gleam he looked the embodiment of cunning and deceit—a wily treacherous fiend, fit subject and able tool of His Satanic Majesty.

"One moment, please," he said, as Satan crossed the room and stood by him. "I am at work on a 'rush order' and do not wish to shut down the machine until it is filled. There," he exclaimed a moment later as he arose and extended his hand in cordial greeting. "That is off my mind. The order was from a big corporation—one of our regular customers. It was for an assorted lot of lies they needed for a new prospectus which is to be sent out broadcast."

Satan grasped his hand and shook it heartily.

"There is no lack of orders then?" he asked.

"No, indeed. There never was a greater demand for lies than now. Nearly every trade and profession has adopted them. They are becoming very critical, though. Once, any lie we happened to have in stock was good enough to send out, but now, to have any market value, a lie must be fresh and attractive," was the reply.

"Well," rejoined Satan, "we have always been able to supply the demand for lies, and as we have a monopoly of the business and can dictate prices, we will go right along with the work. Here is a batch of orders received to-day. Fill them in the order in which they are numbered.

"The first is from the Mayor of a large city," Satan went on. "Before his election he promised anything and everything to those who worked for him, but now he cannot 'deliver the goods' and wants to be helped out. He pays well and we must help him.

"The next is from the attorneys of a man who has appropriated to his own use the savings of the industrious poor. Their client is a wealthy man, and so this request gets a place near the top of the list.

"And so they go on," he continued, handing the papers to the grinning workman. "These requests run the whole gamut of crime and wretchedness; of passion and revenge. Half of the world seems to be running past the signals of Truth, and when the crash comes their souls must be mine."

So saying, he hastened away and I followed him.

At the end of the corridor was a room whose noiseless doors swung easily to Satan's touch. We stepped within to find it a very chamber of horrors, for here were done the

MURDER OF THE INNOCENTS

The fiend in charge of this terrible business wore a grave and professional aspect, as he bent over a long list of names, men and women alike, very many of whom were people who moved in fashionable society. As I turned with a shudder from this den of infamy, I heard Satan say:

"I have given a great deal of thought to the work of your department, and am pleased with the way you handle it. I am confident you will soon note an increase in the volume of business, and that it will come largely from the 'smart set' who are too deeply interested in the pleasures of society to let anything stand in the way of a continued round of frivolous pleasure.

"If you have any difficulty in smothering the voice of conscience in your patrons, call upon the Bureau of Lies for assistance. Its experts can easily convince those who waver in their purpose, that what they contemplate is not murder.

"Be very guarded, though, about one thing," Satan continued. "While I am determined to foster 'race suicide,' statistics regarding it must not be given out, for their publication would raise a cry of horrified protest all over the civilized world."

As I regained the corridor, I could still feel the touch of the invisible hand, and now it led me to a door upon which I saw the words:

MURDER BY ALL METHODS

Underneath, in smaller letters were the words: *Open day and night. Enter!*

As though pressed by the invisible hand of my conductor, the door swung back and I stepped into a room, half workshop, half warehouse. Scores of lamps, each in a colored shade, hung from the ceiling, their rays bathing the entire apartment in blood-red light. Shelves filled with lethal weapons ran along both sides of this room, and upon them were piled bludgeons, axes, pistols, daggers and other tools of the murderer. At the farther end of the room were forges, benches, and machines at which workmen were busily engaged in the manufacture of these implements.

As I stood in the murderous gleam of lamp and forge, shocked beyond power of speech or action, I saw Satan enter noiselessly.

His eyes swept around the room, and took in with satisfaction the busy company and the array along the walls. Then he stamped thrice upon the floor, and, as if in answer to his summons, a fawning fiend appeared, who fell upon one knee in obsequious homage to His Satanic Majesty.

Before the door by which he entered could close behind him there came through it a wailing shriek of such agony as could only have arisen from the throat of one forever damned. As the door swung into its accustomed place I read upon it in letters that shone like bale-fires:

THE ABODE OF LOST SOULS

"Rise," said Satan as he extended his hand to the demon who knelt before him. "Rise, and show me the records of your work for half a century back. I wish to compare it with some figures I have here.

"You know that certain bodies of Christians hold daily services during the period that represents the forty days' fast of the man Jesus, whom, when sore hungered, I tempted with great promises to acknowledge me as Lord of the Earth. At one of these services," he continued—"to-day, in fact, one high in ecclesiastical office gave this to his hearers:

" 'Fifty years ago we had *one* criminal in every *three thousand, four hundred and forty-two* of population. Forty years later we had *one* criminal to every *seven hundred and fifteen* of population, and I dare not look at the figures for the current year for the proportion of crime has increased to an appalling extent. Explain away this disgraceful decadence of the American people as you will, the fact remains.

" 'And bear in mind that these are only statistics of the convicted criminals, but you and I know of many who lead criminal lives whom the law cannot reach. We come in contact with them every day. Again, in every *two hundred and eighteen deaths* there is *one murder!*'

"Now," Satan continued, "of course all these criminals were not equipped by your department, but I want to know how near the bishop comes to the truth of the figures relating to murder.

"On second thought," he went on, "I will not look over your records now; you can bring your books to me with your evening report."

"It shall be as your Majesty pleases," rejoined this ally of the Archfiend. "But I had hoped you would have sufficient time at your disposal to-day to examine an addition I have made to this department. I call it

SATAN'S SUICIDE ANNEX

and it is very convenient to have it close by the main office. Formerly suicide calls, or rather, orders for suicidal materials, were attended to at the office across the corridor, but now, if one wishes, for instance, to do murder and then follow it with suicide, everything necessary for the accomplishment of both deeds can be found right here."

"That has been cleverly thought out," remarked Satan, "and I shall not forget it in the next revision of the pay-roll, but I have an engagement which I cannot afford to break."

So saying, the King of Evil took his leave; and, with unutterable loathing for what I had seen and heard, I passed from the room with him.

SATAN IN THE SCHOOLS

Once more in the corridor I stood still and watched the Prince of Evil as he strode away, but he soon returned in conversation with a fiend who seemed to be giving an account of certain work which had been intrusted to him.

"Well, how did you make out?" asked Satan.

"Only fairly well," was the reply.

"I cannot understand why you only did 'fairly well,'" rejoined Satan. "You had a large supply of choice literature, and with that and the names of students in a score of schools and seminaries, you should have disposed of every book and picture."

"We did the best we could," rejoined Satan's emissary. "We mailed carefully prepared circulars describing the books and pictures to thousands of students. We said the pictures were the most beautiful specimens of 'French art' ever brought into the country. We spoke of the books being superlatively racy, and told how they could only be procured in this way. But in spite of all our efforts, we could not dispose of more than half of our stock.

"You see," he continued, "reading clubs and summer schools are robbing us of our business. It is next to impossible to sow the seeds of sensuality and inculcate evil desires, when the minds of young people are upon their studies and their thoughts are given to the accomplishment of some cherished ambition."

"I suppose you have done the best you could," Satan remarked. "But I have no intention of letting churches and 'Purity Societies' hinder my work in this direction. If necessary, I shall attend to it personally, and not intrust it to other hands. The souls of young men and women must be mine."

At these words of Satan I turned to flee as from the breath of a pestilence, but in a moment I felt the hand of my invisible companion and became conscious that I was being led away from this stronghold of infamy. When we came into the full light of day, beyond the castle walls, I saw my conductor was the Guardian Angel, and that it was her hand which had led me in safety through the Devil's workshops.

SATAN'S LOATHSOME HIRELINGS

As I was about to address the Angel, three of the vilest appearing beings I had ever seen, approached at a rapid pace. Horrified by the demoniacal expression of their faces, I shrank beside the Angel for protection as they came near.

"Fear not, my child," she said tenderly. "Look yonder toward the Cross and they can do you no harm."

The evil ones passed on and entered the castle grounds.

Then said I to the Angel, "Who were those abominable creatures with frightful countenances, and from whence came they?"

"Those are three of Satan's most seductive fiends," explained the Angel; "and they have done great damage to the children of men. Their names are, Evil-Imagination, Self-Gratification, and Sensual Pleasure."

"What is the office of the first?" I inquired.

"To destroy the will, burn out the conscience, and harden the heart of man," she replied.

"And the second?" I asked.

"To bring ruin to the soul by excluding God," the Angel answered.

"And the mission of the third?" I made bold to inquire.

"To destroy the holiness of the truest temple, the body of man, in which the Holy Spirit would dwell," said the Angel in reply.

Kneeling by the foot-path, made smooth by the feet of demons, the Angel knelt by my side and prayed.

"Divine Father, keep those from evil whom Thou hast committed to my charge. Save them from the wiles and snares of Satan. Let me bring them undefiled to Thee at last, when my work is done."

AND A LITTLE CHILD SHALL LEAD THEM

We arose and wended our way down the mountain and came into the Valley of the Cross, where we fell in with Evangelist who was in earnest conversation with a little boy from the City of Worldliness, whom he chanced to meet.

"Thou dost remember me?" he asked tenderly of the child.

"Yes, I remember seeing you in the pavilion where we newsboys had our Christmas dinner," replied the little fellow.

"What is thy name?" inquired the patriarch.

"My name is Theodore," he answered.

"That means a gift from God," explained Evangelist. "Where dwell thy parents?" he asked.

"In yonder city."

"And hast thou brothers and sisters?" continued the old prophet.

"Yes, five brothers and three sisters," he replied.

"What a blessed home thine must be," replied Evangelist.

"It is the best place I know," replied the boy growing more and more confident. "Do you know Miss Sincere?" he asked in his childish way.

"Yes, indeed I do," replied the old man, as he took the hand of the little fellow.

"She's my Sabbath-school teacher at the mission, and a good sweet lady she is too," said the boy.

"What has she taught you?" continued the Evangelist.

"She told me it was wrong to steal, or swear or lie; and said that bad thoughts were poison to our hearts, and that we must not keep them there. The boys all love her. Nothing they would n't do if she asked them," he added proudly.

"She loves you all," explained Evangelist.

"We know she does; she *shows* it. When she formed the League all the boys wanted to join it at once."

"What League was that?" asked the prophet.

"The 'Purity League,'" he replied, as if the old man must know all about it.

"That must be helpful; what does Miss Sincere ask you not to do?"

"We promised that we will not read any more of those bad stories that we used to buy at the news-stands; and each member of the League is to try and persuade some other boy not to buy or read any more of them," he explained in his earnest childish manner.

"You have been well taught, my child?" rejoined the prophet. "Learn to do right in the days of thy youth. I shall see thee again."

So saying, Evangelist went toward the city and the Angel accompanied him. In my vision I was able to see them as they passed into the city and later that they parted before an office upon whose door I could read the words:

SOCIETY FOR THE SUPPRESSION OF VICE

As Evangelist entered, Determination and Whole-Soul were seated in earnest conversation with two officers of the Society, whose names were Integrity and Virtue. As the four rose to greet him, I noticed upon the wall the motto of the Society:

TO DESTROY THE WORKS OF THE DEVIL

Soon the entire company were in conference and during the conversation I heard Evangelist say:

"Satan is more energetic to-day in his efforts to harm the young than he has ever been before. One who has just come from inspecting the workshops in his castle has told me of his latest plan to ensnare and corrupt the youth of this city, and of the world."

"His vile machinations have for their purpose, the blighting of all good in the souls of our youth; and no effort, whatever the cost, is withheld, if he can wrongly signal the youth of each generation," observed Determination.

"It is the old story," replied Virtue. " 'While men slept, the enemy came and sowed tares among the wheat, and went his way.' "

"The entire band of fiends rushed back to the castle."

"If we can only arouse the conscience of God's people to the enormity of the Archfiend's plot to ruin the boys and girls of the land, they can yet be saved," he added.

"There is an increasing demand for more aggressive efforts for the suppression of the subtle beginnings of vice. Satan uses small seed, but the growth is rapid. His choicest ground for sowing it is the child-heart of this age," said Integrity.

THE POLLUTED FOUNTAIN

"The words of the great preacher, Wesley, give us sound advice," remarked Whole-Soul.

"What are they?" Determination asked.

"These," answered Whole-Soul.

" 'In vain do we go about to purge the streams, if we are at no pains about the muddy fountains.' "

"Therein is a great truth," added Evangelist.

Satan had seen Evangelist in conversation with the little boy, but hesitated to draw near. He afterwards stealthily followed the prophet intending to enter the conference and overhear the plans of God's chosen workers.

As he bent to place his ear against the door, he saw the Good Angel who was standing on guard, and was startled by her stern command:

"Begone!"

He remembered the words she had spoken to him at the Bridge of Sighs and slunk away in chagrin.

"The laws which our society has been instrumental in having placed upon the statute books, limit the power of evil," remarked Integrity, "and what we need to-day is men of moral courage to execute them. It is going to be a long and desperate contest, but the Lord is on our side, and therefore we shall win."

"Only the pure in heart can see God," said Evangelist in reply to Integrity. "If God is to be seen and loved by the rising generation, their hearts must be clean. What are your plans for arousing the consciences of God's people, and enlisting them actively in this fight for purity of thought and speech?"

THE DEVIL'S RAPID-FIRING GUNS

"Our society," responded Virtue, "has prepared a message which we are sending broadcast. These are among its words:

"*'The moral cancer planters of the century with fiendish ingenuity are beguiling our children from the paths of sobriety, honesty, virtue, and truth. The rapid firing guns of the Devil's sharpshooters are ever trained upon the youthful mind. Like the fire-serpents of old, they are moving amongst the millions of developing souls, infecting them with moral leprosy—stinging them to death. These insidious foes corrupt thought, debauch the imagination, captivate the fancy, pervert the taste, undermine the character, and turn aspirations of the soul away from God. Like the plagues of Egypt, these insidious foes enter our homes, surround our hearthstones, invade the sleeping rooms of our children, and compass our youths with an environment worse than that of scorpions and adders.'*"

"It is time such ringing utterances were given to the world," remarked the patriarch. "I have been long upon the earth, and with sorrow have seen Satan's activities in these matters."

"Nothing but the blood of Jesus can cleanse the sin-stained robes that many of our youth wear because they have listened to the Devil's foul suggestions," added Determination.

THE PLAGUE OF LEPROSY

Satan was in the City of Worldliness, giving his personal attention to the tainting of the minds of young men and women, as he threatened to do. Passing the church of which Minister Good was pastor, he stopped to read the appeal of the Society for the Suppression of Vice, which appeared upon the bulletin board by the church door.

As he read the warning against the pestilence of impurity that was ravaging the city, his rage knew no bounds.

"That old Evangelist is back of this awakening," he said to himself. "Curse him! I thought I had that Society lulled to sleep. Some new blood must have been infused into it."

Snatching the notice from the board, Satan tore it into shreds which he cast, with an oath, into the street. Then he turned to find himself face to face with the Guardian Angel.

SATAN'S DOOM IS DECREED

Staying his course with an outstretched hand, she pointed her finger at him in scorn, while with words aglow with holy indignation and contempt she thus addressed him:

"Thou art a coward! Thou dost not come forth into the light and appear in open combat with the hosts of the Lord; thou creepest along the slimy track of darkness and iniquity, and aimest to thwart righteousness and truth by thy base and sinister tactics! Thou shalt not prosper! Thy doom is decreed of the Almighty One!"

Lowering her hand, the Angel added:

"Go! and be it remembered of thee, that through Him who died upon Calvary, thy diabolical thrusts at the heart of mankind shall come to naught."

"I once said our paths should lie very much together," said Satan to himself, as he hurried off. "Curse that Angel! Would that I might never behold her again, for she begets within me a sense of fear; and fear is the father of impotence."

BUILDING OF CHARACTER

As the Archfiend passed beyond my sight, the scene faded and my eyes closed in sleep. When I opened them again it was evening and I was looking upon a meeting at the mission where Miss Sincere and other true children of God had assembled a goodly number of youth from the poorer classes of the city.

The meeting opened with song, and a great volume of child-voices rose toward Heaven as they sang:

> "Jesus keep me near the Cross
> There's a precious fountain,
> Free to all a healing stream,
> Flows from Calvary's mountain."

Looking around the room I could discern the form of the Angel invisibly bending low in benediction upon the gathering.

Then Evangelist spoke to the youth there assembled on the danger of "running past the signals," and showed how Satan was endeavoring to get the boys and girls to transgress God's Law, and thus capture their souls.

Emphasizing the love for truth and cleanness of living, he referred to their peculiar temptations and told them that every day was a time when the building of character was going on and asked each child to follow the truths of God as taught by their teachers.

The chorus of youthful voices rose again:

> "Build it well, what e'er you do,
> Build it straight, and strong and true,
> Build it high and clean and broad,
> Build it for the eye of God."

Then with a prayer which the youngest present could understand the exercises closed.

THE ANGEL WITH THE FLAMING SWORD

While the patriarch was praying, I saw in my vision a strange sight in the Valley of the Cross beyond the hill on which stood the castle of the Archfiend.

A company of Satan's most trusted workers hurried down from the castle toward the city, their purpose being to further attack its morals and so imperil immortal souls.

They came onward with great confidence until they reached the spot where the Guardian Angel stood in the midst of the way with a flaming sword in her hand.

"Halt!" she cried. "Ye cannot pass!" and I saw the company fall back abashed at the sight and at her words.

"Ye cannot pass!" she repeated. "The Lord of Heaven hath decreed it!"

With bitter oaths they fell back among the shades of the silent hills.

"It is the Angel," said one of the fiends.

"An attempt to pass her will mean death," ventured another.

"But we are under orders," said a third, "and our master must be obeyed."

A spirit of determined vengeance burned as a fire in the eyes of the Angel, as the band of fiends essayed again to pass, only to fall back for the second time. They would have retreated to the castle had it not been for their leader who was daring in his purpose to carry out Satan's orders.

Giving the Angel a defiant glance, he turned to his associates and shouted, "Forward!" at which command courage seemed to fire their veins, and in a body they rushed on.

It was then that I saw the Guardian Angel become the Avenging Angel, and grasping firmly the hilt of her sword, her person changed to a shining blaze of marvelous light.

She was valiant for the fray. Rushing into the midst of the fiends, she slew them, one by one, and hurled their vile bodies into the ravine, that they might not offend the eyes of men.

Then as she stood upon the edge of the cliff, surrounded by gnarled olive trees, I saw by the light of the moon which bathed her face in holy light, that her eyes were directed toward the Hill of Calvary, which lay but a little distance eastward beyond the Valley of the Cross. Listening, I heard her voice break the silence of the night.

" 'Therefore, saith the Lord of hosts; the mighty one of Israel I will ease me of mine adversaries, I will avenge me of mine enemies!' "

CHAPTER XII

The Broken Cogs

"Evil thoughts are worse enemies than lions and tigers, for we can get out of the way of wild beasts. Keep your heads and hearts full of good thoughts, that bad thoughts may not find room."

—*Sooy.*

"IF I can succeed in placing the wrong persons in office, from the minister down to the sexton," said Satan to one of his trusted assistants, "the church question, so far as I am concerned, will be very nearly solved."

They had been going over the list of Christian churches together, and had made a record of the strong and weak ones. The church of which Minister Good was pastor was under consideration at this time, and the Archfiend realized the difficulty of getting a foothold there under the present management.

"We certainly broke a cog or two in their machinery in the row they had with Hypocrite," said the assistant.

"Yes, it was quite a serious matter at the time, but they have mended them, and everything now appears to be moving along without friction," answered His Majesty.

THE BROKEN COGS 233

"I can tell you how to breed ill-feeling, and often dissension, in the church," ventured the fiend.

"If you can furnish me with a practical idea upon which I can work," replied Satan, "you shall be well rewarded. What is your plan?"

A NEW WAY TO BREED DISSENSION

"Just this," said his assistant. "The minister, the choir, and the sexton are the only ones to whom salaries are paid. Pick out some of the others—the clerks and treasurers, for instance, and have salaries voted them."

"What would happen then?" asked Satan.

"Happen!" returned the fiend, "a great deal would happen. Why, there would be a dozen candidates for each office, ready and willing to do any kind of back-biting and dirty electioneering in order to gain the offices and so enjoy the salaries."

"That idea strikes me quite favorably," said Satan, "and we will try it. My experience has been that the prospect of handling a few dirty dollars will often make a mean man out of a fairly good one."

"We did some good work in the Church of the Redeemer at Longshore," again ventured the assistant.

"Yes, we had things running according to our own ideas, until Evangelist and his company broke in upon us," said Satan.

"That's a fine church, but it's not in condition to hinder us much," was the reply.

"No, not as long as Mr. Please-all is in charge, and Man-of-the-World is a prominent officer," responded the Archfiend.

"What of Mr. Hypocrite? We can depend upon him surely, and every man of his stripe helps our cause," said the fiend.

"I have rather lost faith in him," Satan replied. "He has left me in the lurch several times of late, and excused himself in an ambiguous manner. I don't trust him as I used to do."

"But we cannot afford to lose him."

"That's true," replied Satan thoughtfully.

SATAN GOES ON A JOURNEY

I then saw in my dream that Satan was making preparations for a long journey; and learned that he was about to start on an extended tour, visiting the churches of the earth for the purpose of hindering their work and minimizing their influence.

"See that our plans are carried out during my absence," were his last orders, "and leave no stone unturned to defeat the Church of Christ; for it is to-day, our most gigantic foe. Observe secrecy in all your moves, and so instruct the rest of our hosts."

"I shall diligently execute your orders," answered the governor of the castle.

I looked again and the Archfiend, with his attendant demon had vanished.

Then my thoughts flashed back through the centuries. For two thousand years summer had spread its fair arms over the earth; two thousand times brown autumn had painted it her russet hue; two thousand times the snows of winter had whitened plain and wood; two thousand times birds had built their nests as woods grew green again.

Through all these years, and more maybe—for to whom has it been given to say when these things began? the Antagonist had untiringly plotted for the souls of men. Then I asked, "For how long Satan should have liberty to defy the laws of God? Even now, he has changed his form and will doubtless girdle the globe, deceiving the chosen of God as he goes."

ONLY A THORN IN THE SIDE

"Think not so, my child," said the Guardian Angel. who, standing invisible had read my thoughts. "The Gates of Hell shall not prevail against the Church of Christ.

"The Holy Spirit whom thou hast never seen with the eye of flesh is everywhere present, and to Him has been committed the care and keeping of the Kingdom of Heaven.

"The journey of Satan shall prove but a thorn in the side of the church; its wound shall soon heal, and this devilish fusillade shall but arouse the hosts of the Almighty to more vigorous combat. The Lord shall laugh at the Archfiend's efforts, for He seeth that his day is coming."

"Thou speakest comforting words," I replied.

"Words that shall have a great fulfillment in the achievement of this glorious age," replied the Angel. "I must be gone now," she added, "but I shall see thee again."

"Whither lies thy journey?" I asked.

"To and fro upon the earth, that I may help in the defense of the Lord of Zion against the Devil, by revealing his designs."

"Dost thou know them, then?"

"Yes," she replied, "I saw them written upon the scroll in his hands, as he addressed his helpers."

"Dear Church of the Saviour, no weapon formed against thee shall prosper," were the words of God that came into my thoughts, as the Angel disappeared from my sight.

In my dream I saw much of the visitation of Satan upon the churches and noted that his favorite method of approach was in the guise of men in whose hearts he had become a silent incarnation.

SATAN VISITS THE CONFERENCES

Thus the Archfiend sought to sow the seeds of discord, and to inject his poison into ecclesiastical bodies. He never failed to attend congregational meetings, and with studied design sought to elect to office those whose policy should incite friction in church government.

Then, through the insistence of his dupes he was able to encourage ponderous and unwieldy church machinery; and to insist upon matters, which, as a rule, were not feasible, or for the higher spiritual welfare of the churches.

At one time I saw him in attendance upon the session of a large church, where the congregation were in the act of calling a minister; and noted that he urged the members to insist upon the selection of a man whose theological beliefs were unsound.

"It would not be wise for the church to issue this call," said an aged man, who I learned had been an officer in the church for many years. "The essentials of the man to be called to this church must be that he is sound in the faith, and that he be 'thoroughly furnished of God unto every good work.'"

SATAN IN A CHURCH MEETING

Satan, bending over a trio of his dupes, whispered, "Urge the case. This old man is out of touch with his times. The minister in question is up-to-date in all the learning and philosophy of the age. Push his name."

In turn the trio arose to address the meeting, while Satan, with grinning countenance, sat back of them and encouraged their efforts.

Then a dozen others were on their feet at once, and it became evident that much bitter feeling existed; and that, unless it was checked, harmful dissension would follow.

The Archfiend smiled with great satisfaction as he saw the state of affairs.

It was then, in my vision, that I saw the Good Angel move among the loyal hearts of the church, and, as I noted her pleading, a spirit of peace returned to this body of Christians, as though the Christ Himself had touched the turbulent waters, and whispered His calming words.

Satan felt the changed feeling and turned a scrutinizing gaze in every direction to note the cause. Then he discerned the presence of the Angel and was seized with inward rage.

"What! Is she here?" he gasped to himself. "How has she divined my plan and purpose? Shall I ever succeed in eluding her eyes?" and he sighed as though already suffering the pangs of defeat.

As the Angel bent with hands extended, over the people, she seemed to be pleading before the very Throne of Heaven, that the mind of the Master might rule in their hearts, and that His will might be done.

THE WORK OF RECONCILIATION

Then it was that I saw one rise in the meeting whose name was Reconciliation.

" 'Blessed are the peacemakers,' said I in my soul, 'For they shall be called the children of God.' "

Her face was enshrined in a glory which must have been a reflection from His, into which it was her habit to look constantly.

As she stood before the people, bewilderment and confusion seized the ranks of the Archfiend; as though the Almighty Himself had stricken them with His piercing arrows, while to Reconciliation, there was given, at that moment, an eye of discernment which recognized the Devil where he sat; then with finger pointed directly at him, she revealed his diabolical presence.

A prayer which found its answer in the peace of God which was now shed abroad in the hearts of the congregation, then fell from her lips; and when she had prayed she said:

"He is gone. Let us now conduct this business with the mind of Christ, and may His will be done." As the meeting closed with the Master's thought accomplished, I heard the clear voice of Reconciliation leading in the parting hymn of praise.

The Archfiend had fled in dismay, for the Gospel of Deliverance had again discomfited his hosts, and achieved for Christ's children, a victory over their direst foe.

"The work of the Devil in this world is growing harder and harder," said Satan to himself, as he went his rounds, and heard the voice of prayer and praise at each point where he had proposed to undo the work of God.

SATAN SUMMONS HERESY

Now, in my vision, the Angel revealed to me where Satan had betaken himself, and in a cave deep in the earth, I saw the Archfiend seated, while about him were gathered a score or more of his helpers whom he had summoned to aid in his work of church demolition.

He was seated in the midst of his band and the light from quantities of burning fagots threw over them a ruddy glare, and outlined their forms in ghastly shadows upon the walls.

"Haste thee to the castle," commanded Satan, indicating one of the fiends, "and summon ——" but I failed to catch the name of the demon he mentioned.

"Let no time be lost, for this work demands a more vigorous onslaught. I will meet him here," he continued.

The messenger departed, and seemingly in an instant, I saw return with him, a person of scarred visage who had evidently seen much of religious warfare.

"Sit down Heresy," said the Archfiend, unceremoniously.

Heresy obeyed and they were soon in earnest deliberation.

"Who is this?" I inquired of the Angel who remained at my side.

"This is Satan's most trusted warrior; and one upon whom for centuries he has thrust the responsibility of dismembering the Church of God."

HERESY IS A GRIEVOUS FOE OF THE CHURCH

"His scars show much severe fighting," I replied.

"He has conducted the battles of the ages against truth, and has won many to his side from the ranks of God," answered the Angel.

"Are these battles notable in the history of the Church?" I asked.

"Yes, thousands of the saints have died for the truth. This fiend contended with the Early Church, and in resisting him, countless numbers gave up their lives for the sake of Christ and His message."

"Is Heresy busy in these times?" I inquired.

"Yes, very busy," replied the Angel.

"What are his methods?" I further inquired, "and where does he work?"

"He works wherever Christ's truths are taught and believed," responded the Angel. "It is his direct office to sow the seed of doubt within the fields of faith; and to cast around men the glamour of new theologies."

THE IMPERFECTIONS OF CHURCH MEMBERS

As Satan sent forth his band, it was with explicit instructions that they compass every Christian land, and disseminate all species of error, and especially to call the attention of the worldly classes to the imperfections of church members.

"Pick all the flaws you can, and never cease to publish reports of every church trouble you hear of. Have them put into the papers under glaring headlines. A germ of fact can be extended to an interesting column if you use a trifle of imagination," commanded the Archfiend, as he sent them forth and then retired to the cave.

HERESY ASKS QUESTIONS

"What course would we best pursue?" inquired Satan of Heresy. "How appear the signs of the times to you."

"What 's been your line of procedure in this campaign?" inquired Heresy by way of reply.

"To minimize the zeal of the churches by the introduction of unwieldy methods; to appear interested in all religious work, but insist upon emphasizing the form rather than the essentials. Then, too, as side issues I 've secretly scattered doubt amid the truth, and endeavored to get every energetic David into Saul's armor."

"Hast thou succeeded by such efforts?" asked Heresy.

"Well, not as I hoped. I 've gained a point here and there by

"Vile and grotesque beasts lifted their slimy heads."

inducing the clergy to trust in my methods, and by inducing them to ride some pet hobby, which in time is sure to throw them, but nowadays, they seem shy of a pastoral autocracy and claim to be living by the rule of Him they call Master," replied Satan.

THE BIBLE MUST BE ATTACKED

"Some of our old tactics may still be worked to advantage," asserted Heresy.

"What tactics do you refer to?" asked Satan.

"Attacking the Christians' Book."

"The Bible?" inquired the Archfiend.

"Yes, their Bible."

"That's too solidly set in their hearts and minds to be riddled at this late day. They live by its commandments, and seek its counsels in trouble. I do not think favorably of that plan," rejoined Satan.

"You can twist and snarl the church machinery by disputing the teachings of this book and by dismembering it, more than by any other means," said Heresy consolingly. "Let us bend our united energies towards confusing the faith of Christians in their old book," added the fiend.

"On second thought that appeals to me with great force," replied Satan, and as the flames from the fagots died down into darkness, I saw the two vanish from my sight.

A HOST OF CELESTIAL ONES ARE NEAR

Then my vision changed, and I saw Mr. Man-of-the-World and Mr. Hypocrite in company with a wise appearing man whom I learned was a Professor Philosophy.

He knew the hooks and crooks of rationalism in all its devious ramifications, and spoke with enticing wisdom concerning the exploits of new faiths in these latter days.

As he opened a volume which he had recently written, I saw upon the title page the name of him who had written the book which Mr. Hypocrite, at the Devil's suggestion, had once given to Miss Sincere in the hope of liberalizing her simple faith. He spoke glibly of the side lights recently discovered by modern investigation and science, which had somewhat changed the land marks of historic faith.

PROFESSOR PHILOSOPHY EXPLAINS

"Our strides have made obsolete many forms of thought, and have lighted the way to a simpler religion which finds its source and inspiration in man's reason," said he.

"Is this new?" inquired Hypocrite with apparent interest.

As they were discussing the new form of religion, Evangelist drew near, and was introduced to Prof. Philosophy.

"We have been hearing of the Professor's new book," explained Hypocrite to the prophet.

"What book is this?" inquired Evangelist.

"The Foundation of Faith, as Deduced from Reason," answered Philosophy.

"The results of the most recent research and investigation," explained Man-of-the-World.

"What investigation and inquiry does this refer to?" asked the prophet.

"To matters pertaining to the latest discoveries concerning the Bible and questions of faith," answered the Professor.

"Ah," replied Evangelist, "I see thou hast gotten this new revelation from human sources; from man's inner consciousness."

"From the shrine where God speaks. Man carries the testimony of God, and gathers the record of its truth by the processes of reason—the summing-up of experience," answered the Professor.

NARROW REASON ON HER DOUBTFUL THRONE

"Thou art a disciple of threshed-out formulas. Thy teaching, presumably new, is but an old fad revived. Many times in my long life have I seen its resurrection and speedy death. What thou gathereth from reason, by which little taper thou dost presume to interpret and dismember God's Holy Word, does not satisfy the need and cravings of the human heart. Thou art but one of a sad company, who take the bread from the children's mouths, and hast no means at hand by which to satisfy their piteous cry of hunger," said Evangelist in unsparing resentment

"Thou dost not quite understand the truth of the new teachings, I fear," replied the Professor by way of apology.

"Yes, I do understand, and I have seen the sorrowful plight of hundreds who have been taught to sail by this false compass; and I have rescued them in times of shipwreck.

"Ah, yes I know," added the gray prophet, as the light of indignation flashed from his eyes. "Yes, I know, for I have weighed their sorrow after that faith had been despoiled."

"Thou art prejudiced against our cult," replied Philosophy. "We have but gathered the pure wheat of truth from the chaff in which for centuries it has been imbedded."

FALSE TEACHING IS CONTEMPTIBLE

"Nay, nay," replied Evangelist in tones of contempt for the false teaching. "Thou hast not winnowed the wheat. Thou hast but raked over the cold ashes of man's finite knowledge and hast gathered naught for the yearnings of the soul, but the hard cinders of an unsatisfying dogma. The troubled life of man yet reaches forth everywhere for the bread of life, which the Christ delivered with pierced hands on Calvary; and the soul of man, after intellect has taxed its powers, reaches up for spiritual sustenance to the Lamb of God."

"Our discussion is to no purpose; for thou clingest to the old faith," answered the professor with a sense of discomfiture.

"The old faith? Yes! the precious old faith, on which the human race must pillow its head for true rest. The universal cry of the human heart, is, 'to whom else shall we go, for Thou hast the words of eternal life.'"

THE SIMPLE TRUTHS OF THE BLESSED BOOK

As night gathered round, I saw Evangelist and Determination in the home of Miss Sincere, and shortly these workers for the Master were joined by Minister Good.

"And what report bearest thou from the churches?" eagerly inquired the old prophet, of the minister who had just returned from a conference.

"Good news concerning growth and power wherever the name of Jesus is being proclaimed," was the reply.

"Yes," added Determination, "Satan's purpose to discomfit Zion has failed. The signs of God's promise are everywhere appearing and there shall be showers of blessing wherever the truth is sown."

HOW MANY ATTEND CHURCH?

" 'Zion shall be saved. Mark ye well her bulwarks, consider her palaces; that ye may tell it to the generation following, for this God is our God forever and ever; He will be our guide even to death,' " rejoined Evangelist.

"It is the generation following," said Minister Good, "that is continually before me."

"I have here, statistics," he went on, "which inform us that out of millions of young men, only one-fourth of them attend church; only five out of every hundred are church members; and but three of the five are active in church work.

"It was probably this set of figures, or one like it, that caused a brother clergyman to say during an address to a college audience:

" 'Just as childhood is so assailed by infantile diseases and mishaps that it is surprising to see a child grow up; so youth is assailed with so many sins that it is surprising to see any young man grow up untarnished.' "

THERE IS WORK TO DO

"Whether the figures are correct or not, I do not know," said Determination. "If they are correct, we have plenty of work to do, right at our hand.

"I do not agree, however, with the spirit of the address," he continued, "for I think the normal young man is religiously inclined."

"No one can deny," rejoined Minister Good, "that there are plenty of temptations to evil, but, are there not more temptations to right doing?"

"Paul said: 'I write unto you, young men, because you are strong.' Paul had a great many opportunities to learn what young men could do and could not do. Let us believe that he knew what he was talking about," said Evangelist.

"We must get hold of the young men in some way," said Minister Good, with great earnestness. "We have so much to tell them and there are so many of them, that we must get about our Father's business at once.

TRUTH IS NOT AT THE BOTTOM OF A WELL

"They have been taught," he went on, "when they have been taught at all, that Truth lies at the bottom of a well. We must tell them that neither there nor on heights that must be scaled with bleeding hands is Truth to be found, but right where they can put out their hands and touch it. We must tell them that to acknowledge God is good sense, and that to serve Him is wisdom."

"We must tell them of Jesus, the Wayshower," Determination added, "'tempted as we are,' and yet without a taint of evil in all His years."

"If they ask you for proof," said Evangelist, "remember that Jesus said, 'which of you convicteth me of sin.'

"There was honest Peter," continued the prophet. "He had to say that his Lord was not as other men.

"Judas would have been glad of any excuse to betray Jesus, but could not recall an act that would even help to justify him.

"Jesus' own brother, a man who judged Him by the severest standards, could find no fault in Him.

"Pilate called for water and washed his hands, saying: 'I find no fault in Him.' And there is Jesus Himself, with no sense of sin, no penitence, no prayer for forgiveness, no need of a Redeemer."

"Why not say to men, young and old," cried Determination, while his eyes shone with a desire for souls, "why not say to them, we are in a 'trust,' wider and deeper in its scope than the brain of man could devise—a trust that teaches men to think rightly and to live rightly.

"It is a combine for the better performance of the great work Jesus committed to our care, with directions for its performance that could not be plainer; and you can join it.

"It is breaking down the walls of separation that man has for years been building between God and himself; and all the rhetoric that may be directed against it cannot halt its progress."

"If we tell them this," said Minister Good, "they will join us. Andrew went out and got his brother. We must get ours."

CHAPTER XIII

The Devil's Laboratory

"No sooner is a temple built to God,
But the Devil builds a chapel hard by."
—*George Herbert.*

"In short, if you don't live up to the precepts of the gospel, but abandon yourselves to your irregular appetites, you must expect to receive your reward in a certain place, which it 's not good manners to mention here."
—*Brown's "Laconics."*

IN my vision, my mind dwelt long upon the foolish pageantry of wealth and power, the senseless struggle for precedence of place, which I had witnessed in that great Babylon, the City of Worldliness. Envy and jealousy, which had tortured men's hearts for twelve thousand written years, now seemed to have made them mad.

Then a great longing seized me. Good fortune and success might pass me by, but, that I might share it with mankind, I would know the source and mystery of these twin poisons. Then I would be wiser far

"Than those who thrash their barren thought
With flails of knowledge dearly bought."

THE DEVIL'S LABORATORY

I prayed that it might be said of me:

> "His soul saw through the weary years—
> Past war bells' chimes and poor men's tears—
> That day when time shall bring to birth
> (By many a heart whose hope seems vain,
> And many a fight where love slays pain)
> True freedom come to reign on earth."

As I prayed, my vision cleared and I saw Satan in the laboratory of his castle home.

He was in an apartment on the upper floor. Light streamed through many windows upon lines of retorts from which were steadily dropping into huge receptacles green liquors of varying shades. Bottles labeled Envy or Jealousy were piled conveniently near, and, at a word from the Archfiend, a small army of assistants filled them from the vessels he indicated.

SATAN MIXES HIS OWN POISONS

I marvelled somewhat that Satan allowed no one but himself to mix the poisons that fed the retorts, but now, as at other times in my dream, there came to me what I would know. It was as though one standing by my side had whispered:

"Since time was, he has suffered no hands but his own to mix his death-dealing potions."

As my eyes swept around the room, they now rested upon those who were making up the poisons for shipment. Each package contained one bottle of Envy and one of Jealousy, and bore the name of the person who was to receive it, and the destination as well.

Then I heard Satan say, as he picked up a bottle labelled Envy, "A little of this will poison any heart, and no one knows what ends it may achieve. But," he continued, taking up another bottle, with Jealousy upon the label, "used together, these can neutralize more Christian virtues than any decoctions I have ever brewed. Cain was the first to take them, and from his time to the present day, they have never failed me."

THE THOUGHTS OF CHRISTIANS MUST BE POISONED

Turning to a group of fiends who stood apart from the workmen, Satan said:

"It is time to be about your work! In some way you must get these drops into the hearts of Christians, and it behooves you to administer them with the utmost care, else they will be refused.

"Never mention my name in connection with your work," he went on. "Watch for opportunities, and when people are admiring the blessings and possessions of others, inject these poisons into their hearts.

"This will create a longing for the things they see, and that longing will grow into a wish, and with the wish a spirit of envy, and envy, when it hath conceived, shall give birth to jealousy," he explained.

"Your orders shall be obeyed," the leader of the band answered, and silently they went out upon their unholy mission.

As I wondered if there were any to give warning to the children of men, I was taken, still in my vision, to the home of Widow Faith.

" 'And the Angel of his presence saved them,' " said Widow Faith as she sat in her modest home. Sacrifice on every hand attended her path, and her deprivations in life were accentuated in view of the fact that her younger days had been spent in affluence and comfort.

SATAN'S EMISSARY VISITS THE WIDOW'S HOME

She had that day especially noted the plentitude of the rich, and was longing that her children might have more of the luxuries of life. A spirit which approached resentment, arose unbidden in her heart, and she sought to smother it.

"I must not suffer these thoughts to thus engage my mind," she said to herself. "Envy and covetousness are not the marks of a Christian."

She sat for a moment in silence, as the tears coursed down her face, and fell upon her little child asleep in her arms.

"Father in Heaven give me a clean and murmurless spirit," she pleaded, "for Thou hast filled my life with good things."

THE FIEND WHISPERS A LIE

Then it was that one of the fiends whispered to her: "This is a false way by which to view life. Why should you suffer deprivations while others, less worthy, are having triple their share of good things?"

She listened to the logic of the suggestion for a moment, not knowing from whence it came.

"Why should I and my children be deprived of what I need? Have I deserved it? I've tried hard all these years to walk in God's way," said she to herself. "Oh, that I had—".

The fiend was preparing to inject the poison and would have succeeded had it not been for divine intervention.

THE ANGEL BRINGS CONTENTMENT

"Let your conversation be without covetousness; and be content with such things as ye have," whispered the Good Angel, "for hath He not said, 'I will not leave thee, nor forsake thee?'"

Widow Faith hesitated for a moment, and then arose. As she went to her task, it was with the content that the Angel had given, and she found herself saying: "Be not overcome of evil, but overcome evil with good."

The Angel tarried in the house until the fiend with his hurtful poison had withdrawn, and as he left the home he had endeavored to harm, she heard him mutter:

"I failed because of that Angel's whisper."

"I would have sinned," said Widow Faith to herself, "had God not strengthened me by His words," and, looking up she breathed a prayer of thanksgiving, little knowing the contest that had been waged about her trusting soul.

As the Angel turned to leave this home, I heard her say:

"Dear Father, suffer not the Evil One to corrupt this heart with a spirit of envy. Keep her from the poison of this sin!"

And the Lord answered, "I will keep her as the apple of mine eye."

THE GOOD PROPHET SOLILOQUIZES

As the scene faded from my view, I seemed to be near Evangelist, the servant of God, and to hear him say:

"For many years I have been upon the earth, and everywhere I have noted a marked disposition toward envy and jealousy.

"There is a spirit which lusteth to envy," he went on, "but this should not be among the children of the King."

"Ah, this cometh not of God," he continued, "for God is love, and love envieth not. If there be bitter envying and strife in the heart, its source is not from above, but is earthly and sensual and devilish. The wisdom that is from above is first pure, then peaceable, gentle, and easy to be entreated, full of mercy and good fruits, without partiality, without hypocrisy. No, this spirit cometh not of the Lord."

Then the prophet wended his way toward the city, and as the shades of evening gathered, his form was lost in the darkness, and in my dream I was alone.

THE DEVIL SENDS OUT SLIMY SERPENTS

Yet not alone for I was in the midst of a throng of people of every race. Moving among them were kindly appearing men and women with gracious countenances, and much pity was in their eyes.

As I studied this strange aggregation of souls, I saw, here and there, paths along which the slimy serpents of the Enemy of mankind had wound their way through the mass of humanity, biting and stinging on either hand.

I saw that their poison was in the veins of men and women, and beheld the marks their cruel fangs had made. I heard wails of pain and saw eyes glazing in death, while everywhere the agents of the Archfiend were offering as panaceas, potions brewed in the Castle of All Evil.

The vision to me was a mystery and my soul was moved with a powerless pity.

"What can it all mean?" I asked, as I strained my ear to catch some word which might hold the key, but in the murmur of sound that arose from the throng, not one word was heard which would solve the problem.

THE ANGEL INTERPRETS THE VISION

Then beside me I beheld the Angel of Ministry.

"Pray dear Angel," said I, "what import hath this vision, and what are its teachings?"

"Child," she replied, "Thou art looking upon a scene such as few before thee have witnessed. Thou hast a world vision."

"I need thy interpretation of all this," I replied, "for the finite mind is powerless."

"This which thine eye doth behold represents an envenomed humanity, lost from God, whose hearts Satan's serpents have infected," said the Angel.

"And remaineth there no hope for these?" I asked in great concern.

"..Miss Sincere in the midst of her bitterest enemies."

"Yes, there remaineth yet for them a hope, if they would but cling thereto," said she.

"Where doth this hope lie?" I answered.

THERE IS LIFE FOR A LOOK

"In the Lamb of God, which came to take away the sins of the whole world," replied the Angel.

"Who are the men and women with gracious countenances, whom I behold among this mass of wretchedness?" I asked.

"These are the servants of the Most High who have sacrificed home and friends in order to share and lift the burdens of these miserable ones," she answered.

"Ministers of the precious Gospel?" I asked.

"Yes, thou hast rightly guessed," said she.

"What are they seeking to do?" I asked again.

THE MISSION OF THE GOOD SHEPHERD

"These servants of the Most High, seek to point this sinning throng to the Cross," said the Angel, "and their message is the old one of Jesus:—

"'And as Moses lifted up the serpent in the wilderness, even so hath the Son of Man been lifted up; that whosoever believeth in Him should not perish but have everlasting life; for God sent not His Son into the world to condemn the world; but that the world through Him might be saved.'"

"It is really, then, the voice of God crying in the wilderness of the age; it is He offering mercy and salvation, to the wounded and helpless," I added.

"Thou hast rightly divined, my child. "It is the Good Shepherd seeking to save," she replied.

EVANGELIST IN THE MISSION SCHOOL

Soon I seemed again in the great City of Worldliness, and in my vision I saw the good Evangelist in the mission school of Miss Sincere, where he was to address the children.

The words of the prophet were concerning clean hearts, and he warned the children of the poisons of the Wicked One, naming especially those of envy, hatred and jealousy.

"The Enemy is seeking for little hearts like yours, children, into which to put his poison," he said. "Beware! Oh, beware of him!"

"I thank you, kind Evangelist, for your timely message of to-day," said Miss Sincere to the old prophet, as they journeyed homeward.

"We must train the little ones to despise the blighting poisons of the Devil," answered the prophet. "God bless our labors this day."

"He will bless them surely," said Miss Sincere, in reply.

THE POISON FIENDS TELL THEIR STORY

The Angel in thousands of instances had counteracted the poison of Envy and Jealousy; and the Devil's scheme to taint the souls of men with baneful poisons was now well known abroad.

In consequence a great number were rendered proof against his subtlety.

As the fiends to whom the poison had been entrusted were returning to the castle, I saw that they were much dejected in spirit and reluctant to appear before their master, because of their ill success. Soon they entered the dense shrubbery for conference, and as a result agreed to cover their failure, as far as possible, with a lie.

"We have given these poisons a fair trial," said one.

"We certainly have," added another.

"It is no fault of ours if people refuse to take them," said a third.

"His Majesty must be reasonable in this matter," said a fourth.

Then they set out for the castle with hesitating steps, and Satan met them at the gate.

"What have you to report?" he gruffly asked.

"Rather poor success," answered the foremost one.

"What?" ejaculated Satan angrily.

"It is not our fault," ventured another. "We gave the poisons a fair test, but the people refused to take them."

"By whose advice?" inquired Satan.

"The Angel, and one known as Evangelist, opposed them vigorously," was the reply.

SATAN CALLS UPON HIS RESERVE STAFF

Satan, disgusted, hurried back to the castle, with the poison fiends following him at a safe distance. Soon, however, he appeared with one who was a stranger to me. This stranger was one of the reserve staff, known as Fault-finder.

"Thou hast the art of discouraging Christians, and of breeding dissension among them," said Satan with an air of seductive flattery. "The poisons have failed through the interference of Evangelist and the Angel, and you must now ply your art."

"I shall go at thy bidding," said Fault-finder, "and do all within my power to set them at variance with each other," and with this he moved down the narrow path to the highway, while Satan retired within the walls of the castle and was lost from sight.

THE ANGEL WARNS EVANGELIST

"Suffer not this blighting agent of Satan to ensnare the souls of the people," the Angel said to Evangelist. "Such as follow him learn to be idle, wandering about from house to house, and not only idle, but tattlers also, and busybodies, speaking things they ought not. Go forth to conquer in the name of the Lord, and I shall attend thy efforts."

"I shall obey thee," rejoined the prophet, and went forth as one who was confident of victory.

FAULT-FINDER GOES ABOUT HIS WORK

Fault-finder's first visit was to Mr. Man-of-the-World, but that wily politician refused to have anything to do with him. "It will be detrimental to my business," he told the fiend in reply to his solicitations.

Hypocrite, too, was suspicious of Fault-finder, and, taught by past experience, declined to further any plan of Satan or assist this agent of his.

After Fault-finder had visited a number of churches and homes, only to learn that Evangelist and the Angel had anticipated him and prepared the hearts of men to resist his seductive suggestions, his spirit became dejected.

"My art has been successfullly plied for centuries," he said to himself, "but I have never met such resistance before. Even with those into whose veins envy and jealousy have been injected, I have been unsuccessful. The world is changing."

Pondering upon his failures, I saw that Fault-finder was in great straits, and being at his wit's end, at last he determined to return to the castle and suffer the consequences of his failure. "I am not going to have a pleasant meeting with Satan," said he, as his brawny frame shook with fear.

THE PANACEA OF LOVE

While Fault-finder had been endeavoring to fulfill his instructions from the Archfiend, Whole-Soul and Reconciliation had been to the Cross, and returned with great rejoicing, having with them a panacea called LOVE, which they had obtained by the grace of God. A voice from Heaven had spoken to them and said:

"Love suffereth long and is kind; love envieth not; love vaunteth not itself, is not puffed up, doth not behave itself unseemly; seeketh not her own, is not easily provoked, thinketh no evil."

Evangelist and Minister Good were in conversation as Whole-Soul and Reconciliation met them.

LOVE IS THE ANTIDOTE FOR ENVY

"What is your good news, children?" asked the prophet.

"The King hath entrusted to us an antidote for the pains of envy and kindred ills," they replied.

"By what name is it known?" asked Evangelist.

"The Panacea of Love," said Reconciliation.

"We discovered it by the Cross," explained Whole-Soul.

"And the Lord bade us dispense it as we had opportunity," explained Reconciliation.

"Love is the most wonderful solvent," declared the prophet. "Love is the antidote for all venom. Thou hast a goodly remedy, my children. Go forth and dispense it in the name of the Lord, and may His peace be upon thee."

MALICE AND ENVY CAN BE CURED

Then I saw that Whole-Soul and Reconciliation in the name of their God, went forth to cure, through love, the taint of malice and envy which Satan and his agents had lodged in mankind.

"It shall be well with them," added the Angel, who had joined the prophet and the minister, "for they have the Lord's remedy, and love is as strong as death.

"'Many waters cannot quench love, neither can waters drown

it; if a man should give all the substance of his house for love it would be utterly contemned."

DETERMINATION PLANS A SURPRISE

As the two, bearing the precious panacea, passed out of sight, the remainder of the company vanished likewise, and while I meditated with closed eyes upon what I had seen and heard, I was borne through the air for a moment and then gently let down upon the ground. I opened my eyes, and saw that I was standing where I, myself unseen, could see the spot where the foot-path from Satan's Castle touched the highway which led to the city. There, in hiding, was a company of stalwart youths, and their leader was no other than the valiant Determination.

"Think you we shall succeed?" one of the company asked him.

"We can do all things through Christ who strengthened us," he replied.

SATAN'S FIENDS APPROACH WITH STEALTHY TREAD

Then I saw the band make ready for a vigorous attack, for coming down the foot-path from the Castle, with stealthy tread, were a company of Satan's fiends, each bearing a load of deadly poisons. They had been sent by the Archfiend with instructions to bear it secretly by night to certain of his agents who were to distribute it.

"I will try the children of man again with the poisons," Satan had said, "for I may catch them asleep."

Down the steep incline of the foot-path came the noiseless fiends bearing the venom. Not a suspicion of danger lurked in their thoughts, and as they came to the thoroughfare they laid down their burdens and heaved sighs of relief.

"The worst of the journey is over," said one, with an air of delight.

"It is a hard path to travel; and our task requires steady nerves," added a second.

THE SWORD OF THE LORD AND OF GIDEON

Then, at a signal from Determination, his company rushed forward with a shout, and fell upon the band of fiends, who, seized by fear, rushed back up the dark path toward the Castle, offering no resistance.

"The Lord is with us," said Determination.

"Yes, as with Gideon of old," added one of his band.

Before the fiends ventured to return, Determination and his assistants had destroyed the vessels in which the poison was carried and the vile decoctions ran out upon the path, and were swallowed up by the earth.

"Now that we have destroyed this deadly poison, who can tell how many souls we have saved from the curse of its venom?" said Determination. "Let us be gone, for our purpose is accomplished," and by the light of the stars, I saw them cross the hill toward the city.

"It is a glorious triumph," said Evangelist, as Determination related the victory. "Thou hast done valiantly and thy reward shall be great."

"I did it not for reward," replied Determination.

"Thou didst it for the King, and for the salvation of man They who contend with such purposes shall be blest," replied the prophet.

THE HAPLESS FIENDS ARE INCARCERATED

Satan's fury was unquenchable upon learning of Determination's exploit, and he immediately incarcerated the band from whom the poisons were taken in a vile dungeon, and from their prison I heard horrible wailings and gnashings of teeth.

"Fools! This shall be their lesson, neither shall they come forth to the light until their cursed fears are burned from their souls," said the Archfiend, as he made the door secure by turning the ponderous key.

"There!" continued he, still in violent passion. "Let them suffer for their cowardice!"

ANOTHER OF SATAN'S PLANS IS RUINED

Then I beheld Satan retire to a room in the Castle and open a great book which lay upon the table. He scanned the pages carefully, after whch he closed it angrily, and pushing it aside said to his attendant:

"By their bungling work those cowards have ruined one of my most cherished plans."

"Cannot you commission more reliable ones to do such work?" asked the attendant.

"More reliable! Those were the choicest and most trusted of

my force. It 's getting to be a problem to know who can be relied upon," Satan answered with disgust, and as the vision faded, I last saw him on a bench in a corner of the room with his eyes resting upon the floor absorbed in meditation.

Then, in my dream, I beheld the Angel pass over Calvary, and learned that her mission was to be a long journey among the sons of men.

"For what purpose?" I inquired.

"She hath gone to give unto men the 'touch of love,' and to further the blessed work of Whole-Soul and Reconciliation."

EVANGELIST HAS A VISION

When Evangelist learned of the Angel's departure, he received a vision which he gave to me, saying: "Write it down, for the fulfillment is at hand.

"I saw a craft upon an angry sea which threatened to engulf it, and noticed that the rowers toiled with difficulty in keeping the ship afloat. A number of vile and grotesque beasts lifted their slimy heads out of the sea and would have devoured them.

"Then I beheld that an angel was sent forth by one whose face I beheld in the storm, and walking upon the billows she passed by the beasts with no sense of fear. She extended her hand and the beasts sank suddenly from view and a great calm fell upon the sea."

THE SIGNIFICANCE OF THE VISION

"And what signifieth this vision?" I asked the prophet.

" 'T is the foregleam of God's day which is at hand, when love, at the touch of the Divine messenger, shall work the miracle of redemption."

"Whose face was that thou didst discern in the clouds?" I asked.

" 'T was that of the Christ, who ever watches the work of His anointed," replied the prophet.

"And who are those that toiled at rowing in the little craft?"

"These are the children of God in a world of sin and tribulation," he replied.

"And the beasts?" I continued.

"They," replied Evangelist, "are the schemes of the Enemy of Souls by which he would quench the faith of the redeemed."

"And shall he succeed?"

"The Angel of His presence saveth them," answered the prophet.

Then I realized the meaning of the vision, and saw that the Angel's mission at that moment was to have a share in its fulfillment.

SATAN TAKES THE AIR

It was late in the day, when my eyes were turned toward the Castle, and there within its spacious grounds, I beheld the Archfiend regaling himself in the cool of the evening.

Then I heard the voice of Jehovah, but was not permitted to see His form. As the voice fell upon the ear of the Archfiend he shrank back as though fearful of harm, and hid himself among the dense shadows of the trees. Terrible in judgment were the words of the Almighty and His voice reverberated throughout the depths of the chasm which lay below.

"Thou accursed of God! The Almighty hath measured thy days. The time fast approacheth when thou, with all thy hosts, shall be cast into the lake of fire and brimstone, where the beasts and false prophets are, and thou shalt be tormented day and night forever and ever."

A great silence fell upon the shadows in which the Enemy of Souls sought to hide from the face of God.

Then the lights went out in the Castle and all was dark.

CHAPTER XIV

The Devil's Poisoned Arrows

"I shot an arrow into the air,
 It fell to earth, I knew not where;
 For so swiftly it flew, the sight
 Could not follow it in its flight.

"I breathed a song into the air,
 It fell to earth, I knew not where,
 For who has sight so keen and strong
 That it can follow the flight of song?

"Long, long afterward, in an oak,
 I found the arrow still unbroke;
 And the song, from beginning to end,
 I found again in the heart of a friend."
—*Longfellow.*

DURING the night a terrific storm passed over the hill, and jagged rocks which had withstood the tempests of centuries crashed into the dark ravine. Sharp flashes of lightning rent the sable robe which screened the hills, and outlined for a moment the gray walls of the castle.

Satan and his workmen, busy within, were oblivious of the storm, until an intense peal of thunder, following a piercing flash, shook the castle and held it for a moment trembling in its grasp. Satan shuddered, for the judgment of Jehovah was yet fresh in his mind.

"The thunders of the Resurrection seem to be let loose," said he, as he walked to a window and peered out into the darkness.

THE SHEETED DEAD LEFT THEIR GRAVES

"That storm was the most memorable in all history," ventured one of his helpers. "The graves on the hillside were opened, and many of the old saints were said to have appeared in Jerusalem and vicinity."

"Yes, that was a memorable day," responded Satan.

"Think you this forebodes a similar victory to the children of God?" asked one who stood near the Archfiend.

"It is to be hoped not," replied he, "for we have never quite recovered from the cataclysm of that day."

"That was many years ago," added the fiend.

"Yes, *twenty centuries*," replied Satan.

As the storm receded, their fears subsided, and as the stars came forth to keep vigil over the earth, Satan and his fiends resumed their tasks.

They were in a little room close by the one where the poisons of envy and jealousy were concocted. The haste with which they all labored attracted my attention; and I listened to their conversation, seeking to learn the intent of such urgent activity.

THE DEVIL'S POISONED ARROWS

SATAN ISSUES HIS ORDERS

"These arrows must be pointed, poisoned, and on their way to their destination before morning," said the Archfiend to an assistant.

"Why such great haste?" asked the latter.

"There is need for them this very moment in the city where Hypocrite lives. There is a tangle in Minister Good's church, and the more acrimonious we can make it the better," replied Satan.

"They shall be pointed and poisoned in time for shipment," rejoined his assistant.

Then I understood they were speaking of words, which were intended to blast friendships, and, if possible, despoil character. These were spoken of in the castle as "arrows," and were suggested in such a form as would give them, when spoken, a deadly influence.

In a short time Satan summoned a number of fiends and gave them orders to enter the homes of Minister Good's people, and incite them to gossip, backbiting, and slander. Faultfinder was in charge of the force, and his manner was most determined.

"We shall have to redeem ourselves this time," said he to his band, "for our master has placed upon us a great responsibility."

"If tact and subtlety are worth anything, we shall win this time," answered the second in command.

IN THE SILENCE OF THE GREAT CITY

As Faultfinder and his demon crew stealthily left the castle, I followed them to the City of Worldliness.

This great Babylon, with its untold opportunities for good or evil, always fascinated me. Now in shrouded splendor it lay, outstretched like some slumbering giant, waiting for the first touch of dawn to wake it into activity.

Its basilisk eyes were dimming in the faint flush that was climbing the eastern sky, as Satan's shadowy horde passed within its boundaries, conferred for a moment, and then separated to strive for the ending of Minister Good's faithful work.

Here and there belated devotees of Bacchus or Belphegor, or both (for their shrines are never far apart), wan-eyed and furtive, slunk past me as though afraid of God's sunlight.

The indescribable voice of the city began to be heard, as men and women with pallid faces, aye, and little children, too, with no mark of childhood's happy time upon them, filled the thoroughfares, crowding, jostling, pushing on to where the iron arms of great factories and workshops stood open to receive them.

THE INVENTIONS OF CASUISTRY

I thought of the endless and nameless circumstances of everyday existence; of how, to most, life goes round and round in one beaten path; and how man manacles himself with the supposition that, a little money, a little food and sleep, old age and death, are all the future holds for him.

Might not something be drawn from past or present knowledge, science, or faith, whereby to shape million-handed labor to an end, an outcome, in which sunshine and flowers should have a part?

"'I saw Belial and Faultfinder approach a house.'"

FORGIVE US OUR DEBTS AS WE FORGIVE

Then, as if in answer to my unspoken question, a voice beside me, which I recognized as that of the Angel of Ministry, said:

"When men acknowledge the supremacy of the commandment to love God and man; when they accept the doctrine of the fatherhood of God and the brotherhood of man; when they agree to the abrogation of the law of retaliation, and assume the obligation to love even one's enemies—then, and then only, shall all tears be wiped away."

THE TONGUE IS AN UNRULY MEMBER

I turned to greet her, but met only the light touch of her invisible hand, which now led me along the busy streets until we came to the home of Minister Good. The faithful priest of God was in earnest conversation with his wife, and as we entered unseen by them, I heard him say:

"It is too bad that such things should happen among the followers of Jesus."

"The tongue is an unruly member; and no man has yet been able to tame it," replied his wife.

"It will take years to neutralize the venom of these hurtful words, I fear. Where the mind is wrought into a fever, cruel and cutting words are spoken and every such act is harmful to the Master's cause," said the minister.

WE DO THE THINGS WE SHOULD NOT

"I have often thought," rejoined Mrs. Good, "how sad it is that we start off so full of zeal to serve the Master, only to find ourselves repeating old blunders and allowing the same besetting sins to retain their hold on us when but a little way along the road."

"Yes," replied her husband, "men seem to compromise with themselves in these days. They will not do murder, but they hate, and, according to the divine standard, that is murder.

"They will not steal," he went on, "but they covet their neighbor's goods, or, perhaps, cloud his reputation, and that, by the same standard, is theft."

"That is true," responded his wife, "but it seems to me that what we need most, at this time, is to have a clearer understanding about the beam and the mote—the one in our own, the other in our brother's eye. It is very easy to criticise another's life, but how pitiful it all seems when we realize that our own lives are not ordered any too well."

WE GRUMBLE AT ANSWERED PRAYER

"I often think," said the minister, "how we pray every day 'forgive us our debts, as we forgive our debtors,' and then are disappointed because our prayer is granted *exactly as we asked that it should be.*

"But we can pray for understanding," he continued, "and when we practice in life whatever we pray for, God will give it to us more abundantly. Then, 'Be ye therefore perfect, even as your Father' shall not be a fair vision which recedes as we go on, but we shall come up to it one day.

"I pray for the tongue of an angel when I think of the work

that is laid upon me to do, the words that I must speak to this generation," he still went on. "Would that I could gather them together and by the 'white light of potent words' convince them that they stand fronting their own shadows, and that, seeing only this darkness, they are denying the glory of that 'Light which lighteth every man that cometh into the world.'

THE NEW OLD STORY

"I would say to them, 'I have no dogma to offer you, no ritual, no church polity, no creed; but what I have for you is the truth that was put in words two thousand years ago, and yet thrills through the world's heart to-day as never before:

" 'Christ is at hand! Truth is here, within touch!

" 'The gospel is vital and glowing; no longer an abstract theory, but a moving force, a beautiful, living verity."

THE INANE TUMULT OF HEARSAY

The immediate subject of the conversation between Minister Good and his wife was the fact that two societies which had been organized for the material benefit of the church had fallen into a tumult of hasty words because one had outdone the other in the success of an entertainment. Mutual friendships of long standing were blasted, and the matter which began with unkindness of speech assumed a personal character, and ere long a spirit moved in many hearts which gave expression to resentment and retaliation, that bore neither the mind nor the marks of the lowly Nazarene.

276 THE DEVIL'S POISONED ARROWS

Bitter as the sting of that old serpent, the Devil, were the utterances of those who had upon them a vow of holiness unto the Lord, and, in consequence, a stain was placed upon the church, which led the Angel to weep.

Hate and rancor polluted the springs of finer feeling in many hearts, and the poisoned streams which issued from them carried the venom direct into unsuspecting souls.

VOWS OF HOLINESS ARE FORGOTTEN

Stinging insinuations were made by thoughtless hearts, and bitter words, pointed with intent to injure, flew thick and fast, until the minister's heart fairly bled, because of conditions which he seemed powerless to change.

Gossip and evil-speaking ran into slander in many instances. People took sides, and the war of words went on, until the minister felt that his work of years had fairly come to naught.

"Why can they act thus if they have learned of the Master?" he inquired to himself. "The spirit of Christ, which esteemeth others beyond self, and which thinketh no evil, seems to have been obliterated by that of backbiting and hatred."

He was thinking of Mrs. Hypocrite and the unkind things she had said of Miss Sincere. Both were presidents of church societies, and the former was intensely jealous of the latter's success.

"Yes, one little word, poisoned and aimed to injure, has defeated the cause of the Master more than once. Would they could realize the harm their reckless speech is doing," said he, opening his Bible. As his eyes fell upon the words, "He was oppressed, and he was afflicted, yet he opened not his mouth," Miss Sincere came to his mind; and also the way in which she persistently adhered to what she considered her duty notwithstanding the bitter accusations made by Mrs. Hypocrite. "She hath learned of Him," he thought. "Yes, it is true, 'He that is slow to anger is better than the mighty; and he that ruleth his spirit than he that taketh a city.'"

From the parsonage, the Angel led me to the home of Miss Sincere.

EVANGELIST COMFORTS MISS SINCERE

"There is a soul-sorrow in being misunderstood," she was saying to Evangelist, who had come to her home upon hearing of the trouble.

"Yes, dear child, when our best motives are questioned, it is not an easy cross to bear, but trials in life bring the Christian into fellowship with the Master's sufferings," answered the prophet.

"I had never thought to look at these problems from that point of view, but I believe you are right," she replied.

"Thou needest not fear the issue when an illuminated conscience approveth thee," said Evangelist.

"That is so, but one longs to be at peace with all men, especially with those of the household of faith; and to endure the stings of envy and untruth calls for more grace than we sometimes possess. It is hard to do as Jesus did," Miss Sincere replied.

LET US FOLLOW HIM

"Yes, it is, and no one appreciates this fact more than our Lord, who bade us follow in His footsteps," added the prophet.

"Yes, it must be so," responded Miss Sincere.

Then I saw the aged servant of God lay his hand upon that of this much disturbed child of faith, and I heard him speak in the tones of a father:

"Let not these arrows of malice and untruth pierce thy soul. Maintain the integrity of thy motives and fear not; for coming days shall exalt thee as one who needeth not to be ashamed."

"I will endeavor to do so," she answered.

"It is well," responded the prophet, and as he spoke, the rays of a great goodness lighted up his saintly face.

Ere Evangelist retired for the night, he opened his Bible and read as the evening's lesson these words:

"The lip of truth shall be established for ever: but a lying tongue is but for a moment. Deceit is in the heart of them that imagine evil: but to the counsellors of peace is joy."

FAULTFINDER HEARS THE REPORT OF HIS BAND

After leaving the home of Miss Sincere, I walked along until I came to the Church of the Disciples. I paused for a moment to admire its architectural beauties, and while standing there, saw Faultfinder approach, unseen to any mortal eyes save mine. He was apparently there by appointment, for he peered up and down the street, at short intervals.

Soon his band of demons appeared, and a gleam of satisfaction appeared upon his repulsive face as he saw that they were empty-handed.

"If you have succeeded in sowing a good crop of personal words in the hearts of the members of this church," indicating the edifice with his hand, "I shall be satisfied," was his salutation to his band.

THE DEVIL WILL SMILE IN APPROVAL

"We have finished our task and the work has been well done," said one with assurance.

"That will gratify His Satanic Majesty, surely," responded Faultfinder.

"How far did the supply of arrows go?" he inquired.

"We covered the two societies with the exception of one person," answered the leading fiend.

"Who is the exception?" asked Faultfinder.

"The one with whom the prophet tarries," said he.

"Do you mean Miss Sincere, one of the presidents?" asked Faultfinder.

"She is the one," was the reply.

"Well, the crop is sown; now we shall see what comes of it," observed Faultfinder. "Back to the castle!"

As the emissaries of Satan hurried away, I heard the voice of the Angel say to me:

"The soil of many hearts in the church had been long ready for the arrow-words, and from them shall be ripened a harvest of lies, slander, revenge. But Satan's triumph shall be of short duration."

MISS SINCERE FACES HER ENEMIES

In my dream I seemed to take no note of time, for the next scene that appeared before me was the vestibule of the Church of the Disciples at the close of the morning service. Invisible to all, Satan and Faultfinder watched the congregation passing from the church to the street.

"Watch those glances," said Satan, as he pointed to Mrs. Hypocrite. "They speak volumes."

"There certainly is plenty of venom in them," responded Faultfinder.

"Listen! listen!" said the latter, a moment later, as he pointed to a small company just within the church door. There was Miss Sincere in the midst of several of her bitterest enemies, who had loitered in order to "have it out with her," as they said.

"That is what we want to hear," said Satan, "that is the work we intended to do. Listen to that caustic scoring. That sarcasm is superb."

"She seems entirely defenseless," said Faultfinder, "she opens not her mouth," and he laughed with great glee. "We have won in this game, all right."

"I am not so sure of that," replied Satan.

"Why, certainly we have; see how they have her cowed, and every one of them paying off old scores with a vengeance," Faultfinder rejoined.

"I know," replied the Archfiend, "but that woman is defending herself by the silence of Truth. She is a disciple of Evangelist, and the Angel dwells under her roof."

"Why are you so pessimistic? She is the only one who remains untainted by our poisons," asked Faultfinder consolingly.

"Ah, that is just it, only one, but this is one whom I have striven to ensnare for many years. There is no telling but that she may blight this entire harvest by her spirit of meekness," rejoined Satan.

"That is impossible," said Faultfinder, "for our work is too far advanced. Revenge is both sweet and contagious."

"That is true, but you have not contended with Truth as long as I have. I have seen strange things happen on the eve of fulfillment of my hopes. I shudder with fear at the sight of one who hath learned to master her spirit by silence," replied Satan.

THE ANGEL SPEAKS TO MISS SINCERE

Then I saw the Angel suddenly appear in the very midst of the tempest of hatred and ungoverned speech. None of the company recognized her presence but Miss Sincere, whose eyes were filled with tears.

"Thou hast honored the Lord this hour," said the Angel to her. "Thou hast borne His image; for 'when He was reviled,' He 'reviled not again;' and 'when He suffered, He threatened not; but committed Himself to Him that judgeth righteously.'"

"I thank thee for the strength of thy presence and for thy comforting words," Miss Sincere replied.

"The Christ hath also prayed for thee that thy courage and strength should not fail; thy spirit at this hour shall be blessed of God," the Angel replied, and turning her searching eyes in the direction of Satan and Faultfinder, her lips moved as though in speech, but I heard no sound. Suddenly the two departed with hatred upon their faces.

THE MINISTER IS COMFORTED

Later in the day, Determination and Whole-soul, who had attended the morning service and afterward witnessed the scene in the vestibule, called upon Minister Good. Falling in with them on their way to the parsonage, I entered it with them. Evidently both the minister and his wife were dejected over the occurrence in the very gateway of the house of God, for the first words of the pastor were:

"Your coming is a great comfort to us."

"We have come in the name of the Lord, and are glad to be here," replied Whole-soul.

"Your visit is most timely," added the minister. "Satan's thrusts at the church are especially subtle, just now."

"We think we can see our way to baffle him," said Determination.

"It is time something was done, for our church is in a sad plight," rejoined the minister.

"So it seems," assented Whole-soul. "Satan's onslaught to-day was both cruel and vigorous."

"We are prepared to give the old fiend a tussle. We have met him before this, and know something of his ways," added Determination.

THE GREAT SOUL OF THE WORLD IS JUST

"Most enmities in life spring from some misunderstanding, and often the bitterest of foes, when they come to know each other, become the closest of friends. I tell Mr. Good," said his sweet-faced wife, "that this sorrow will be but temporary, for we have the Lord on our side."

"Yes, it shall be well with thee in a little while. Be of good courage," said Whole-soul.

Then the two departed upon their mission.

"They are true friends," said the minister.

"They are, indeed," replied his wife.

LET US KNOW HIS WILL

"Let me read this to you," she added, taking a book from the table:

> "Let us labor for an inward stillness,
> An inward stillness and an inward healing;
> What perfect stillness when the lips and heart
> Are still, and we no longer entertain
> Our own imperfect thoughts and vain opinions,
> But God alone speaks in us, and we wait
> In singleness of heart, that we may know
> His will, and in the silence of our spirits,
> That we may do His will, and do that only!"

"That is the secret, no doubt, of the calm life," replied the minister.

YE SHALL BEAR AND FORBEAR

"Yes," assented his wife, "for the servants of the Lord must not strive; but be gentle unto all men, apt to teach, and forbearing."

"The pain of these arrow-words has been very poignant, but I am sure that the Lord whom we serve shall heal the hurt," said the minister.

"Yes," responded his wife, "and 'a soft answer turneth away wrath.' In all of this cruel contest of words, I am thankful that we have maintained a peaceable attitude."

"That is indeed a satisfaction," replied Minister Good, "but it is difficult to remain silent when one's good intent is assailed."

"It is hard," said Mrs. Good, "but He did it, and those who follow Him must walk in His steps."

" 'The meek will he guide in judgment: and the meek will he teach his way,' " added Minister Good.

THREE GATES OF GOLD

"I have thought for some time," said the minister's wife after a few moments of silence, "that a few well-chosen words, judiciously circulated, would go far toward healing the fault in the church. If you agree, I should like to try my plan."

It was not long after this, that a little card found its way among the congregation of the Church of the Disciples, and on it were these words:

"If you are tempted to reveal
A tale some one to you has told
About another, make it pass,
Before you speak, three gates of gold—
Three narrow gates. First, 'Is it true?'
Then, 'Is it needful?' In your mind
Give truthful answer. And the next
Is last and narrowest—'Is it kind?'
And if, to reach your lips at last,
It passes through these gateways three,
Then you may tell the tale, nor fear
What the result of speech may be."

The little card justified Mrs. Good's belief in its efficacy, for time and again it found its way where spoken words could not have gone, and many of those whose speech had been intemperate were touched by its message.

MR. HYPOCRITE APPLAUDS SELF-POISE

"That hits the nail on the head," said Hypocrite to his wife, as he handed her one of the little cards.

"That is some of Miss Sincere's sly work," replied his wife contemptuously, as after reading it she threw it on the floor.

"Good for Miss Sincere, then," replied Hypocrite. "It is a clever reply to her enemies, and certainly offers wholesome advice to every one. What has been gained by this battle of words? I don't know but what it is an excellent plan to return good for evil."

"Good for evil? I do not think so," responded his wife, with great bitterness.

"Self-poise in controversy is a grace, however," said her husband, "and that is what Miss Sincere has kept through this affair."

"Oh, yes. She's one of your good sort," sneered his wife.

"Perhaps she is," said Hypocrite as he left the room.

IT IS LAID UPON ME TO SPEAK

Again, and without having taken note of intervening time, I found myself in the home of Minister Good, and saw him arise from his chair to welcome Evangelist, who had just entered.

"The Lord be with thee," said the prophet in salutation.

"And with thee, also," returned the minister.

"I hear the Enemy hath wounded many of thy flock of late," continued the prophet.

"Yes," answered Minister Good sadly, "and I fear the injury to their religious life is irreparable."

"The sin of guile in speech shall be atoned for, and I am come at the Lord's bidding to set this matter right. Sin must no longer reign in their mortal bodies."

"To what work has His spirit prompted thee?" inquired the minister.

"Even to declare the plain truth of God concerning the sin of evil-speaking, this coming Sabbath, in thy place. The truth must be told, and it must be first told in the house of God " answered Evangelist.

"Do you think that the congregation will submit to the truth being told them at this time?" asked the minister. "There is yet much rancor and enmity in the church."

"The message of truth may cut to the quick, and for the time enrage the sinner, but in the end it will lay bare to him his guilty heart," replied the patriarch.

"Yes," assented the minister. "Truth alone can set us free from the bondage of sin and death."

EVANGELIST PREACHES WITH BOLDNESS

"In just a few more years each soul, here gathered," said the prophet in the pulpit of the Church of the Disciples, "must appear before the God of Judgment, and give an account of every idle word. 'Let us not therefore judge one another any more: but judge this rather, that no man put a stumblingblock or an occasion to fall in his brother's way.' 'Grieve not the holy Spirit of God, whereby ye are sealed unto the day of redemption. Let all bitterness, and wrath, and anger, and clamour, and evil-speaking, be put away from you, with all malice: and be ye kind one to another, tenderhearted, forgiving one another, even as God for Christ's sake hath forgiven you.'"

TEARS OF REPENTANCE FLOW

When Evangelist had finished his address, a mighty hush fell upon the audience. Tears flowed freely, and the Angel, who, unseen, hovered over the assembly, saw that the tears were of repentance.

Minister Good prayed for the sealing of the prophet's message to the souls of all, as the closing hymn ascended from the lips of the congregation:

> "So let our lips and lives express
> The holy gospel we profess;
> So let our works and virtues shine
> To prove the doctrine all divine."

THE FERVENT, EFFECTUAL PRAYER

"There shall be peace after the storm; for the sun of God's favor is beginning to break through the clouds," said Mrs. Good to her husband, after the service.

"The Lord was in His holy temple to-day, and the marks of Jesus shall be restored to His people," answered the minister.

"Showers of blessings were falling unseen throughout the entire service," said Whole-soul, who had now joined them. "The coming of the prophet was God's answer to your fervent prayer."

"It seems as though Jesus was again walking on the dark waters of angry Galilee. One almost saw Him there, and heard His 'Peace, be still,' " replied the minister's wife.

"There can be no doubt that He was there," assented Whole-soul.

Then I heard by my side the voice of the Angel, saying:

"Child of the vision, the Lord has wrought mightily this day through his servant, Evangelist; He has silenced and cleansed a host of venomous tongues; He hath purged malice from the hearts of many, and put an end to slander and lies in this fold of His people."

"The Court has decided to grant a bill of divorcement."

THE DEVIL'S POISONED ARROWS

HYPOCRITE AND MAN-OF-THE-WORLD DISCUSS MATTERS

On the following day, I saw Hypocrite and Man-of-the-World seated in the former's office.

"That was a most wondrous meeting last Lord's Day," Hypocrite was saying to his friend. "I have not joined in the altercations that have been going on in the church these past months, but if I am able to judge, the Almighty was in that gathering."

"How does your wife feel regarding it?" asked Man-of-the-World.

"She has been very quiet since then. At first she appeared troubled, but yesterday she called upon Miss Sincere, and the two societies may yet work harmoniously," answered Hypocrite.

"That is indeed wonderful," said his friend.

"Yes, it is, and do you know," said Hypocrite, in a tone of confidence, "I'm coming to feel that there is more in the religion of Evangelist than I have been willing to admit. Life is too short for many of the feelings you and I entertain, and the principles we strive to follow."

"Well, you may be right," replied Man-of-the-World, "but those are matters I know very little of, and I'm too busy to be troubled much about them."

"The possession of a soul is a matter of grave responsibility, though," added Hypocrite, as they turned to the business that was to engage them.

SATAN FALLS INTO A RAGE

When the Archfiend learned of the prophet's sermon and was told by his fiends that it was an antidote to the arrow-words, his rage was terrible to behold. Rushing back and forth through the corridors of his castle, he heaped oath after oath upon Faultfinder, and refused to be satisfied with any explanation he could offer.

"Shall nothing that I undertake succeed?" he cried out in his passion. "Shall this man Evangelist and that Angel hold sway over all the earth in the name of the Almighty?"

"It is only ill success in one church," Faultfinder ventured to say.

"Ill success?—failure! utter failure! I say," rejoined the Archfiend, "and if those two can beat us when our plans were as well laid as they were in that church, they can do it everywhere throughout the world."

"You need not take the matter so much to heart," replied the fiend, seeking to pacify his master.

"Take it to heart! Where else can one take such galling reverses? All of you that were concerned in this shall suffer," cried Satan, as his rage increased.

Faultfinder skulked away in fear, as Satan, gathering bundle after bundle of newly pointed and poisoned arrows, threw them in a heap on the floor and then jumped upon them in a paroxysm of fury.

LOVE AND FORGIVENESS IS THE BETTER WAY

As the vision faded away, I beheld Miss Sincere seated in friendly conversation with Mrs. Hypocrite, and knew that they were planning for the mutual good of their societies, which had for their object the extension of Christ's kingdom on earth.

Toying with a little card which lay on the table, Mrs. Hypocrite said: "This was handed to me by my husband last evening. It seems to me that it forms a little bridge over which we can both cross to reconciliation, and perhaps see life from its nobler side. Then she read these words:

> "Thou hast, dear heart, no time for bitter hatred;
> Life's little day is all too short for tears.
> Live in the love whose magic touch gives healing,
> Where words unkind cut deep along the years.
>
> "Then lay aside each little hurt and foible,
> Let not revenge enthrall thy heart to-day;
> Life is too brief for aught which breeds contention,
> Love and forgiveness is the better way."

CHAPTER XV

The Divorce Bureau

"The kindest and the happiest pair
Will find occasion to forbear;
And something every day they live
To pity, and perhaps forgive."
—*Cowper.*

ONCE more I visited the little glade from whose friendly seclusion I had witnessed the rage of Satan at the escape of Artful.

The red and golden glories of sunrise were touching the grim walls of the Castle of All Evil, as I reached the spot to which I had bent my steps, and soon the sky was a dome of blue velvet mottled with fleecy clouds.

How long I stood regarding the scene, as nature bloomed afresh, I know not, but letting my eyes fall on the path in front of me, I saw one Belial by name, in earnest conversation with the Archfiend. They were seated upon a little knoll near my retreat, and their words came easily to my ears.

"We must do something," said Satan, "to make up for the reverses of the last few days."

"Have you formed any new plans?" inquired Belial.

"Nothing definite," replied the Archfiend.

FAULTFINDER REDEEMS HIMSELF

Just then a fiend bearing a sealed note came on a run to where the plotters were seated. Satan tore open the missive and read:

"To His Satanic Majesty.

"Greeting: I have been stirring up trouble in the home lives of men and women, and have succeeded, during the last year, in having four thousand six hundred and sixty-nine divorces granted in one state alone. It strikes me that this is a matter worthy of your most serious thought. If we can break up homes at this rate, we are doing a great deal to retrieve our losses in other directions.
"Your faithful servant,
"Faultfinder."

"This is the very thing we want," said Satan with a smile. "Faultfinder is again in my good graces.

BELIAL GRASPS THE SITUATION

"It certainly will open a large field for operations," continued Satan. "I have heard that all matches are made in Heaven, but from what I have seen I'm quite sure that this is not the fact."

"Ha! ha!" shouted Belial. "Well, I should say not! There are hundreds of men and women whom I know, who are unequally yoked together, and with many it would take but a trifle of interference to dissolve the relation. In fact, they are anxious to dissolve it, but are restrained from taking the step by a false sense of respectability."

"I think your views are correct," replied the Archfiend. "The more I dwell upon Faultfinder's suggestion, the more it appeals to me. I think this is a capital time for action."

"His suggestion is certainly worth trying; and the success he has already attained is in itself a guarantee of future success," replied Belial.

"The work shall be attempted at least," said Satan. "I place the matter in your hands. See to it that you keep up your reputation for good work."

With this, I saw the pair walk slowly toward the castle, and noticed the gleam of gratification which lit up the face of the Archfiend, as they passed through the massive doorway and were lost from sight.

But only for a moment were they beyond my vision.

IN THE DIVORCE BUREAU

Again I saw Satan and Belial, and this time they were seated at a table in the Archfiend's Divorce Bureau, with a number of large books open before them, over which they were conferring. Several fiends were searching in other volumes for certain records, while another compiled with great rapidity a long list of names from Satan's dictation. Still another, who was no less a person than the Archfiend's private secretary, was drawing up what appeared to be a set of rules.

"There," said Satan to the fiend who was compiling the list, "that will do for to-day. Make two copies; file one for reference

THE DIVORCE BUREAU

and send the other to Faultfinder." Then turning to Belial he said:

"The marriage bond used to be regarded with great sacredness; and only for certain reasons, as stated in the teachings of Jesus, was it possible for Christians to secure letters of separation."

BOTH CHURCH AND JUDICIARY ARE LAX

"We broadened the way for divorce when we induced the statesmen to relax the statutes somewhat," answered Belial.

"When people see money in a thing, you can have any law, however rigid, annulled or amended nowadays. It's only a question of knowing how and when to pull the wires," Satan replied with a grin.

"Laxity on the part of the church has also helped this divorce business," responded Belial.

"I know it," said the Archfiend, "but at this time the church is greatly agitated over the question of divorce."

"It takes a long while, though, to restore sentiment when once it has been tampered with, and you know our manipulations have been pretty effective," Belial replied.

"There is no question of that," said Satan, "but there is now such an awakening of conscience regarding this matter that our plans must be well laid if we are to have any success in our undertaking."

HOME DESTRUCTION IS CAREFULLY PLANNED

At this moment the secretary handed a paper to the Archfiend.

"Read it aloud," said Satan, returning it to him.

"Yes," rejoined Belial, as he settled himself comfortably to listen, "we have spent considerable time and thought on this divorce business, and I am quite anxious to know the result of our conference."

The secretary began to read:

"CASTLE OF ALL EVIL:

"RESIDENCE OF HIS SATANIC MAJESTY:

"*Memorandum of rules to be observed in handling divorce—*"

"Never mind all that!" ejaculated Satan impatiently. "Read the rules!"

The secretary read again:

> "*1. We shall tempt all law-makers and judges to further amend existing laws concerning marriage and divorce, in order that both may be matters of convenience.*
>
> "*2. We shall tempt the legal fraternity to stir up the question of divorce, wherever feasible, by offering them exceptionally large fees.*
>
> "*3. We shall fence off certain states where, by reason of this adjustment, divorces can be readily obtained.*
>
> "*4. We shall use every possible means known to our craft, to deaden the consciences of men with reference to the moral side of marital separation.*
>
> "*5. We shall tempt youth, and such as are unfit for conjugal union, to speedily enter that state.*

> "6. We shall persuade all ministers, in so far as possible, to install private marriage bureaus, whereby all classes and conditions may be more easily joined in matrimony.
>
> "7. We shall give special attention to 'Society People,' and by encouraging platonic friendships, reach the same result—home destruction—as by methods which already obtain."

"That sounds all right," said Satan as the secretary finished the reading.

"Yes," replied Belial. "I think that covers the ground."

"Despatch a copy to Faultfinder at once," said Satan to the secretary, "and express my appreciation of his suggestion."

"It shall be done," was the reply, and so saying, he took his leave of the pair, who, soon after, arose and left the room.

Darkness closed around me, blotting out the vision, as an invisible hand led me from the place and beyond the castle walls.

THE ANGEL'S MISSION IS TO WARN

The touch of my conductor seemed familiar, and I was not surprised to find the Guardian Angel standing beside me in the grounds that surrounded Satan's stronghold.

"Child of the Vision," said she, "thou hast again been within the walls of Satan's home and hast once more heard him plot to ensnare the souls of men and women.

"As the very breath of his nostrils," she went on, "is this disturbing of the marriage relation. But it shall not be!" she cried.

"It shall not be! Now I know the plan of his attack upon the home, and I must impart it to those whose mission it is to sound the note of warning that must ring with no uncertain sound throughout the City of Worldliness. Come with me!"

As we entered the home of Minister Good, Evangelist and Determination were seated in his study, deep in conversation. To them the Angel revealed herself, while I, unseen, heard what they said.

"Whence comest thou, kind Angel?" said the venerable prophet.

"I have come from Satan's Castle of All Evil," replied the Angel, "and there I heard him and his familiar demon, Belial, plotting new harm to mankind."

Then she told them of what we had seen and heard in the castle, and of the Archfiend's latest plans to disrupt and dismember the home, by encouraging and facilitating the divorce evil.

THE ANGEL'S NOTE OF WARNING

"This is the message that you shall bear to the people of this city," she then said:

"The sanctity of married life must remain hallowed, and the home must continue to reflect the love and righteousness of God."

"This divorce evil is one of Satan's sharpest spears, which he has thrust secretly into the vitals of humanity," said Evangelist.

"The Lord of Heaven hath sent me to arouse the churches and all Christian people to the enormity of the guilt of those, who, without excuse, disrupt the relations consummated by marital vows," rejoined the Angel. "He hath sent this word of warning by me, and commands the co-operation of His people in safeguarding the home from the wiles of the Devil. Love must be kept pure at the fountain."

"It is a time for prayer, and then for untiring activity," said Evangelist, breaking the silence that followed the words of the Angel.

Determination then knelt and led in prayer for light, direction, and power, whereby to co-operate with God in thwarting this gigantic evil.

A GAME OF PROGRESSIVE POLYGAMY

"The voice of the Church of Christendom must be specific," said Evangelist, "and its deliverance must strike a death blow to this curse. Divorce, as now permitted, is but a game of *progressive polygamy,* and while hundreds dally in this sin, the Archfiend is blasting their future and damning their souls. No! This unrighteous procedure must no longer be tolerated in the Church of Christ."

"The Angel hath spoken the eternal truth concerning the sin of divorce," said Minister Good. "The Church has been lax in teaching and enforcing the sacredness of the marital vow. The words of the Angel are but a reiteration of God's ancient command."

"His commands are yea and nay; times change, but God and His work never," replied Evangelist.

POLITICAL DECAY FOLLOWS LAXITY IN MORALS

"There are lands where the population has decreased wofully in recent years," said Determination, "and their rulers have recognized and pointed the people to the violation of the laws of marriage as the alarming cause."

"Any effort at race suicide runs counter to the divine laws of nature; and upon the individual and upon the state which suffers this breach of holy orders will ever rest both a curse and a shame," replied the Angel.

"If a man would keep the sacred relations of his life clean, and make them a blessing to the race of which each generation is but a unit, he must obey the laws of God," said the minister.

THE LICENSE OF A DEAD CONSCIENCE

"In so-called 'Society Life,' there is an atrophy of conscience which leads people to break any divinely constituted law of life, when seeking to reach the goal of their perverted passions," Determination added.

"Only to-day," said Minister Good, "I was reading a sermon in which the preacher, a bishop in a fellow-denomination, said:

"'Men are losing respect for the home and caring less for the family, the unit of our civilization. On the shoulders of the husbands and fathers of the land rests the responsibility for the low estate to which the family has fallen in this country.

"'This great evil—the most frightful danger of our age—is divorce and the breaking down of the family institution. If it is not stopped, the women of this country and our race will be degraded within fifty years.' "

THE PENALTY OF ILLICIT PASSION

For some time the Angel had stood before the company in silence, with the air of one who is deciding a matter of importance. Now she said:

"I will describe to you what mine eyes have seen this day.

"In the dungeons of the Archfiend's castle, I saw gruesome cages in which were incarcerated for eternal misery the souls of those, who, for the sake of gratifying their illicit passions, had wrought revenge and indescribable sorrows and murder.

"The wailing of their plight was unending; for the light of hope had been extinguished by their keeper ere they entered. I saw them thus, and pitied them, but my arm was powerless to save, for the tears of repentance were dried up in their souls.

SATAN ALWAYS MOCKS HIS VICTIMS

"The Archfiend, in passing, mocked their piteous cries, and tauntingly reminded them of their chains, as he laughed in derision."

"For what offense were they in these hideous cages?" inquired Determination.

"They," answered the Angel, "lost their souls by following the evil suggestions of the Devil regarding love and marriage. Thus they wrote the record of their doom."

"It is indeed sad," said the minister, "that there are yet those of a like persuasion."

"There are many who will risk their very souls in defiance of the laws of God, to achieve their ends," answered the Angel.

"The way of the transgressor is hard everywhere; he must ever reap the harvest for which he sows," said Evangelist.

PREACH THE CURSE OF VIOLATED VOWS

"We must bend every effort," said Determination, "toward ushering in the day when the true light of God shall illumine all men with the truth concerning the hallowed relations of marriage."

"Yes, toward this urge all Christians to strive vigorously, for Satan vaunteth himself concerning his recently conceived action," urged the heavenly ministrant.

"How shall we proceed?" inquired Minister Good.

"Give instant heed to having the sin and curse of violated martial vows proclaimed from every pulpit in the land; and secure the co-operation of the religious and secular press.

"Urge Christ's people to safeguard this sacred ordinance of God, by right and just love; and make it reprehensible for the clergy of all faiths to unite in marriage those unjustly divorced, or those whose physical conditions would render this hallowed estate a menace to the race," declared the Angel.

"Thou speakest the words of God," said Evangelist.

THE ANGEL TEACHES GOD'S LAW

Then I beheld the Angel, upon swift wings, crossing the earth, and where men and women regarded God, she taught His law concerning marriage and the sacredness and purpose of this bond.

Her message was voiced in all the churches in the exact words of the Lord's command, and much heed was given to it.

Thus did the Angel advise and plead everywhere for the observance of the divine rule as to marriage; warning all in this particular, however, that ye be "not unequally yoked together with unbelievers."

Throughout her world journey she denounced the evils of divorce, clearly stating the only case in which it was justified, and quoting the Nazarene teacher as authority for her unqualified words.

Minister Good, from his pulpit, proclaimed the message which the Angel had brought, and throughout the entire City of Worldliness the same message was given by Determination and Wholesoul under the direction of Evangelist. The conscience of the Church was awakened, and its power was soon felt in all walks of life.

The Judiciary, as well as the Church, now began to see the disintegrating influence of the divorce evil upon the state; and unsubsidized periodicals took up the note of warning, until the protest of the right-minded against the Archfiend's plan to corrupt the home became universal.

BELIAL AND FAULTFINDER ATTACK A CHRISTIAN HOME

In my vision I saw Belial and Faultfinder approach a home known for its happiness, which was situated in the Valley of the Cross. I marked the evil intent that burned in their souls. Disguised, they knocked at the door and entered the modest cottage.

Then it was that I saw an engagement with the King of the Bottomless Pit; for, with Belial and Faultfinder, there suddenly appeared a company of satanic beings who were taught of Beelzebub himself to destroy domestic happiness.

"They had breast-plates, as it were breast-plates of iron, and the sound of their wings was as the sound of chariots of many horses running to battle. And they had tails like unto scorpions, and there were stings on their tails; and their power was to hurt."

With hellish fierceness they assailed the home upon which the sunshine of Heaven had fallen for years, while their fiendish cries rent the air.

"What will the end be?" I asked myself. Then I beheld the Angel enter the contest and knew that the hour of victory had come. With the Sword of the Avenger she slew the vile horde and then burned their bodies in the pit of Gehenna. None escaped her vengeance save Belial and Faultfinder, who vanished as she appeared.

Then I beheld the Angel in the midst of this family which she had saved. Lifting her hands in love, while a smile such as Heaven alone can kindle lighted up her face, she repeated the words of Jesus:

"Peace be within this home."

SATAN'S EMISSARIES WRECK A HOME

Prior to their attack upon the laborer's cottage, Belial and his partner had despoiled a home among the aristocracy of the city. They had blasted faith by a base suspicion, and in hearts prone

"'Knees are calloused from the worship of other gods.'"

to unforgiveness their hellish poison lodged and accomplished its work. The Angel sighed in spirit as she watched the sorrowful ending of what was begun as a lifelong blessing; but her hand was powerless to expose the base lies of the enemy, for neither husband nor wife would consent to hear the truth.

As I watched these two misguided souls between whom the fiends of Beelzebub had come with the baseness of hell, and witnessed the death of love in their souls, I said:

"The life they lived led up to this; for it was a hand unnerved by the giddy swirl that unbarred the door of the heart to suspicion."

"*Cursed be the social wants that sin against the strength of youth!*
Cursed be the social lies that warp us from the living truth!
Cursed be the sickly forms that err from honest Nature's rule!
Cursed be the gold that gilds the straiten'd forehead of the fool!
Comfort? Comfort, scorned of devils: this is truth the poet sings,
That a sorrow's crown of sorrow is remembering happier things."

HYPOCRITE'S WEDDING ANNIVERSARY

Whatever else were his faults, Hypocrite was a believer in the purity of the home; and the elimination of any evil that threatened domestic happiness appealed to him.

I saw him seated in his library in pleasant conversation with his family on the anniversary of his marriage, and a few friends, among whom were Minister Good and his wife, and Evangelist, were there by invitation.

During the evening Minister Good spoke to Hypocrite concerning the blessings of home, for which he had great occasion to be grateful.

This reference furnished an occasion for Evangelist to speak of the divorce evil, and of the Church's effort to defeat the purpose of Satan.

"Those who appreciate the joy and comfort of home should unite with us in an effort to suppress the evils which encourage family dissolution," said the prophet.

Mr. Hypocrite immediately warmed to the subject, and became intensely alive to the importance of the movement.

"I am so glad that the ministers and churches are awaking to the enormity of the divorce evil," said he. "Old Satan will gnash his teeth, when he realizes that spiritual forces are again opposing him."

"A man in your position in political life must have had occasion to see the enormity of this sin," said Minister Good.

BEELZEBUB'S LITANY IS SUNG IN COURT

"Yes," replied Hypocrite. "It would surprise you to see what is going on in the courts. It's a light matter nowadays for people to brush up some excuse for annulling marriage. Of the hundreds of divorces yearly granted in this city, very few are gotten upon legitimate grounds."

"What do you consider legitimate grounds?" inquired Evangelist.

"The law as announced by Jesus Christ," answered Hypocrite.

"Then we stand together in this matter, and why not stampede the Devil at the point where he least suspects?" questioned the minister.

"What point is that?" queried Hypocrite.

"The law-making and the executive centres," answered the minister.

"Well, we have much influence there, if the plan is rightly presented," replied Hypocrite.

"It is well to leave no stone unturned," added Evangelist, "but to me it seems that the truth concerning God's law as to marriage and its attending responsibilities must be plainly taught in our churches, that Christians may rightly instruct their families, and that those who contemplate entering that holy estate may do so with an intelligent conscience."

THE DIVORCE MILLS

"You have hit the nail on the head," was the reply. "Do this, and the rest must follow as sure as day follows night. The young people of these times enter marriage thoughtlessly. The prospect of social advancement, or wealth, leads them to take steps which a little later they seek to undo upon the most flimsy pretexts. They seek the divorce mills of some unregenerate state, and by feeding the hoppers with fees and falsehood, they disrupt their God-appointed union."

"That is true," responded the prophet; "court records abound with the names of such as have perjured themselves into freedom."

Belial and Faultfinder had been at work in the city, and now I saw them seated within a massive stone edifice which I learned was the Court of Justice. The judge, attired in his robe of office, sat in his judicial chair, and with him were two of his colleagues. They had reached a conclusion concerning a case, and the judge, with unquestionable authority, announced that:

"Having weighed the evidence, the court has decided to grant an annulment of the marriage in question, and grant the said parties a bill of divorcement."

Belial and his friend chuckled with great glee as this decision was declared.

"What a feather in our caps!" said Belial. "Church members, too, with no more real ground for divorce than for jumping into the river."

"There will be more of our victims here," said Faultfinder. "So we'll wait awhile and help to keep matters moving."

"Good," rejoined Belial.

THE DEVIL IS VERY POLITE

Then I saw Satan join the smooth-tongued attorneys who had pleaded the case, and noted their jovial conversation.

"We are very much obliged for your interest in our business," said one of the attorneys.

"The obligation is mutual," replied Satan. "We consider you our most efficient co-laborers in this branch of our enterprise."

"That's a great compliment, indeed," added another, bending low out of respect to His Satanic Majesty.

At this moment Satan introduced them to Belial and Fault-finder, and in turn the attorneys introduced the three friends to the Court.

Before leaving, the Archfiend divided among the attorneys a large sum of money as a further retainer, and I heard him say:

"See that those mills keep on grinding; for we shall be needing new material right along."

"We shall certainly look after your interests," they replied.

THE DIVORCE MILLS ARE DESTROYED

Not long after this, however, Whole-soul and Determination gathered a number of faithful souls for an attack upon the Divorce Mills, whose location Hypocrite had given to Evangelist.

When I saw them go forth on their mission, the righteous indignation which fired the great reformer of Galilee as he scourged the money-changers from the temple burned in their veins, and when they reached the Divorce Mills, the entire band, at the command of Determination, rushed in with the weapons of law and truth, and demolished them. Their patrons, and all who were supported by the unholy trade, fled in confusion to escape both shame and punishment.

"In the name of God and the home, we shall yet rid the world of this damnable business," said Determination to the valiant band, as they returned after purifying the entire valley from the accursed thing.

ALL 'S WELL WITH THE WORLD

As the last of the company passed me, I beheld Evangelist and the Angel together, while just behind them, against the evening sky, was outlined the Hill of the Cross.

"What are the signs of promise?" inquired the prophet.

"The Lord is in His Heavens and all is well. The work of His servants hath been followed with His blessing. The Archfiend has failed in his diabolical design," answered the Angel.

As the Angel parted from him, the gray prophet returned to the home of Minister Good, and conveyed to him the words of the Angel; and together, with glad hearts, they thanked the Lord for the tokens of blessing and power He had shown to them.

When the news of Determination's achievement reached the castle, Satan's wrath was withering in its fury. He raved as one given over to madness because his plans had miscarried.

JEHOVAH LAUGHS AT SATAN

Rushing forth, he climbed a rock in the midst of the spacious grounds about the castle and stood boldly upright. The dense woods with their umbrageous shadows clasped the hills back of him, as, with face turned heavenward, he pointed his finger in defiance toward the Throne of the Omnipotent, and, in oaths known only to the Pit, began to vilify the Creator of the Universe, man's only friend.

In his rage, I beheld the Archfiend stand as one pinned to the rock, until the night hid his vile person from my eyes. Then his wrath seemed to lack the power of speech, and silence rested within the great void which stretched toward the heavens.

At last a sound like unto the tremendous notes of a mighty thunder-peal interrupted the silence; and I asked the Angel, who now stood by my side, to teach me the meaning of it.

"The sound is that of the Lord laughing at the rage and blasphemy of the Archfiend," she replied.

CHAPTER XVI

The Worship of Other Gods

"Among those who hear the wise, four species may be distinguished—the sponge, the funnel, the filter, and the sieve. The sponge swallows up everything; the funnel allows that to escape at one end which it receives at the other; the filter allows the liquor to escape and retains the dregs; the sieve rejects the chaff and retains nothing but the wheat." —*Jewish Proverb.*

EASTER morn had again dawned upon the earth. As the first streaks of dawn shot up the sky, the chimes in the tower of the Church of the Disciples rang out exultingly the ancient choral of the Resurrection:

> "Jesus Christ is risen to-day,
>   Alleluia!
> Our triumphant, holy day,
>   Alleluia!
> Who did once upon the cross
> Suffer to redeem our loss,
>   Alleluia!"

Then came the clang of bells, and other chimes; and as their diverse tones combined in one faint, misty harmony, I thought of the multiform and many-colored creeds which men wrap around the one living truth God gives them—Himself. Might not these varied forms, at last, reach His perfect ear in the clear monotone of love?—

"Glory in the highest—on earth, peace!"

SILENCE THAT DREADFUL BELL; IT FRIGHTS THE ISLE

The melody of the morning bells was wafted to the ear of Satan in his castle home, and as the music rose and fell, he exclaimed to Deception, who sat near him:

"Those cursed bells will awaken in the thoughts of the people a recollection of the meaning of this day. We must devise some plan to change all this."

"Nothing will so soon accomplish our end as to captivate the people by erecting certain gods to which they already incline, for them to worship," replied Deception. "I have worked among them and am fully acquainted with their whims and proclivities."

"You have given me a good suggestion," assented Satan. "What further plan have you in mind?"

THOU SHALT HAVE NO OTHER GODS

"My thought," continued Deception, "is to build along the Road of Life a number of gods such as the gay and worldly-inclined secretly worship, and thus divide the interests and thoughts of these Christians ere they reach the church.

"The tendency will then be to create in their churches the

spirit and form which best ministers to their tastes and self-seeking. We can control the clergy through the insistence of the people.

"We have made remarkable headway in many other matters in this age, and your suggestion covers a question which has given me much anxiety and concern."

"What gods do you propose as best suited to the majority of mortals?" rejoined the Archfiend.

"The gods of Gold, Fashion, Ambition, Self, Covetousness, and a number of others which the hearts of the people easily suggest. For the worship of these, they will quickly trample under foot their former ideas of honor, of conscience, and religious duty; but in rearing these gods, care must be taken to make them attractive."

NOW DOES MY PROJECT GATHER TO A HEAD

Then I beheld Satan summon his henchmen, and a vast number of horrible fiends appeared, to whom he gave orders concerning the immediate erection of the gods, and with ready obedience they set forth to carry out His Majesty's plans.

Then my heart was bathed in sorrow to behold how along each path of life these false gods arose to tempt the souls of the multitude. Some were new, the creation of the present age, while others were old ones—regilded gods which men and women for centuries had worshipped with adoring souls.

"The work is done," said Satan, as he beheld the gods of his own fashioning stationed at every point, and kneeling before them, a concourse of deceived devotees.

THE WORSHIP OF OTHER GODS

HE IS RISEN. HE IS NOT HERE

Evangelist had spent the night upon a hill outside the city, from which the Cross of the Crucified could be seen, watching for the dawn of the morrow, which should recall to men the resurrection of the sinless Saviour.

As the day awoke, he kneeled in prayer, and then rose to find the Angel standing by his side.

> "Jesus Christ to-day has risen,
> And o'er death triumphant reigns,"

were her words of salutation.

> "He has burst the grave's strong prison,
> Leading sin itself in chains,"

was the reply of the prophet.

"But why is there a shade of sadness on thy face this blessed morn?" he asked.

THOU SHALT NOT BOW DOWN THYSELF TO THEM

"Satan is setting up more of his false gods along the Road of Life," she replied. "He has chosen this, of all days, to delude the souls of men and cause them to forget, or lightly pass over, the significance of this blessed morn. Thousands who bear His name will this day bow down to other gods, thus making Him second in their devotions."

Passing her hand to and fro as though to part the veil of sense, the Angel pointed toward the City of Worldliness.

"Look, servant of God," she said; "look yonder along life's

pathway by which this generation journeys to the grave. Yonder lies the goal," as she pointed to a distant spot on the horizon, "and these columns in the path are the waymarks of years. How heedless the soul is to the religion which places Christ upon the heart's throne."

"I behold the vision," replied the prophet, "and see the gods before whom so many of the world vainly worship. To them, religion is but a form. The Enemy hath blinded the eyes of the people, and they bow down as though their visible gods were the eternal."

I MAY NOT STOP TO SEEK REPOSE

Then the Angel pointed the prophet toward a distant garden, where was situated still, the grave from which the shining ones had removed the stone. Turning until he faced the Cross, the patriarch knelt for a moment in prayer, and then, with the Angel, passed on to the city.

"Our Lord hath much for us to do this day," I heard him say, "for the Enemy purposeth to substitute forms and follies for the true worship of the risen Jesus.

"The Lord grant us power to undo the works of the Devil! The Lord give victory to the work of His saints," he exclaimed.

"Fear not," replied the Angel, "for the Lord of Heaven will this day endue with righteousness and might the hearts of the believing. His spirit, inbreathed, shall vitalize the life smothered by the empty forms of the Enemy. The songs of His angels shall restore harmony where satanic discords abound."

As the Angel and Evangelist entered the city, Satan spied them.

"Curses upon that Angel!" he raged. "She hath again divined my purpose, and even now goes to stir up the zeal of those I most fear."

Once within the city, the Angel noticed that the false gods were built along the way which led to the sanctuary and that they were even set up within the sacred edifice itself, in the hope that some souls would worship form and ritual rather than the Christ. Calling the attention of Evangelist to the subtlety in this, she said:

"Behold the deception of man's Enemy. He hath set these pitfalls at every weak point in human nature."

"So hath he wrought since the Fall," replied Evangelist, "only in these latter days his skill and subterfuge know no bounds in his determination to capture souls."

THERE SHINES ONE DAY IN SEVEN

Then I saw that the Angel and Evangelist sought the home of Minister Good, and found him in preparation for the day's work. To his soul the Angel whispered helpful words, and gave strength for the day's mission.

"We have prayed and shall strive," said Evangelist, "to demolish the false gods of the Enemy and point the souls of mankind to the risen Saviour."

Then placing his hand upon the shoulder of the minister, the prophet continued, "Be of good courage and give unto thy flock the vision of the Christ; for all must behold Him this day.

"These gods which Satan has erected, but reflect the wish of the worldly worshipper wrought out into pleasing form," continued

Evangelist. "Satan, nowadays, does not so much invent new ideas, as he reproduces the gods which embody the whims and foibles of a selfish heart. The temples of time are filled with such idols, and each life has some god, secreted within the cloister of the soul, which it has canonized, and to which it gives conscious or unconscious obeisance."

FOR I, THY GOD, AM A JEALOUS GOD

"For some, I fear it may be too late," replied Minister Good, "for when the knees are calloused from the worship of other gods, it is difficult to bend them in loyal supplication to the Christ."

"That is true," admitted Evangelist, "yet to such as these, pressed of the Devil by wealth and fashion and whims of many sorts, His patience and forbearance is infinite. He wills not that any should perish. He has paved the path of life with hope, up to the hour of departure. His eye is ever watchful for the return of a prodigal—and there are prodigals from faith—and to such, after the sorrows of waywardness have driven them home, the Christ is most tender and forgiving. Yes,

> "'There's a wideness in God's mercy,
> Like the wideness of the sea.'"

"I pray it shall be so," answered the minister, as Evangelist passed from his home, after leaving a blessing.

"What a beautiful morning it is," said the minister to his wife, who had entered the room in time to hear Evangelist's last words.

"It is indeed a beautiful day," assented Mrs. Good, "and no

day is empty of blessing; for His benedictions are falling somewhere all the while.

"No bird yet sang with all its heart but that his fellows were made the happier; no flower yet bloomed but that the air around was laden with its perfume; no sun ever shone but that the whole world in some way felt the healing of its beams; so, no life ever fills its true meaning without leaving some lasting good with the race.

"There is help we may each give to these disturbed conditions of life, if so be we have seen the face of Jesus, and read therein the message of God's love for mankind."

"That is true," returned her husband. "We each have our work to do, and our word to speak. They will fit in somewhere, however much we sometimes regard our efforts from a discouraged standpoint."

"There is really no discouragement," replied Mrs. Good, "to such as live and abide in the Life Giver; joy is but the sunlight of God's smile falling upon the opening flowers of the garden of the soul, while our little sorrow is but his loving hand thoughtfully pruning the vines during a cloudy day.

"All days run close together and carry the same divine thought. The Christian must go on singing to all his brightest hopes, as by faith he sees that completion of life which lies for each friend of God within the atoning merits of His Son."

SURE ALL THINGS WEAR A HEAVENLY DRESS

Bright skies bathed in azure, air laden with the perfume of blossoms, and paths bordered by flowers newly risen from the grave, gave to this Easter morning a halo of blessedness to all who beheld it through the Angel's eyes.

Vast throngs of people hastened toward the churches, and as Satan beheld the tide of the populace entering the sacred edifices, he realized how effective had been the services of the heavenly ministrant.

"That Angel has turned the thoughts of hundreds, upon whom we wrought, to the Church and the recollection of the day's teaching," said Satan to Deception in a tone of disgust.

"I have been tinkering somewhat with the service in the churches," replied the latter, "and have planned to hide the real import of the day's teaching under a cloak of outward form. We may have better results than you are hoping for."

"That was a bright thought," admitted Satan. "Those on pleasure bent will not slip from our grasp; so let us haste to the churches and see that our plans are consummated."

WE SAY THE PRAYERS AND HEAR THE WORD

As the hour for morning service drew near, the streets of the City of Worldliness were thronged with men, women, and children. Throughout the year, Sundays were not regarded as other than days of amusement and recreation, but to be absent from the house of God on Easter was to commit a flagrant sin.

The Church of the Holy Passion was the centre of attraction for a large portion of the well-dressed company on this occasion, for the Rev. Mr. Please-all, a celebrated pulpiteer, had recently been

"'T is Man-of-the-World!" Determination cried. "He calls for help!"

called from Longshore to become its pastor, and was to deliver his initial sermon.

In my vision, I beheld Evangelist and Determination enter the church with the crowd, and take a position from which they could study the scene and grasp the spirit and form of the service.

Other things were given me to see, as from the place I had chosen I watched the multitude fill the beautiful auditorium. Satan and Deception were conversing in a corner, and the Good Angel was standing by the side of Mr. Please-all.

SO FROM MY LIPS THY SONG SHALL FLOW

Soon the great organ in rapturous exultation responded to the touch of the master at its keys, and then the choir, easily the first in the city, began the rendition of the musical program of the day.

"Certainly no one understood a word of that," said Satan to Deception.

"They are doing it just as I intended they should," was the smiling reply.

"They can entertain the mind, but such performances are pretty sure of never awaking the sympathies of the heart to the real truths of the day," returned Satan. "You have done your part well."

"I have striven to suppress all religious emotions or sentiment, which thoughts of the Resurrection excite, by prompting the singers to pay more attention to technique than to the sentiment of truth the words should convey," continued Deception.

HOW FAITHLESSLY I DID MY LITTLE PART

"I understand," said the Enemy of Souls. "That was indeed a masterly stroke. If we can only keep Please-all from getting to the heart of the day's teaching, we shall have won our ends."

"Don't worry about Please-all. I was with him in the preparation of his sermon; and he is going to read it just as he wrote it. There will be no heart-glow born of the occasion, thrown in—yes, I 've fixed him," asserted Deception.

"You have gone further into the matter than I thought," admitted Satan.

"We must attend to every detail nowadays if we want to deceive mankind," was the reply.

Then I saw how earnestly the Angel pleaded with Mr. Please-all to break from the cold, philosophical formalism of his discourse and, with soul bathed with holy unction, enter into the practical truths and lessons of the day, and thus touch souls with the loving and gladdening message of the Resurrection.

A FAITH THAT SEEMS NOT FAITH

She pleaded in vain, for the Rev. Mr. Please-all knew what would please his audience, and though it was an angel from Heaven who solicited him, he refused either to suffer his cold ritualism to thaw, or to depart an inch from set forms. The Angel sorrowed, for she saw that the great truth of God's triumph from the grave — humanity's greatest boon — was not to be expressed, either in song or sermon, that day.

The sweet flowers with which the church was profusely decorated were the true messengers of the Resurrection, as with uplifted faces they seemed to say:

"He is not here. He is RISEN."

The great organ thundered forth the postlude as the congregation passed out, and I saw the officers of the church, among whom was Man-of-the-World, congratulate the minister upon the success of the service; and pointing to the burdened plates, I heard one of them say: "That is a fine offering. The congregation has been generous to-day."

Within the choir-room, the singers were complimenting themselves over the perfection with which they had all rendered their parts, and I heard the leader say: "The most exacting critic could not find fault with the music this morning."

But the Angel knew that because the great stone of form, and worship of art for art's sake, had been rolled against the sepulchre, the soul of the congregation had not been fed; that it had not met the risen Christ.

As she departed, she whispered to me, "The people have not learned the lessons of the day. In their hearts the Saviour did not rise."

OH, WEARISOME CONDITION OF HUMANITY!

Leaving the Church of the Holy Passion, I passed into the street, and as I threaded my way through the crowds, I particularly noticed how a host of Satan's adroit fiends were pulling the Juggernaut of fashion over the forms of the gay multitude.

Seemingly the true conception of the Resurrection, which nineteen centuries of touch with Christ had sought to teach, was not yet grasped. All were making of the day a Saturnalia, when the goddess of fashion was devoutly worshipped; and the joy with which souls should abound in contemplation of the Redeemer's triumph over death was to this host of pleasure-seekers an empty thing.

Satan smiled with great satisfaction as he strolled hither and thither among the crowd and saw the ease with which he had diverted it from the thought and teachings of the day.

"Never before in the city have I seen such relaxation, nor such abandonment of regard for the worship of the risen Christ as this day," said the Archfiend to Deception, as the two watched the passing show.

OH! SHOW THAT SIN TO ME

But not all in the great City of Worldliness worshipped false gods that day. In the consciences of thousands, the voice of the Angel had awakened a sense of personal duty, who otherwise would have forgotten to fulfill their pledges to Christ that day.

At her solicitation the eyes of thousands whom Satan had blinded by the glare of other gods gazed with sorrow for their mistakes into the face of God's Anointed; and the dayspring of a better life began to revive where the soul's love had long been dead.

With the Good Angel, on her mission of awakening, were a host from above, who had concern for the household of faith, and who gave to the Lord's children the touch of quickening.

THE WORSHIP OF OTHER GODS

NEW OBSTACLES ARISE AND OMENS ILL

Later in the day, Evangelist and Determination were in the study of Minister Good, and, unseen by them, I heard their conversation.

"Times have changed. The idea and habit of keeping the festivals of the Church lack the old-time reverence. I can record great changes here, within my own lifetime," said Minister Good.

"Yes," answered the prophet, "times have changed, and with this change, the expression of Christian faith has been recast. The old truths, which are rock truths, of our religious faith are not regarded in these days as of the same importance as in former years. Religious festivals are not now accorded the personal sacredness they received from the Fathers. The truths these festivals then conveyed wrought with much feeling upon the soul. Now we have these festivals in forms which gratify the æsthetic side of our nature and from them comes very little of transfiguring vision to the life. Art has been lifted up as a false god, and the age applauds it."

THY FAIR WHITE FAITH IS SOILED

"You have spoken a great truth," admitted the minister. "The Christians of this age are guilty of going no deeper in their devotion to Christ than the form their selfishness approves."

"What didst thou think of the service this morning?" inquired Determination of the prophet.

"Oh, it was so cold and bare of the real spirit which should have gladdened the occasion of the Saviour's Resurrection. To my heart's sorrow, I saw again exemplified the attempt of man to emphasize the form and ceremonial of religion, at the sacrifice of the clear utterance of the truths the Church was instructed to proclaim.

"The Church was organized to declare God's eternal message, rather than to express a form which delights the fancy. Such a service is but man's foolish and futile attempt to make bread for the soul from the stones of art and hackneyed dogmatism."

"This is the tendency of the times in many places," observed Minister Good. "The forces of our advancing civilization seek through the social influence of modern times to construct not only a church, but a doctrinal form also, that shall regale the tastes of the fastidious and querulous, and with the advent of this product of the age has gone the soul's keen craving for the essential truths which were once sought after and given prominence."

FALSE AS THE DESERT'S SHINING SPRINGS

"Rev. Mr. Please-all is one who emphasizes the æsthetic and formal elements of religion. So long as the Church lives to please the fancies of the people it abides successful, but I have often wondered what its membership would be if it were stripped of the draperies of fad and fashion which are made so conspicuously essential," answered Determination.

"These are the gods many worship instead of the true One, and with their demolition would depart the religious expression of their lives. There are too many Christians nowadays who attend the church to be entertained, and their devotion is to the thing which affords them mental delight, rather than to God, their Maker,'' added Minister Good.

"Thou hast indeed touched the fact,'' replied the prophet.

"Hundreds of Christians are afraid of the evangelistic spirit in this age. Soft-cushioned pews, brief and restful sermons, plenty of operatic music—in fact, an hour of diversion, is all a large proportion of the church seek. The heathen abroad and the heathen at home give them little concern, and conscience is easily put to rest if a degree of religious form is maintained.''

"This modernizing of the Church is the work of the Devil; and too often the eyes of the elect are blinded by the gilt with which the Enemy veneers the weaknesses and idiosyncrasies of the saints,'' replied Minister Good.

ONE LOOK BROUGHT PETER BACK

"The truth is,'' added Evangelist, "the Cross is kept too far in the background; and the reason for this is that the personal sacrifice it enjoins is greater than the pleasure-loving and selfish are willing to make. If Christ should appear to-day in our modern churches, and insist that those alone could bear His name who are willing to break in pieces all other gods they worship, and follow Him, bearing their cross even to the point of denial of self, church membership would be materially reduced. That law, however, marks a man as either a Christian or one of the world.''

"The Master drew a distinction which thousands are not

acknowledging in their religious life to-day," replied the minister.

"We shall have to bend our energies to flooding the cold and ceremonial centres of religious life with the light of the Cross of the Son of God," continued Determination. "We shall have to resort to methods that shall banish from the land the false gods of the Devil's substitution."

Then Minister Good, Evangelist, and Determination left the home of the former and sought the centre of the city.

E'EN SUNDAY SHINES NO SABBATH DAY TO US

Places of amusement under license of the city government were open, and were doing a profitable business. Excursions were being run to various parks within easy reach of the city; street cars carried tens of thousands to base-ball grounds and golf links. The marks of Satan's hands were upon everything.

"These are the gods they worship," said Evangelist sadly, "and the Lord's children look on supinely, uttering not a word of protest, while Satan is hurling soul after soul for whom the Redeemer died, into perdition."

While the prophet was speaking, Rev. Mr. Please-all went by with a party of friends on their way to take a train for one of the pleasure parks. Recognizing Evangelist, he looked back, and then turned to the one beside him and said in ridicule:

"He's the old erratic who ran the beach meetings a year or two ago at Longshore. What do you suppose he's up to now?" With these words the pastor of the fashionable Church of the Holy Passion passed on to seek his recreation.

PERVERTS THE PROPHETS AND PURLOINS THE PSALMS

"That man," said Evangelist, as he pointed his staff at Rev. Mr. Please-all, "has let down the bars of Zion. He is of the world, worldly. The Lord shall require much at his hands; for it is his spirit of indulgence that has encouraged others of his class, and together their influence reaches a wide area.

"Please-all hath forgotten the divine injunction: 'Ye shall burn no . . . honey in any offering of the Lord made by fire, . . . and every oblation of thy meat offering shalt thou season with salt; neither shalt thou suffer the salt of the covenant of thy God to be lacking.' Let us go hence."

HE HATH A SERVICE FOR EACH ONE

In the gathering twilight, as the sinking sun threw its golden light in soft effulgence over the Hill-lands of Faith, I saw Evangelist standing with face turned toward the Cross, while by him stood Determination looking out in pity upon the great mass of thoughtless and transgressing humanity. The countenance of the prophet shone as one inspired. He had spoken with God, and I saw that the Angel stood near him with outstretched hands.

Then, in my vision, I saw her direct Evangelist to the steps of an old weather-beaten church, long deserted by reason of the migration of its congregation to other parts of the city.

Crowds were hurrying homewards from the afternoon's amusements and sports, among which was Rev. Mr. Please-all and his friend, Mr. Man-of-the-World.

"Stand thou here," the Angel said to the prophet, "and cry

out in the name of our God against such flagrant and wanton desecration of the Lord's Day. Speak thou the burning words of judgment! Spare none; for all these have sinned. Many of them under the cloak of religion are deceiving themselves, and this day have been the source of stumbling to others of weaker wills. Speak! and the Lord give thee power!"

Then I heard him hurl the anathemas of his God into the very teeth of the sin-cursed city. The surging throng stopped, and standing silent, a sea of faces faced his, as though listening to a sentence of doom.

ENTER NOT INTO THE PATH OF THE WICKED

With the boldness of one empowered from Heaven, he decried the lax spirit of Christians, and each sentence cut deep into the sinful worship of self-chosen idols which for pleasure and revenue were exalted before the people in defiance of the laws of Jehovah.

Fearlessly he enunciated the irrevocable judgment of the Almighty against such as caused the innocent to sin by their artful and arrogant perversion of truth.

"Turn ye! turn ye! Why will ye die? The night hastens in which for you, steeped in sin, the stars of repentance may never shine. The night cometh, in which the memory of wasted years shall be in thy soul as quenchless fires of remorse."

TAKE FAST HOLD OF INSTRUCTION

Thus did I hear the prophet address the multitude, and as with bated breath the sin-stained souls hearkened, I saw the Angel, who stood by his side, turn the light from the Cross on the Lonely Hill upon the hearts of the motley crowd.

Then for the moment, as Evangelist stood in silence before them, did they see the vision of the Crucified, whose teachings they had that day trampled under foot in their eagerness to worship the gods of the world, the flesh, and the Devil.

HE DEVISETH MISCHIEF CONTINUALLY

"He's at it again," said Please-all sarcastically, to Man-of-the-World, as they passed on. "I trust he will not upset things as he once did by his fanatical words at Longshore."

"I should be sorry," answered Man-of-the-World, "for I lost a good round sum through his troubling of men's consciences on that visit."

"I still hold," continued Please-all, "that the authorities should put him away. He is both a babbler and a disturber of the peace."

"I wish it might be done," replied Man-of-the-World, "but our hands are tied in that matter by the sentiment and attachment of a great number to him."

"It is strange that such a nuisance should be permitted here in the City of Worldliness, and that the hands of the law are powerless," persisted Please-all.

"It is strange, but resistance would only lead to greater trouble," replied Man-of-the-World.

SO COMES A RECKONING

Hidden behind each false god was a fiend, placed there by Satan, to keep record of the number of its worshippers, and now I saw Satan interrogating each in turn.

The god that had the greatest worship was that of Self.

"This signifies loss of power," said Satan. "How fared we in the churches?" he asked of Deception, who came up just then.

"The Angel turned the hearts of the people toward thoughts of the Resurrection in all save in the Church of the Holy Passion," was the reply.

Crestfallen, Satan burst forth in a fearful anathema upon the Angel, at whose door he laid his defeat.

Turning away from the Archfiend's awful blasphemy, I came in my vision to the home of Minister Good, whither Evangelist and Determination once more had come; and the three communed regarding the work of God during the day past. The Angel also was there.

HAVING EARS THEY HEAR NOT

"How can they hear such words and not become convicted of their sins?" asked Minister Good, as he heard of the prophet's message.

"The eyes of the multitude have seen the light of the Cross," said the Angel. "They alone who feel the permanent claims of the Christ will tear down the false gods before whom they bow."

"Good Angel," entreated Determination, "let the light of the Cross shine; let it guide the wayward hearts of this city to a pardoning and forgiving Saviour."

"Thou shalt go with those of like spirit," enjoined the Angel of Determination, "throughout the land to kindle the fires of a greater devotion to Christ. The false gods of the human heart must be thrown down before the appearing of the triumphant Lord."

Later, upon the Hill-lands of Faith, I saw Evangelist again kneel for prayer, and I heard the Angel say: "The toil of the past day hath been blessed. Many are even now departing from their false gods. It shall be a long struggle, but the reward shall be worthy of the sacrifice. The Enemy shall also resist, but the beginnings of a true faith have this day had their birth."

FROM SEEMING EVIL STILL EDUCING GOOD

Once more that day I saw Satan in his castle.

"What are you doing there?" said Satan to Deception as he passed by a room in which the latter sat.

"I am trying to offset the damage done our projects by old Evangelist," answered Deception.

"What is your plan?" inquired Satan.

"I am devising excuses with which to supply all weak Christians, and thus save them, if possible, from the damaging appeals of the prophet to which they gave heed."

"That is a good idea," assented Satan. "Hurry them up and deliver them as speedily as possible."

"I shall do the best I can. It takes time and thought to frame excuses which will satisfy consciences quickened by such burning words as he spoke," continued Deception.

"You have been in this business many years and should be a master at it," replied Satan, flatteringly.

"I've been at it a long while, but Christians are not deceived as easily as they used to be before the Angel and Evangelist appeared. Still, as a wise man once said, 'No man is happy without a delusion of some kind.' Delusions are as necessary to our happiness as realities. I'm working on that line and hope to catch a few souls anyway."

"Good! Good!" laughed the Archfiend. "Only lose no time in sending out the excuses. I will furnish you with all the help you need in their distribution." With these words, the Enemy of Souls left him.

HIM HAVE I PIERCED

The last vision of the day took me into the study of Rev. Mr. Please-all. In his hand was a book, and this is what he was reading:

"The one burden of His preaching was conduct. He laid down no dogmas. He invented no formulas. He made no metaphysical definitions. Questions which used to keep Christendom in a frantic state of turmoil were never even suggested by Christ himself. The so-called Christian Church has spent the best part of its energy in discussing subjects which are almost unintelligible and altogether unpractical."

"This is true," whispered the Angel within his soul, "and thou art one of those who cloak the truth, that thy people may burn pleasant incense to the false gods of their own choosing."

THE WORSHIP OF OTHER GODS

Please-all opened his eyes wide in thoughtful amazement, and as my vision passed, I saw the Angel pointing him beyond the gods which he allowed his congregation to worship unmolested.

His eyes rested upon an empty tomb in an ancient garden, before which appeared One with hands extended, in which the scars of a crucifixion were healing. Beaming with a love which constrains even the erring to the truth, I heard Him say to Minister Please-all:

"I am He that was dead and am risen again. Preach me! PREACH ME!"

CHAPTER XVII

Wrecks Along the Shore

"I protest that if some power would agree to make me always think what is true and do what is right, on condition of being turned into a sort of clock and wound up every morning, I should instantly close with the offer." —*Huxley.*

I STOOD on the shore of a vast sea—the "Sea of Social Swirl," and saw that its alluring and invigorating appearance tempted thousands to enter it.

Farther out, in the embrace of the full swell, were other thousands whose predilections for social excesses were being amply gratified. All was merriment and self-gratification, and in not a soul was there found an ambition for anything more substantial than fashionable follies.

As the Archfiend watched the scene from the shore, I heard him say:

"How innocently they accept the pleasures we have provided. The older ones lead on the younger set, and an ample crowd of

"Tireless fiends sorted and labeled bribes."

venturesome ones are always in waiting to take the place of those who are carried beyond their depth."

"Yes, very little solicitation is needed in this phase of life, if we keep the attractions brilliant," replied Belial who stood by his side.

THE OTHER SIDE OF THE PICTURE

The pursuit of pleasure so absorbed the time and ambition of society's devotees, that they saw not the reverse of the scene, but it was given me to see the merciless tides lash their helpless victims, and then, with means and strength gone and souls shriveled, I saw them hurled upon the scorching sands to die as wrecks upon the shore—mere semblances of their former selves.

Depleted and worn by the life they had been leading, I saw their bleared faces and bloodshot eyes upturned to the sun, which, kinder than their convivial associates, kissed these pitiful remnants of life, as though wishing to save them. But the day of hope had sped and could not be overtaken.

Among those who had paid the penalty of this exciting yet exacting life I saw, as I walked past them, the forms of two whom I had once seen in the glory of social position.

Satan had won, and there, in the embrace of untimely death, lay Presumption and Incredulous, two of those whom Evangelist had warned of the dangers that lurked by the Primrose Path.

A great shout of merriment mingled with the murmurs of the sea, and I noticed that those enjoying the gayety of the hour were unmoved by the death harvest strewn upon the beach.

Then I saw the prophet weep as his eyes swept over the scene. He had come to speak the "word in season" if not too late.

SIN'S PROMPTINGS EVER ENTHRAL US

"Pleasure and death," said he, as his keen sense of perception grasped the scene. "Pleasure and death, what a narrow strip of life lies between them, and yet, thousands rush to certain doom."

"The fascinations of the hour seem to be overmastering," I replied.

"Yes, but this is because people will not think. They rush forward to their pleasures and then are thrown back by the merciless sea to die along the shore," remarked the prophet.

Walking among the dead and dying, Evangelist's eyes fell upon the two whom he had kindly warned while on their way to the Pavilion of Pleasure, and a great desire to save such as oppose themselves to right living seized his soul.

BRIGHT, SHARP DEATH SHINES EVERYWHERE

"Would that my God might give me a voice that should appeal to the so-called society life of this age. Its path is that of death—death not only of the body, but of the soul," he exclaimed.

"This wreckage is a sad commentary upon it," I replied.

"Yes," he continued; "there is a way which seemeth right unto a man, but the end is death. 'What shall it profit a man, if he shall gain the whole world, and lose his own soul?'"

WRECKS ALONG THE SHORE

Then I saw how Satan massed his forces on the shore to foster new fads and diversions among the "Smart Set."

"They will follow every fad we suggest," said the Archfiend, "for they are always eager for novelty. There is no place where customs so soon grow commonplace as among the gay set."

WHEN SINNERS ENTREAT THEE

"It is an easy matter to gratify them in this particular," replied Belial. "We have an abundance of ideas to work out, and every suggestion they fall in with will lay them stark along the shore, sooner or later."

"These wrecks of humanity prove that," answered Satan, laughing. "See there," he continued, as he pointed to the dead and dying. "Every one of them thought himself safe from harm."

"What a gullible throng there is here," said Belial with a smile of gratification, as his eyes swept along the shore.

"And all will follow us if they are left alone," replied the Archfiend.

"Yes, but there are numbers we cannot catch, however gilded the trap," Belial rejoined.

GOD'S GRASP IS RELENTLESS

"Yes, God's grasp is relentless when men once yield to him," Satan asserted.

"It is our business to see that men do not yield," replied Belial.

"You 're right," answered Satan, "and we must push our business among this set with all energy and despatch."

I saw the two walk along the beach to a spot where the most frivolous of the set were basking in the joys of sensuality and dissipation.

"Here is the place for action. Those wrecks we have left behind are safe," said Satan.

"Yes," replied Belial, "they are beyond the pale of hope."

THE ANGEL'S APPEAL

The Angel of God had been studying the scene, and was at that very moment mustering the hosts of Heaven to defeat the Enemy of Mankind in his purpose of soul-destruction.

"It shall not be! It shall not be!" she cried, and then I heard her passionate appeal for saving power approach the Throne of Jehovah.

At times her voice was shut from my ears by the incoming tide, which, surging shoreward over this scene of sin, dashed its spray heavenward, to be jewelled for the moment by the kiss of the sun, and then falling upon the blood-stained sands, moan its way back again.

In a moment of calm the voice of the Almighty was heard upon the deep; and His message was an answer to the Angel's prayer.

"How often would I have gathered thy children together, even as a hen gathereth her chickens under her wings, and ye would not!"

Then fell what seemed to be a word of doom—"Behold, your house is left unto you desolate."

Tears came to my eyes, and sorrow for the heedless multitude I saw before me filled my soul. Then came a word in which the Almighty left both hope and promise.

"For I say unto you, Ye shall not see me henceforth, till ye shall say, Blessed is he that cometh in the name of the Lord."

"These have come in the name of the Lord," pleaded the Angel. "These would bring salvation to such as, forgetful of Thee, and have been ensnared by the Devil. Save! oh, save the perishing, Almighty God!"

She spoke of Evangelist and Determination, who stood by her side.

"They shall be anointed with the Holy Ghost and with power. Guide thou their steps," replied the voice of Jehovah.

THE TRUTH SHALL MAKE YOU FREE

"Thy blessed name be praised, O Most High," whispered the Angel.

Then I saw, with Determination, a band of young men, among whom was Light Heart, who, heeding the prophet's message at Longshore, had turned to God. He and Whole-soul were laboring together for those whose hearts God had touched. Now they sought for guidance in their attempt to cleanse the social world of its besetting sins.

"The Lord hath enjoined," Evangelist advised them, "that you be 'wise as serpents, and harmless as doves.' Resort to drastic measures only in extreme cases. Teach men the truth, for the truth is to make them free."

Turning his gaze toward the "Sea of Social Swirl," Determination recognized one, who, having ventured beyond his depth, was now struggling for life in a current known as the Whirlpool of Wine. Thousands since the days of Noah had ventured into its vortex and perished.

The waters near its edge were most invigorating, and Satan had given to the whirlpool such a peculiar fascination that when their eyes were once fixed upon it, men and women plunged into it, heedless of all warnings. Thousands from the fashionable set of every city in the land had gone to their destruction in the pool upon which Determination was now looking.

WINE IS A MOCKER

"'T is Man-of-the-World!" he cried. "He calls for help!" and so shouting, he sprang into the treacherous pool, while thousands of the "Smart Set" laughed at his efforts, as with superhuman power, bestowed by the Angel, he laid hold of Man-of-the-World and dragged him from the waters that were carrying him down to death.

A hush fell upon the giddy crowd as brave Determination laid down his burden—one of their own set, whose death would have been to them but the sensation of an hour; then, the excitement over, all returned to their merrymaking and frivolity.

"Curse that man, Determination," growled Satan in his fury. "I've struggled for years to get Man-of-the-World where he was at that moment. He's escaped me again and again; but I thought I had him in my grasp here."

As Evangelist looked down into the opening eyes of Man-of-the-World, saved from death by the very hands he had often studied to weaken, he saw that he was torn inwardly by emotions of shame and chagrin. But when the prophet pointed him to the Hill of the Cross, saying, "Man-of-the-World, 'Go, and sin no more,'" his treacherous eyes looked mockingly at the prophet, as he jumped to his feet and hurried back to join his set, who welcomed him with much shouting, in which Satan and Belial joined.

"He hath a thankless spirit," said Light Heart.

> "'Blow, blow, thou winter wind,
> Thou art not so unkind
> As man's ingratitude,'"

quoted Whole-soul.

"I fear he hath forged the chains which bind man to destruction," said Determination.

"He hath long spurned the will of God, and the Almighty hath given him over to his desire. He hath walked in paths of covetousness, excess of wine, revellings, banquetings, and abominable idolatries," explained Evangelist.

Then I beheld a number of fiends stir up the whirlpool, while another vile company, with seductive voices, whispered into the ears of those who sat at the card tables and filled the gambling halls situated close by the sea. Fascinated, absorbed, eager to win, they all became easy subjects of the Archfiend's subtleties.

UP! IT IS JEHOVAH'S RALLY

"The course of all these thoughtless souls," said the Angel to Determination, "is toward the Whirlpool of Wine. Go ye forth to arouse the conscience of the Christian Church throughout the world, that coming generations may be taught to escape its perils."

"Ah," said the Archfiend, who had overheard her words, "she's looking a good way ahead."

"I suppose she calls it taking up arms for Jehovah," added Belial.

Then the Angel turned towards these demons of the Pit, and, with flashing eyes, she cried:

"Dost thou not recall, O Snarer of Souls, the judgment pronounced upon thee by the Most High? Dost thou not yet hear the Almighty laughing at the fury of thy defiance in the castle grounds? And thou, O Belial, lawless and worthless son of evil, remember this: 'The gates of hell shall not prevail.'"

As her words fell like thunderbolts upon the scheming pair, both fled from the scene.

GOD'S ARM HATH NEED OF THINE

Determination soon set to work against evils that were plainly to be seen, and I noticed in him an enthusiasm, as well as a spirit of athletic Christianity, which feared not to attack social wrongs nor hesitated to call sins by their right names.

"Every social sin we propose to attack," said Determination

to himself, "is a scorpion in the breast of society, and each of these before me, clothed in ermine and silk and bedecked with jewels, has an immortal soul to save."

The prophet sought the Angel in the home of Miss Sincere that he might learn God's thought concerning the surest way of destroying Satan's seductive snares for the souls of men.

WEAN THE HEART FROM LOW DESIRES

"How may we best save the people from the whirlpool?" asked Evangelist of the Angel.

"By teaching the children of this generation the dangers of the wine-cup, and by instructing them to avoid the temptations which lead to it," replied the Angel.

"Temperance principles are hard to inculcate when men and women thirst for strong drink," said the prophet.

"A thirst for strong drink is Satan's millstone hung about the neck of this age. The people of God must arrest this appetite, else the foundations of the home and state shall perish," rejoined the Angel.

"The Archfiend sets his gilded traps for each new generation; and the laws of this Christian land help to damn it by legalizing the dram-shop," said Miss Sincere.

"The Lord's people have done little to suppress this evil," added the prophet. "Thousands upon thousands of inebriates die yearly like dogs, under the thraldom of the drink habit, and the prisons hold their thousands more, whom this curse has driven to crime. The battle is truly against the mighty."

SENTIMENT IS AGAINST THE DRINK EVIL

"The sentiment of the world is changing as to the drink evil," replied the Angel, "and with the Church aroused, and youth protected by truth, a better day must soon dawn."

Then I saw that Evangelist set on foot a movement for the destruction of the drink evil; for he cried out fearlessly the anathemas of Jehovah against this sin, and instructed the hosts of the Lord to carry the campaign to the very bounds of Christendom.

Belial and his helpers trembled with fear as they witnessed the universal activity of God's people, and I beheld them hurry to the castle for conference, lest this curse should be blotted from the face of the earth.

YOUTH IS DAZZLED BY THE GILDED PATH

Within the City of Worldliness Satan had caused to be constructed a secret passageway to the Whirlpool of Wine. Its entrance was gilded, and along its entire length were such alluring pictures that hosts of venturesome youths were daily dazed by its attractive appearance. This path led through the club-room, then through the saloon, and so on by devious ways until the whirlpool was reached. One of the Archfiend's artisans, known as Deception, had constructed this way in early times; but in latter days he had renewed the pavement and supplied it with a wealth of satanic charms.

"The temptations of this way must remain a secret, lest the Christians start in to oppose us," said Satan to Deception.

"We shall say as little as possible, and leave the rest to the protection of the law," was the reply.

"Yes, but their influence may change existing laws. It requires a philosopher nowadays to elude those Christians, among whom is that enthusiast, Determination," replied Satan.

THE GROG-SHOP IS PROTECTED

"The path is safe from harm, and will be thronged for years if we can but induce the youth to enter it," replied Deception.

"See to it, then, that society folks set the pace, and you will find hundreds aping them," said the Archfiend. So saying, he and Deception went forth to add new touches of splendor to the Gilded Path.

"There lies the sin which menaces this age," said the Angel to Determination, as she pointed to the door of the club-room through which thousands were taking their first steps toward the whirlpool. "Seduced by social fads, they take chances with iniquity; and yearly, out of Christian homes, a great number choose the road which leads to death."

"Where is the end of the Gilded Path?" asked Determination.

"Yonder upon the death sands of the beach. There lie the wrecks cast forth from the Whirlpool of Wine by the merciless tide," answered the Angel.

HIDDEN THINGS SHALL BE REVEALED

Following in the steps of Evangelist, Determination conceived a plan and set forth with his helpers to execute it.

"We must save the youth of this generation from taking the Gilded Path," said Determination, "for it leads to eternal destruction."

"We shall follow thee in the name of the Lord," answered his valiant company.

Then I saw the Angel give to Determination a light called the Lamp of Truth, which had power to reveal the hidden things of darkness; and with it, praising God, these heroes of the Cross went forth to expose the subtleties and dangers of this path of death.

TEARING AWAY THE MASK

With the aid of the wonderful lamp, they revealed to the eyes of men the hidden sins and dangers associated with the gaming-tables of fashionable society; and by its searching light they also revealed the secret doors of aristocratic clubs and crystal saloons. Its beams also discovered Satan's most affable demons guiding the young and uninitiated into the Gilded Path which led to shame and ruin.

"Look! look!" cried Determination to a crowd of young men who had been attracted by his words. "Behold the infamy of the Devil." So saying, he turned the Lamp of Truth upon a gilded door, which Whole-soul then opened and held back. As its rays lighted up the way beyond, he cried again:

TO MEET THIS LATTER END

"Behold the horror of this way, all ye who have yielded to the tempting proposals of Satan! Every sin you enjoy brings you nearer to the whirlpool that shall suck you down to everlasting damnation! All such paths as this lead to it."

The young men stood aghast as they perceived, by the aid of the penetrating light, that the path back of the gilded door led direct to certain death; for the light in the hand of Determination revealed also the dying wrecks upon the sands that bordered the Sea of Social Swirl.

OUR SPIRITS BREATHE INFECTED AIR

But this was not all. In the hands of Determination, the merciless rays of the Lamp of Truth swept the horizon, and then fell once more upon the City of Worldliness. To the right and to the left they flashed and burrowed, everywhere exposing death-in-life to the awe-struck group that stood by God's stern-faced messenger.

Blear-eyed patrons of the grog-shop turned their backs to its piercing beams; painted wantons fell upon their faces in their brothel homes; evil-doers of every kind hid themselves in holes and corners as the pitiless light wrapped them in its white embrace. Curses and blasphemy, piteous cries for succor, wails of anguish, arose on every side.

"It is too terrible to behold!" cried Whole-soul, covering his face with his hands, as he with others turned from the hideous spectacle.

WHERE THE DEVIL REAPS HIS HARVEST

"Hold!" entreated Determination. "Once they were as you; now they are bound in Satan's chains, and hopeless damnation is written upon their souls."

Then, as the faces before him turned white with fear, his passionate appeal rang out.

"Behold the Devil's harvest! the harvest which the Destroyer of Souls reaps behind doors which swing open to the lightest touch. These, alive, yet dead, which you see, passed these portals and are doomed. It is your turn to enter now!"

IN SATAN'S FETTERS

With an infinite tenderness in his voice he went on:

"Oh, shun the jeweled gateways of pleasant sins. Once they close behind you, Satan's grinning demons will shackle you to your lusts, and clasp the arms of wan remorse around your necks. The gibbering spectre of what you might have been shall mock you, as your feet now tread easily in passion's well-worn paths.

"And then the end!" he cried in tones that swept even past his hearers and echoed down the busy street. "Not as the righteous die; no peaceful passing to Him who made you, as the purple shadows of closing day fall around your couch.

ONLY ONE LOOK BEHIND

"No! fiends shall stifle your cries for help as they bear you swiftly to your doom. Will they never stop? Yes, once. You shall have a look behind, and you shall see a shape set upon and beaten, time and time again, to the ground until it can rise no more. It is your better self, and in your hand is the weapon that struck it down. With this before your eyes, you shall be swallowed up in the eternal night of God's wrath."

SATAN SENDS FOR REINFORCEMENTS

The exposures made by the Lamp of Truth, in the hands of Determination, enraged Satan to such a pitch that he sent for a band of his most desperate fiends to help him, by every means known to the powers of Hell, to extinguish the light. But God strengthened the flame, and every attempt upon it utterly failed. Held aloft by the servant of God, its rays pierced the walls of mansion and hovel alike, revealing to all who would look the lust and sins that the Archfiend had made pleasant to the eye.

Deception was with Satan, and I saw him quail as the steady searching of the light laid bare the plans for soul capture which had taken him centuries to conceive and execute.

DECEPTION WOULD KILL WHOLE-SOUL

Rushing into the saloon he shut to the door which Whole-soul had kept open; and made a violent attempt to do him bodily harm. Doubtless he would have slain him had it not been for the intervention of the Angel, who now thrust herself between the two, as she thus commanded the fiend:

"Stay thy cursed hand, thou infamous viper of the Pit! Thou canst not harm those who reveal to the eyes of men the damning work conceived in thy iniquitous heart. Begone!" and so saying she turned to Determination and his company.

Satan and Belial, and the rest of the fiendish band, had sought to conceal their presence from the eyes of the Angel by changing their forms, but she had marked their presence and knew their purpose was to extinguish the Lamp of Truth. As they slunk away she said to Determination and his helpers:

"'Their feet run to evil, and they make haste to shed innocent blood: . . . wasting and destruction are in their paths.'"

As the last words of the Angel fell upon my ears, one by one the lights of the great city went out, and men, and women, too, sought their homes, wherever they might be, in the great Babylon.

AT THEIR FEET THE CITY SLUMBERED

Then I saw the rays of the Lamp of Truth fall upon the ground and run along it until they rested upon the steps of the Church of the Disciples. For a moment they lingered there, then rose past sculptured façade and painted window, until they rested, high above, upon the frieze that girdled the stone finger pointing to the home of the Living God. There, in the diamond-white light, the effigies of the disciples of Jesus—those who had known and loved the Son of Him for whose worship this temple was reared looked out over the sleeping city, and to me they seemed to say:

"We, too, have been living, suffering men. We chose the good and were rewarded by broader outlooks from higher slopes.

LO! THE RIGHT'S ABOUT TO CONQUER

"Men, to-day, are at the turning of the ways, and because they, too, shall choose the good, they shall achieve mental health and vigor, clearer vision, and the keen pleasure that comes from

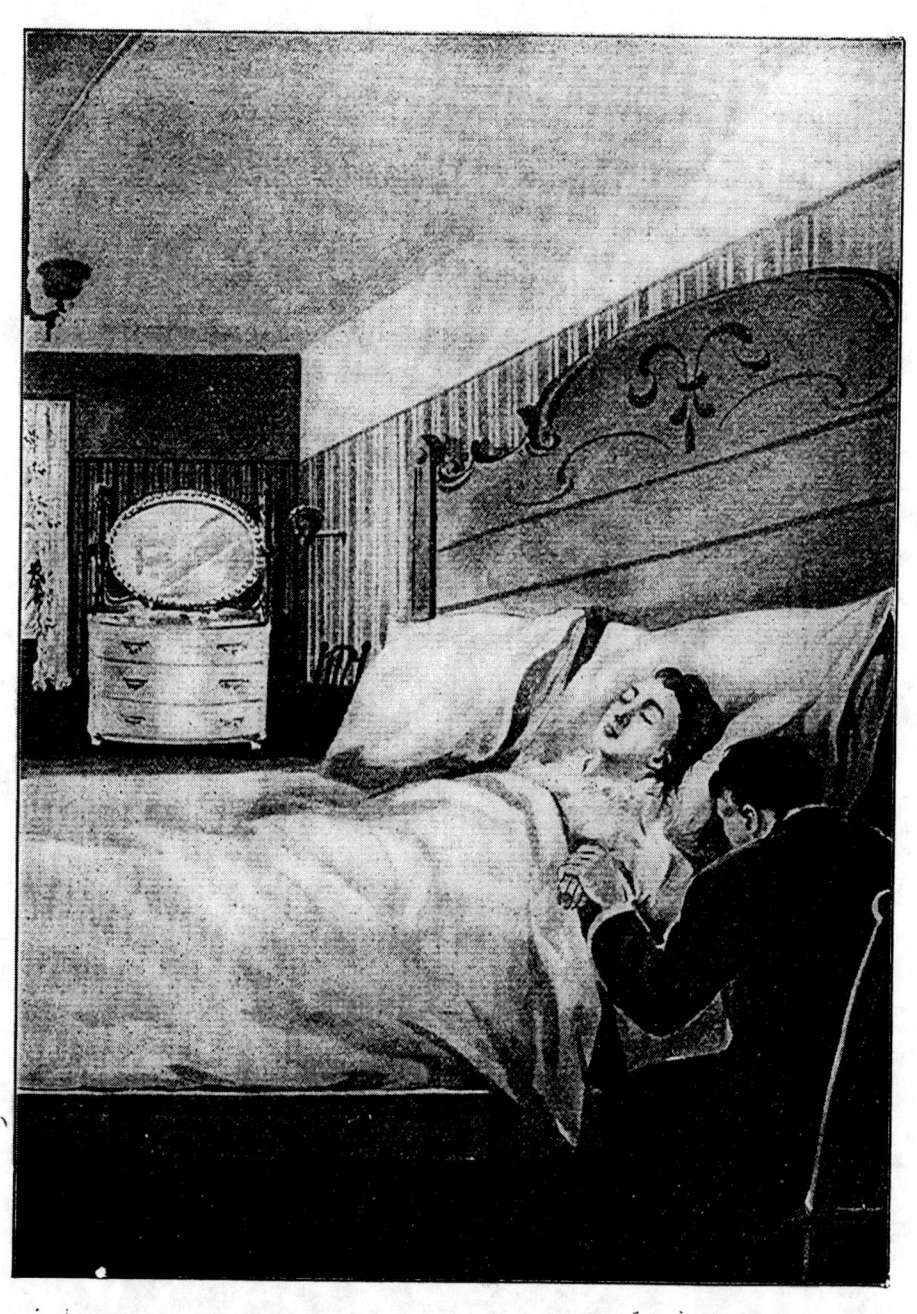

"With face buried in the pillow, he wept bitterly."

the sense of awakened faculties. They shall do noble things, not dream them."

The beams of the wonderful lamp fell again to the ground, and then were extinguished. I was alone in the silent street, tired in body, but happy in mind, for the drab miseries of humanity seemed well nigh fallen away, for now it was given me to know beyond peradventure that, His "fan is in his hand, and he will thoroughly purge his floor."

The night won her coronal of stars, sparkling beyond dreams of splendor, and as I gazed into the vast blue above my head, a warm wind folded me in its embrace and wafted me away.

THE BANQUET OF THE SELECT

Vaguely I seemed to know that my course was along the city's streets, and soon I was set down before an imposing building, ablaze with light, through whose open doors the élite of the city were entering to participate in the Banquet of the Select.

Unseen, I gained entrance to the hall, where thousands of dollars had been squandered upon the decorations alone, for the night's revelry. Obsequious servants passed choice viands and choicer wines to the laughing guests sitting at the glittering tables; from palm-hid recesses, strains of sensuous music lured to the dance; and soon the company, old and young alike, were whirling along the polished floor.

Man-of-the-World, the political boss of the City of Worldliness, bribe-giver, bribe-taker, had planned the banquet to further his predatory schemes, and now I saw him, in company with Hypocrite and other convivial associates, complacently beholding the debauch which had swiftly followed the feast. Behind them, unseen by all eyes save mine, stood Satan with his mocking smile, and Belial with his baleful eyes.

ONCE MORE, THE LAMP OF TRUTH

And so the night wore on. Then when the eyes of the revellers were dimmed with wine, and when its fumes had weighted the atmosphere already heavy with the breath of dying flowers, the piercing rays of the Light of Truth flashed around the hall and rested upon the centre of its floor.

"See how the Destroyer of Souls has you in his power," cried Evangelist, who had entered with Determination, as he stepped to the spot where Satan, hitherto invisible, now stood in his proper form—as every presence must in the Light of Truth.

Touching a spring in the wall, close by the Archfiend's hand, the prophet pressed it, and the central portion of the floor fell back on hinges, revealing a hideous pit. Then, as the white-faced throng huddled upon the narrow space that remained, he cried:

"Behold the trap which Satan had cunningly arranged for you! See how he holds your souls in his hand!" pointing to wires which led to the spring by which the mechanism was operated.

DOWN! DOWN! TO HELL

"Soon, with dulled senses and heavy eyes, you would have stood upon the fatal spot, and once there, the lightest touch of his hand would have sent you to eternal destruction."

"This hall is but an anteroom of hell!" now came in the clear tones of the Angel, as she manifested herself to the scared revellers.

"Flee from this place as from a pestilence! Flee while yet there is time!" she entreated.

Ere I realized it, the sobered company was gone, and then the Angel, turning to where the King and Prince of Evil stood in the full blaze of the Lamp of Truth, thus commanded them:

"Begone! Thou fools who fancy Christ mistaken. Not one hair of these, my children, canst thou harm. Begone!"

The discomfited fiends vanished, and only darkness remained.

NEVER A NIGHT WITHOUT A DAY

Upon the wings of the wind the Angel now visited the churches throughout the land, everywhere speaking by the mouths of God's ministers against the social sins which Satan made so alluring. Great unrest followed, and as time swept along, thousands upon thousands, thus warned against the pitfall of the Gilded Path, chose the safe way.

Besides these, wastrels, gamblers, reprobates of all sorts, were induced to forsake their easily besetting sins and turn to the Cross.

Minister Good resolutely repelled each fresh attack of Satan upon the souls of those committed to his care, but with Determination—in whose eyes the fires of righteous battle always glared—and Whole-soul, aided by the counsels of Evangelist, waged an incessant warfare upon the Enemy of Mankind, as well.

HIS MIGHTY ARMS UPHOLD THEE

At the close of a day spent in work for the Master, the faithful band sat in the study of Minister Good.

"We must not be ignorant of this one thing," Whole-soul was saying, " 'that one day is with the Lord as a thousand years, and a thousand years as one day.' Our impatience at results is due to our limitations."

"Truly so," answered Evangelist. " 'Nevertheless we, according to his promise, look for new heavens and a new earth, wherein dwelleth righteousness.' "

"That promise shall be realized," said Determination, "for our God is marching on."

"Then," suggested the minister, "let us pray for more of the knowledge God gives his children when they feel their ignorance and are eager for His light to shine upon their way."

CHAPTER XVIII

HIS MAJESTY'S CHARITY FUND

"Unquestionably there is a personal Devil, full of malignity, perversity, and falsehood. He seeks his prey 'as a roaring lion'; therefore, watch. He is 'your adversary'; do not believe him.

"Some there are that will go from Rome to England to make proselytes; but the Devil will go from one end of the world to the other, and walk from pole to pole, till he hath put a girdle about the loins of the earth, to make a man the child of hell like himself."
—*Adams.*

ONCE more, still in my dream, I found myself within the forbidding walls of Satan's Castle of All Evil, and saw, as if with actual vision, a mammoth vault filled with gold and silver and costly treasures of every description. Beings bearing lights were hurrying to and fro within the vault, and drawing nearer, I saw the Archfiend himself, directing the movements of a busy company of his fiends.

While I meditated upon the scene, trying to discern its meaning, these words came to my ears:

"Child of the vision, canst thou interpret what thou seest?"

"Nay, Good Angel," I replied, for I recognized the voice.

"This vault contains Satan's Charity Fund," she replied. "According to the computation of this world, there are millions upon millions of wealth in its keeping."

"Why does Satan hoard up treasure?" I asked. "How can he use it?"

AND BID YOU LIVE ADMIRED FROM AGE TO AGE

"He does not hoard it," was the reply, "but uses it to secure the souls of men, making them believe when they accept it, that they are doing good to their fellow-men."

"Satan's Charity Fund?" I repeated, in the confusion of the moment.

"Dost thou still fail to comprehend?" asked the Angel.

"Truly I do," I answered.

"It is a good name for a means which serves a bad purpose. Satan's gifts are given to men, that he may get their souls," she explained.

"Do riches then come from the Devil?" I asked.

"Many times they do," she answered.

"I thought true riches were from God, and that He gave unto men the power to get wealth."

"All *true* riches come from Him," replied the Angel, "and such possessions harm no one."

Then the Angel vanished and I was alone before the great vault where tireless fiends still sorted and labelled bribes for the souls of men. Soon both vault and demons vanished, as the Angel had done, and I was borne away to the parsonage of the Church of the Disciples.

In the many hours I had spent, an unseen listener, in the study of Minister Good, I had learned much from the conversation of those gathered there from time to time. A spirit of genuine piety and love for mankind was ever present, and the views expressed showed that the speakers had made a careful study of prevailing conditions in the City of Worldliness. I had come to love the very atmosphere of the place, and now prepared my mind to grasp and retain what I was to hear.

TRUE RELIGION AND UNDEFILED

"What, then, are we to count as riches?" asked the minister. "Character first, for that is the foundation of all commendable wealth.

"Next," he continued, "I would place the love of others and the desire to do toward them as we would have them do to us; then, cheerfulness, faith, knowledge, and the respect of our fellow-beings.

"Take down the dollar mark, and set up in its place something of this kind."

"Life would then be much more sweet," observed Evangelist, "and more simple. Then what we gained should be ours forever, and with it we should have gained eternal wealth."

"It seems to me," said Mrs. Good, "that it is not the amount of a man's possessions, so much as the spirit and purpose with which he wields his wealth, that is the vital consideration."

"True, my dear," replied her husband. "It takes a very great man so to handle riches as to save his own soul in the process, and to spread only beneficence among his family and fellow-men."

"There is certainly a close connection between plain living and high thinking," commented Evangelist. "Human character cannot flourish in an atmosphere of luxury."

HIS MOUTH FULL OF LOUD FUTILITIES

"We are constantly hearing," said Determination, who had been listening intently to the conversation, "of men who are noted for two things: first, their wealth, and then their religion—which may also be said to contain their philanthropy.

"Now, in spite of the fact that these men have donated many millions of their money to charitable and educational purposes, the world at large seldom regards them with much favor."

"Religious emotion and sentiments of charity, propriety and self-denial seem to have taken the place of notions of justice and regard for the rights of others," replied Evangelist, to whom Determination had addressed himself. "And I believe," he went on, "that no amount of religion or riches can save such men as you have described from the just estimation of their fellow-men."

TEACHING BY EXAMPLE

"There is something fine and satisfying in a man who is consistent in his churchmanship—who lives up to the tenets of his belief and is as regular in his sacred as in his secular duties," said the minister, "but there is little to admire in one who forgets 'the weightier matters of the law,' and no matter how great may become his bank account, and how high his position in the world, he is poor."

LINKED WITH ONE VIRTUE AND A THOUSAND CRIMES

"Such people remind me," said the minister's wife, "of the robber barons of the Middle Ages, who, when brought under Christianity, salved their consciences by splendid gifts to the people, of churches and public works."

"To me there is something almost brutal in a multi-millionaire putting his hand in his pocket and tossing out a church here, a hospital there, and endowments, libraries, fountains, parks, as one might throw pennies to children in the street," replied her husband.

"Sometimes it is the following generation that seeks to make atonement," said Mrs. Good. "Only yesterday I was reading of two men who were admiring a handsome structure—a recent gift to the city.

" 'Who did you say was the donor?' asked one.

" 'The children of Mr. ———,' naming a very wealthy citizen then deceased, was the reply.

" 'I knew him,' rejoined the other. 'They are evidently trying to make up for their father's delinquencies. Probably the next generation will want to canonize him.' "

THESE THINGS WELL DESERVE MEDITATING

"Among the dangers which threaten those who apparently care for nothing but the accumulating of wealth, is this," observed Evangelist.

"The cares, distractions, and social ambitions which riches and power and place bring with them; the rounds of visits and dinners and functions, make it difficult for the rich parent to give the child its due—to fulfill the impulse of the true parents to live with and for their children.

"The child can thrive only in an atmosphere of love and heartiness and companionship. The children of the rich are deprived of this too often.

FOR THE PERIL-HOUR HAS COME

"Let the modern man with a genius for money-getting beware," he continued with great earnestness, "lest in his eagerness for riches, the souls of his children as well as his own perish at its blighting touch."

With these words, Evangelist and Determination took leave of the minister and his wife, and left the parsonage together. As they did so, I seemed to fall asleep. When I waked, I saw Mr. Hypocrite sitting in the familiar room in earnest conversation with Minister Good.

AN INSTINCT FOR REAL DUTIES

I was not altogether surprised to see him there, for of late he had been much in my mind, and I had fancied him weary of the life he had been leading.

All of the man's good impulses had not been stifled. His association with Man-of-the-World in dishonest enterprises had seared his conscience severely, and the love of wealth and power was still strong within him.

Yet, Mr. Hypocrite had been, of late, in some degree heeding the promptings of his better nature, and as a sort of compromise in the matter had now called upon the minister, vaguely hoping that he might hear something that would help to settle the inward disquietude which was his hourly companion.

Something of this occurred to me as I remembered his stand for the right in the matter of the Divorce Mills. I recalled, too, that his term of office as mayor of the city had expired, and that, although he appeared as a guest of Man-of-the-World at the Banquet of the Select, his political relations with the "boss" were a thing of the past.

IN VAIN THOU WEEPEST, IN VAIN DOTH YEARN

"I am coming to believe," Hypocrite was saying, "that the love of money is the curse of thousands."

"It is 'the root of all evil,'" replied the minister. "Many a soul is so weighted to earth by the burden of wealth that when the hour comes to depart, this treasure is a matter of sad concern. I have seen hundreds pitifully idolizing their gold in the very hour of death."

"I cannot think it was intended to be a curse," insisted Hypocrite.

"It was not intended to be a curse. Man made it so," was the reply.

"The sin, then, seems to be in setting the heart so upon riches as to exclude thoughts of the higher life?" asked Hypocrite.

"Just so," the minister replied, "and what a picture of the vanity of trusting in material things Job gives:

"'Though he heap up silver as the dust, and prepare raiment as the clay; he may prepare it, but the just shall put it on, and the innocent shall divide the silver. He buildeth his house as a moth, and as a booth that the keeper maketh. The rich man shall lie down, but he shall not be gathered: he openeth his eyes, and he is not.'"

IN THY GIFT IS WISDOM'S BEST AVAIL

After a moment of silence, Hypocrite said: "I hardly know, Mr. Good, why I came here to-night, unless it be that I am led to do so in the hope of receiving advice regarding the disposition of a part of my wealth."

"I am very glad that you came to me, Mr. Hypocrite," replied the minister, "for I can help you. If you have among your possessions wealth honestly come by, wealth upon which there is no taint—no widows' tears or orphans' cries, endow with it the mission enterprise started by Miss Sincere here in this city. Forgive my plain-speaking," he added.

Hypocrite's face crimsoned, as the minister's words whipped his blood like a wind from the hills. For a moment he was silent, and then he said:

"I thank you." Then, rising, he extended his hand to the minister, who had also risen. Without another word the two men parted, and as the door closed behind Hypocrite, I saw the faithful servant of God kneel beside his chair and thank the throne of infinite mercy that his words had touched the heart of an erring brother.

WHEN FORTUNE SHEDS HER FAIREST BEAMS

As Hypocrite attended to the ordinary concerns of his business during the remainder of the day, his thoughts often recurred to the faithful words of Minister Good. He was now possessed of an immense fortune, and as the day wore on he reviewed, from time to time, the sources from which it was acquired.

Nearly, if not quite all the money he had accumulated by connivance at the robberies of Man-of-the-World and his political associates during his term as mayor, he had invested in an enterprise which was housed in a collection of mammoth buildings covering a full square on the outskirts of the city.

Late in the day he left the office, and entering his carriage, he instructed his coachman to drive past these mills, instead of taking the more direct way to his residence in the fashionable section of the city. Why he did this, he could not have answered even to himself.

As his carriage rolled noiselessly along the streets, he abandoned himself to thoughts which ran through his entire term of office in the great city where his whole life had been spent. This transaction had brought him so much money; that had enabled him to gratify this ambition—but always with dirty money—money that was tainted, tainted.

Darkness had fallen when the great works were reached, and, obeying a sudden impulse, Hypocrite signalled the coachman to stop, stepped to the street, and then sent the carriage home.

The section of the city where he stood was deserted, save for pacing policemen on their lonely beats, and the watchmen about the large mills and hulking warehouses that stood dark and grim against the sky.

TREAD THOSE REVIVING PASSIONS DOWN

Were not these great buildings his? he asked himself. The product of the untiring machines they contained—was it not his to do with as he liked? To whom need he account for the wealth his scheming brain had brought him?

Nervously, he walked along one side of the great quadrangle, unable to dismiss from his mind the means by which he had been able to acquire this goodly property. With ceaseless iteration these words rang in his ears:

> "Heavy to get and light to hold,
> Hoarded, bartered, bought and sold."

A cloud which had hidden the moon, sailed past, letting its light fall in a silver glow upon the scene.

"What shall I do with all this when death shall come to tell me the story that we all must hear?" he said half aloud, and turned away.

THIS IS THE PORTION OF A WICKED MAN

Turning, as he reached an intersecting street for one more look at the great works which were his pride, Hypocrite saw a tongue of flame leap from one of the buildings, blood-red against the sky. Black smoke began to ooze through the windows, and then a rush of swirling flame burst from windows and doors alike.

Clouds of pungent vapor arose as swift flashes of flame sprang from one building to another, and then the red spires and pillars of fire united in one vast sheet of flame. Dull, heavy clouds of smoke now spread over the scene, and under their pall, scarlet gleams, changing to purple and blue, flashed continuously.

In this huge, flaming pit, enclosed by outer blackness, Hypocrite read the answer to his questions, and as the full meaning of it swept across him, he reeled and fell to the ground as consciousness left him.

" 'The fool hath said in his heart, There is no God!' " said the voice of the Angel beside me.

THOU WILT SHOW ME THE PATH OF LIFE

On the following day, I saw Hypocrite in his office, waiting the arrival of Evangelist, for whom he had sent. He was somewhat shaken in body and mind by the event of the night previous, but his face revealed the presence of a fixed resolve.

"My son," said the prophet, by way of greeting, "the hand of the Lord hath been laid heavily upon thee, but it is given me to know that a blessing shall surely follow."

"I have sent for you," Hypocrite began, "to say that I am a man who has persistently closed my heart to good. With wide-open eyes I have accepted the suggestions of Satan and blindly followed where he led.

"Time and time again," he went on, "I have done the will of Satan, conscious that my actions would militate against thy labors and those of the Angel of Ministry. I will not catalogue all my offenses against God, but I wish to say, now that my eyes have been opened, that throughout it all your face has been constantly before me in reproach, and has helped to make my life a bitter one."

AND WINGED FOR YOU THEIR BENEDICTIONS RISE

"Hath Satan approached thee recently?" inquired the prophet.

"Only yesterday he proposed a scheme by which he said I should receive great approbation, not to say honor," was the reply.

"And thou didst not yield?"

"The Angel strengthened me to refuse. When Satan offered me an immense sum, saying, 'Thou art welcome to distribute this among the poor. It shall procure thee the distinction of being not only rich, but of being a man of generous heart,' she whispered in my ear:

"'Give thy gold as the Lord shall direct thee. Give only as Love prompts, and seek always to conceal thyself as the donor. Let not thy right hand know what thy left hand doeth.'

"'The act will add great glory to thy years,' Satan went on, 'and thousands shall rise up and call thee blessed.'

"'See thou do it not!'" persisted the Angel.

"But now an host of shining guards surrounded it."

"And thou wert able to say, 'Get thee behind me, Satan'! I thank the Lord for this!" cried the prophet.

MY STEPS HAD WELL-NIGH SLIPPED

"I have just written a letter to Miss Sincere," Hypocrite went on, "offering to endow her mission enterprise among the poor. I have made the offer in acknowledgment of God's many blessings to me."

"This act of thine shall be blessed," replied the prophet.

"Man-of-the-World hath accepted the Archfiend's gold and endowed the Art Museum," continued Evangelist, "and is receiving much commendation for his generous gift."

"But what shall it profit him?" asked Hypocrite.

"It will but bar the door of the vault," replied Evangelist. "Dost thou remember the door seen in thy dream?"

"That vision has never been erased from my thought; and your words have been engraven within my heart through all these years," confessed Hypocrite.

"The vision was of the Lord for thy salvation; and my words of warning were His repeated. It is hard to oppose the will of the Almighty," said the prophet.

"And God alone knows what I have suffered here, even in moments of wrong-doing," added Hypocrite as he laid his hand upon his heart.

> "The ill-timed truth we might have kept—
>   Who knows how sharp it pierced and stung?
> The word we had not sense to say—
>   Who knows how grandly it had rung?

> "Our faults no tenderness should ask,
>   The chastening stripes must cleanse them all;
> But for our blunders,—oh, in shame,
>   Before the eyes of Heaven we fall,"

quoted Evangelist.

THE WICKED IN HIS PRIDE

As they parted, the Angel, unseen by them, lifted her hands above them as her lips moved in benediction.

I then saw in my vision a company who were treading with iron heel upon the poor, and noted the cries of the helpless, and the stolid indifference of the masters who marched boldly on, with no sense of feeling or manifest sympathy. I marked how the Good Angel followed, and stooped often to lay a kind touch upon the downtrodden. She sighed within her soul as she looked upon the heartless taskmasters.

Drawing near, I asked of her who these tyrants were.

She replied, "These are they who in their haste to obtain riches, oppress the laboring class by whom their riches are gathered."

"But those who tread upon the men and women of toil bear the beautiful name of the Christ," I answered in surprise.

THEIR HOPE OF DELIVERANCE IS YET SMALL

"It is true in many instances," she answered. "Refusing them just compensation, they reduce those who toil for their enrichment to want and penury, and often remain untouched in heart by the hungry cry of little children."

"Is this, then, the 'Christian Age' we boast of?"

"Man calls it thus, but as yet it is much mixed with evil. Covetousness is to-day the world's greatest sin."

"Yes," I answered, "but it seems so strange that men should gather fortunes and yet have no conscience as to the manner by which it was gathered."

"A change is being wrought as time wears on. Man is prone to exaggerate the importance of those whose name is a synonym for millions; and, forgetting the rich in faith and good works, imagine God to be asleep," said the Angel.

"The new earth and the new Heaven seem so far away to such as view spiritual advance by the eyes of sense," said I.

"It is true," she replied, "but, hidden beneath the undergrowth of this materialistic age, the patient flowers of God's planting are making preparations to bloom, and their fragrance will be recognized and their beauty seen, when the Angels of righteousness shall rake away the dead leaves of man's avaricious self-seeking."

"That time seems so far off."

IN THE HUNGER TOWER STERN THINGS HAPPEN

"Nevertheless it is coming," replied the Angel.

"The Lord shall break in pieces the oppressor. 'I will come near to you in judgment; and I will be a swift witness . . . against those that oppress the hireling in his wages, the widow, and the fatherless, and that turn aside the stranger from his right . . . saith the Lord of hosts.'"

As the Angel sped on, I found myself alone, and as I looked away toward the Hill of the Cross, in my heart was the prayer:

"Thy kingdom come. Thy will be done in earth, as it is in heaven."

Again I found myself in the parsonage, where a little company was discussing Hypocrite's gift to the mission school.

"Scores of these children will carry the blessing of this gift with them out into life, and no one will ever know about the endowment, either. That to me is the divine way of giving," said Miss Sincere to Minister Good.

"God knows all about it," interjected Evangelist.

"Yes," answered the minister, "even the cup of cold water given in the name of a disciple is recognized and blessed."

THE CRUSADE FOR CONSECRATED WEALTH

"There are too many of our churches and religious institutions to-day who are taking gold from the hands of the inglorious rich," said Evangelist.

"Many give for the sake of notoriety, and others to cover up some sin of craftiness; the world is yet full of scheming, and the Devil passes out many dollars for holy uses, and laughs to see the eagerness with which the Church grasps them," added the minister.

"I never yet saw an unconsecrated dollar do any good. It comes of the Devil, and he is shrewd enough to see that he is not the loser in his own transactions," replied Miss Sincere.

"His vault is full of unconsecrated dollars," said Evangelist, "and they have been doing damage to the kingdom since the world began. The Lord in whose name we serve insists upon consecrated wealth."

At this point in the conversation Whole-soul and Determination entered, and were welcomed by the three.

"We just heard Deception say to Satan that one could do more with a dollar nowadays than with the Bible," said Determination.

"Yes," added Whole-soul, "and Satan informed him of one who had covered up a great theft by his generosity to a school of learning."

WHO HAS IT ENRICHED?

"What a blessing honestly gotten wealth may be; and on the other hand, what a curse the gold taken from the Archfiend's treasury may become," added Minister Good.

"We can close the Archfiend's vaults forever," said Determination, "if the conscience of God's children is aroused. We have thwarted the Enemy before, and we can do it again in the name of the Lord."

"'Consecrated wealth' shall be the ringing watchword of God's servants. We are living in the day when upon the bells of the horses must be inscribed 'Holiness unto the Lord,'" answered the prophet.

"Christian people must be taught the sacredness of possession; and be shown how God honors the gift which is honestly won and reverently used," replied Determination.

WORK AND DESPAIR NOT

Then I saw this band of valiant souls go forth to liberate the world from the thraldom of greed and perverted impulse, and marked that the Angel led the way; that their message was seasoned with the spirit of Jesus; and that assurance of victory reigned supreme in their hearts.

As they passed through the land the Church became conscious of her sin, and a sense of individual responsibility for the wiser use of riches in the maintenance of Christian philanthropy entered the heart; and the cause of Christ, which had languished, began to receive a portion of that which the Giver of All Good had bestowed, but which had been withheld.

"The Lord's people must arise. The Lord's people must welcome the privilege of furthering the interests of the Cross; and thus render the gift of unconsecrated wealth both a shame and a disgrace," was the warning message of Determination and his band.

PROVE ME, SAITH THE LORD

"There shall be no lack," said the Angel, "when the Lord's people bring their tithes into the treasury; then, too, shall the windows of Heaven be open, and the showers of divine blessing shall descend."

Thus did I behold the word of God going forward; and in the distance I saw the foregleam of a new day in which the disciples of the Nazarene should distribute their gold according to the necessities of the Messiah's kingdom. In that day, they who believed should be of one accord, and, continuing in gladsome co-operation with the plan of their Master, they would eat their meat with gladness and singleness of heart.

The praises of God were heard throughout the land, and the signs of the coming kingdom everywhere appeared; for the wilderness and the hitherto solitary places became glad, and the Rose of Sharon began to bloom in the desert of man's covetous heart.

THE KING HAS NO LACK

Satan sat in the doorway of the great vault that held his Charity Fund, awaiting the return of Deception and Belial, and the report of what they had been able to do with his accursed gold.

"They preach a gospel of 'consecrated wealth,' and, in consequence, the treasury of the Church more than suffices the need of their King," said Deception as they approached.

"It is no fault of ours," added Belial, seeing Satan was angry. "No one would take any gold but Man-of-the-World."

Without a word of reply, Satan barred the door of the vault, and passed down the corridor, cursing furiously.

WHAT SHALL IT PROFIT A MAN?

Man-of-the-World sat in his office counting a pile of money recently pilfered from a helpless public, with a smile of satisfaction playing upon his face. Then, as he placed the banknotes in a safe he said to himself: "I'll keep this. Yes, I'll keep it, and not a cent will I give again to philanthropic objects.

376   HIS MAJESTY'S CHARITY FUND

The honor of the other gift was very short-lived, and has not compensated for the ridicule and abuse that have been heaped upon me."

"Thy gold shall perish with thee," whispered the Angel. "Thy ill-gotten gold and silver are as vile in the sight of the Almighty as the treasures within the vault of the Archfiend. It was from his fund that thy gift to the museum came."

Man-of-the-World shuddered for a moment at the words of the Angel, but gaining his composure passed from his office saying, "It all goes in a lifetime."

MY ONE DESIRE SHALL BE

Then I listened to a familiar voice. It was that of Hypocrite.

"It is never too late to mend, and it may be true that 'we always may be what we might have been,'" he said. "I will at least make restitution, and begin again. The long, wasted years! the long, wasted years! All I have and am shall be consecrated to God."

The message of Evangelist had found its way to his heart, and at last was preparing the soil for a better harvest.

Within a lonely cottage I saw Widow Faith in the attitude of prayer, and heard her say:

"'Silver and gold have I none; but such as I have give I Thee.'" She was giving herself in loving devotion to the work of teaching the youth in the mission school founded by Miss Sincere and endowed by Hypocrite.

Evangelist and the minister were reviewing the cause of the Master whom they served; and as the latter closed a book in which the record of his service was kept, he said, "The better day is coming," to which the prophet replied:

> "Each tribute and expression
> With an holy radiance shine,
> Lighting up earth's lower levels
> With a light which is divine."

CHAPTER XIX

THE PILGRIM'S SCARS

"'A bruised reed shall he not break'; that is, He will not bear hard upon a wounded and contrite and truly humble heart, bowed down with a sense of its infirmity. 'And the smoking flax shall he not quench'; the faintest spark of returning virtue he will not extinguish by severity . . ." —*Bishop Porteous.*

A GREAT sorrow, the greatest of his life, was tenting outside Hypocrite's home, and though he looked through polished windows, his eyes saw it not. But the Angel knew that it was there, and when God marked the hour, it entered with silent step and laid its hand upon the man's heart. It was to be a new experience in Hypocrite's life, and he was to profit by its stern teachings.

I saw him seated by the bedside of the wife he idolized, and in my vision noted that a fatal disease was slowly extinguishing the fires of her life, and that Hypocrite realized that the passing of a soul long trusted and cherished was now but a matter of moments.

Taking her frail hand in his, he pressed it, as he looked tenderly into the eyes which had grown oblivious to the things of time. A life all unconscious of his presence was crossing the bar; and in the agony of his grief he was conscious of emotions which for years had lain dormant within his cold and materialistic nature.

"Must we part, and part forever?" he sobbed, as, with face buried in the pillow by her side, he wept bitterly. Hypocrite had reached his first real life-sorrow.

Then he was alone, and the stars seemed to have burned out with the departure of the one he loved. The burden of his grief pressed heavily, and his soul cried out to God from the depths of its despair.

"O God, give to me thy sustaining grace. Suffer not this great sorrow to crush me."

The mansion was hushed in darkness out of respect to the dead; and in an upper room, all alone, sat the helpless and broken man, his soul struggling 'twixt hope and fear, 'twixt love and sorrow, as he sought in vain to solve the enigma of the trying hour.

Then it was that I saw a white-robed one, whom I thought to be a stranger, approach the dwelling. As the moonlight fell softly upon his snowy beard, I knew it was Evangelist, and that he had come to minister in God's name to the stricken man.

I saw him linger for a moment before the door; placing his hand upon his brow, he breathed silently a prayer for the Father's guidance in this work of love. The door yielded to his hand and then closed behind him. Slowly he ascended the stairs and passed into the room where sat the bereaved one. Taking a seat beside him, the old prophet laid his hand upon the stricken man's shoulder and said:

"Now thou hast sorrow, but in each affliction God conceals a blessing."

Hypocrite sat silent.

PASS UNDER THE ROD

"Where our treasure is there our hearts will be tending. The stairway to our Father's house grows clear to our vision when once, through tears, we have seen our loved ones ascend," continued the prophet.

"It is all dark, so dark," answered Hypocrite.

"'At evening time it shall be light,'" responded Evangelist. "Thou must have faith. The Lord doth not willingly afflict the children of men. He hath comforts for their bruised hearts. What God doeth we cannot now explain; but we shall know in His good time."

So saying, I saw Evangelist kneel by the side of the sorrowful man; and in the hush, broken only by the sobs of a smitten heart, he prayed:

"Divine Master, Thou who didst sorrow with the sorrowful; and mingle Thy tears in sympathy with such as mourned, abide in this home, and speak again Thy message of love, of peace, and life immortal. Point the darkness with the stars of promise; and give to Thy servant the comfort and blessing of

Thy immediate and constant presence. May his heart be opened to hear Thy voice in this bereavement; and may his soul be freed to follow the beckoning of the life which was so much a part of his own."

IN THE PREPARED, APPOINTED WAY

When the prophet arose, Hypocrite remained kneeling, still moved by his great emotion. Laying his hand again upon the stricken man's shoulder, Evangelist then said:

"The Lord shall make all things clear. He will not give thee a burden greater than thou canst bear. The Lord bless and keep thee."

So saying, the prophet departed, and in his stead the Angel came and tarried.

When Miss Sincere learned of the prophet's visit and his words of comfort, she said, as she recalled her visit in his company to the home of little Theodore, where sorrow had also entered: "It is just like him; for even as his Master, he goeth about doing good, and the comforts of God are in his keeping. It is a blessed office, that of giving joy for sorrow, and discovering to saddened hearts the flowers of blessing which grow beneath the briars in the valley of the heart."

MEMORY STILL KEEPS CARNIVAL

Hypocrite rose from his knees, and crossing the room, threw open the shutters of a window that faced the west. Standing there, he forgot the folded hands, the awful calm in his home, and lived again the "bright days when gayly sings the world."

In the glow that bathed the evening sky, tender memories floated in, and he saw only the soft eyes and heard the name of that dearer self now lying with her white face turned toward the skies.

Then the air seemed still, as dull, heavy clouds spread along the rim of the horizon and blotted out the glories of the dying day. A vivid flash of lightning dazzled his eyes, and then, for an instant, everything seemed of pitchy darkness. Before his eyes recovered from the blinding glare, he was conscious of a shadowy presence beside him, and shudderingly knew it for that of the enemy of souls.

WHEN THE ACCUSER FLINGS HIS DARTS

"Canst thou reconcile a loss so great as thine with faith in a just God?" it whispered. "Thou hast been cruelly treated, and art justified in meeting this blow with a rebellious spirit."

" 'Though He slay me, yet will I trust Him,' " whispered the Angel.

Torn by mingled emotions, the soul of Hypocrite was as wheat upon the threshing-floor under the strokes of the flail. Remembering the counsel of the prophet, he struggled to repeat the words of the Angel, making them the language of his feeble faith.

" 'Though—He—slay—me—yet—' " and then could go no further.

"Trust Him when He hath torn from thy breast one whom thou lovedst?" still inquired Satan. "Trust one who has struck thee down by so heartless an act?"

" 'Our light affliction, which is but for a moment, worketh for us a far more exceeding and eternal weight of glory; while we look not at the things which are seen, but at the things which are not seen: for the things which are seen are temporal; but the things which are not seen are eternal,' " whispered the Angel.

"Thou art entitled to a life of peace, and thy years should have remained undisturbed. Hadst thou not broken with me, I would have given thee the desire of thy heart, but now thine hands are empty, and thou art left in pain and sorrow," taunted Satan.

LOOK DOWN ON ME, FOR I AM WEAK

Hypocrite seemed surrounded by a mist of torment, as within his soul he was striving to master his oppressor. Again slowly came the words:

" 'Though—He—slay—me—yet—' "

Then I saw the Angel lay her hand upon him, and with her touch came an unction of power.

"Defy the Archfiend," she whispered. "Suffer him no longer to tempt thee to doubt."

With the feeble beginnings of a faith which was born of God, Hypocrite cried out:

"Get thee behind me, Satan, for thy words are as sharp

arrows to my soul. I have broken my allegiance to thee; yes, broken it forever!"

Satan stood abashed, for these words, born of a new faith, spread terror in his soul.

"The Enemy would sift thee as wheat, but the Lord, thy Redeemer, prayeth for thee, that thy strength shall not fail. Cast thy burden upon Him, for he careth for thee," persisted the Angel.

ON THE CROSS OF CHRIST RELYING

Then I saw a wondrous sight; for, at the Angel's command, a strange, but beauteous light came streaming into the soul of Hypocrite from over the Hill of the Cross. It came from the door of an open sepulchre which stood in a garden, wherein once lay the World's Redeemer and whence He arose, bringing life and immortality to light. Satan saw it, too, and fled.

Then I heard the Angel say:

"It is by this light that all souls must interpret their sorrow." And as she spoke the light arose, and for a moment seemed to rest upon the peak of the far-off mountain, while within its divine effulgence the faint outlines of a celestial city could be traced.

"Thou hast now seen a part of the road of faith, along which, by means of thy grief, thy soul must journey," said the Angel. "But the best is yet to be," she added.

"I will follow the road and may God give me grace," answered Hypocrite.

"It shall be well with thee," was the reply.

"'I behold the Cross!' cried Man-of-the-World."

THE PILGRIM'S SCARS

EACH CONFLICT WITH INDWELLING SIN

Then I understood that it had been given me to look in upon the unseen battlefield which lies in every human heart; that field on which meet, at some time, the two opposing forces—doubt and faith—and which, in some lives, occasions constant unrest. I saw that, though to mortal eyes the struggle remains unseen and its fierceness of combat unreckoned, God ever watches the conflict and crowns the victor when the fierce fight for good is won.

"Yes," said Evangelist later, "each pilgrim shall have his scars; and if those scars be the evidence of a victorious faith, they are known in Heaven as the marks of the Lord Jesus; and to wear them is distinction and honor."

EACH AFFLICTION IS GOD'S MESSENGER

"Everything hath worked together for my good," said Hypocrite, as he sat with the minister some days after. "The path was both rough and steep, and on either side were the temptations and chidings of the Enemy; but it led to the open ground."

"Yes," replied Minister Good. "Thou canst take this message to thyself, now," and so saying he opened his Bible and read:

"'For thou, O God, hast proved us: thou hast tried us, as silver is tried. Thou broughtest us into the net; thou laidst affliction upon our loins. Thou hast caused men to ride over our heads; we went through fire and through water: but thou broughtest us out into a wealthy place.' "

"So it has been with my soul; and I now believe with the Angel that, 'the best is yet to be.' "

"The way grows brighter as we near the perfect day," assented the minister.

Soon Hypocrite, with a new spirit, was much in the company of Evangelist, and I began to see them together helping those whom sorrow had overcome.

"They who wear the cross can carry the oil of sympathy," answered Hypocrite.

"Yes," responded the prophet, "we are to comfort others with the same comfort wherewith we have been comforted of God."

"That not only makes our service tender, but very real," added Hypocrite.

IN THE SEAT OF THE SCORNFUL

Man-of-the-World and Rev. Mr. Please-all laughed in derision as they spoke of the new rôle of Hypocrite.

"He's a fine specimen to undertake religious work," said Man-of-the-World.

"Surprises never seem to end," commented Mr. Please-all. "Probably the prophet has turned his head."

"Certainly his heart cannot be in the work," added Man-of-the-World.

Within the hearts of both the Angel whispered, "Judge not," and hurried away.

At last Satan met Mr. Hypocrite and sneeringly accosted him. "So thou, too, hast become one of His followers?"

"I have sworn allegiance to Jesus, and may God forgive the past; henceforth our ways part, and as a disciple of the Nazarene, I despise both thee and thy works," answered Hypocrite with great emphasis.

"Ha! ha! Thou art a unique disciple. Who will believe in thee?" ejaculated the Archfiend, and with a mocking laugh he passed on.

" 'The Lord bless thee, and keep thee: the Lord make his face shine upon thee, and be gracious unto thee: the Lord lift up his countenance upon thee, and give thee peace,' " prayed the Angel who, though invisible, guarded the steps of Hypocrite, redeemed.

THE CONSECRATED CROSS I 'LL BEAR

An errand of mercy had brought Evangelist and Hypocrite into the Valley of the Cross, and at sunset, with the sky crimsoned by the touch of Nature's pencil, I saw the two looking intently toward the Cross upon the Lonely Hill.

"Yonder He died for our sins," said the prophet.

Then in the silence of reverent meditation, their eyes wandered far beyond Calvary till the scene was interrupted by the hills and mountains of Galilee.

"There remaineth yet a cross for each who would follow Him," said Hypocrite.

"Yes, a cross for each, but 'faith has still its Olivet.' "

"'And love its Galilee,'" answered Evangelist.

As night wore on, the two wended their way to the city, and at the home of Minister Good met with Determination and Whole-soul, who had a wonderful discovery to relate.

THE DESTRUCTION OF SATAN'S CASTLE FORETOLD

"We have seen a strange thing to-day, while tarrying for rest upon the Hill-lands of Faith," said Whole-soul. "It should inspire great valor in the heart of every Christian. I will ask Determination to relate it; for it was he who made the discovery."

Then Determination told how that day while turning the Lamp of Truth upon the castle of the Archfiend, he had discovered by its light a great crack in one of its walls; which predicted the doom of the place which hitherto had been thought impregnable.

"Art thou sure of thy vision?" asked the minister.

"I am positive; for both mine eyes and those of Whole-soul saw clearly the rent."

"Why should such a fact be considered incredible?" asked Evangelist.

"Did the Archfiend also detect it?" asked Hypocrite.

"We saw him gaze upon the place where our light shone; and then, shielding his eyes, he, together with a number of imps, hurried within," answered Determination.

"We spoke of it to the Angel," said Whole-soul, "and she informed us that the day should come when the place shall be destroyed."

"How fares the work of the Mission?" Determination now asked of Miss Sincere, who was one of the company.

"The Lord has been very gracious," she replied. "We have gathered the poor and neglected, until now the place is filled. The endowment has been of the greatest help to us, and we are very thankful for it," she added, as her eyes turned toward Hypocrite, who made no reply, however.

"The Lord always provides," observed the minister.

"He 'shall supply all your need according to his riches in glory by Christ Jesus,'" added the prophet.

THOUGH THE WICKED FLOURISH

Ere they parted, the Angel came into their midst and said:

"The Lord has laid his hand heavily upon Man-of-the-World. Great reverses have visited him, and with his treasures gone from him, he sits in the toils of despair. The Almighty hath shorn him of his strength, if perchance, detached from worldly things, he might be saved."

"I will go to him quickly," responded Hypocrite, "for once we were friends; and may God give me the power to point him to the Cross."

"And I shall go with thee," said the Angel.

"We shall follow you in our prayers," Evangelist added.

Hypocrite and the Angel found Man-of-the-World alone, and in great perturbation of mind.

"Hearing of your trouble, we have come to be of service, if possible," said Hypocrite, "for our gospel teaches the duty of bearing one another's burdens."

THE SKY IS CHANGED—AND SUCH A CHANGE!

"All, all, has gone, and left me in wretchedness and poverty," lamented Man-of-the-World.

"There are worse conditions than poverty," replied Hypocrite. "I have had reverses, and have learned that a man's way is ordered of the Lord. He hath some better possessions for thee."

"This disaster is the work of Satan. I followed his advice; and now the earnings of a lifetime have been swept away. Wretched man that I am!"

"We have both suffered," said Hypocrite, "from adhering to the advice of Satan. His paths are those of sorrow, his policy is defeat, and the purpose he seeks is death. I bear on me the scars of wounds which he has inflicted, but I thank God I have been able to help in the healing of hundreds who have likewise suffered."

THE NEEDFUL DISCIPLINE OF LIFE

During the silence which followed, Man-of-the-World sat in misery and refused to be comforted. The ploughshare of the Almighty was tearing up the hard sod of his heart and the furrows seemed to stretch interminably down the years.

"I can see no hope. I am not only deserted by friends, but poverty, absolute poverty, confronts me. No, there is no hope! What is such an existence worth? I might as well end it all," cried he in despair.

"Speak not so," replied Hypocrite.

Man-of-the-World raised his eyes and looked into the face of Hypocrite, whose tenderness of speech had opened his heart to learn, for the first time, that sympathy abounded for such as he, and that it was not all an empty idea as he had always supposed.

MY TIMES ARE IN THY HANDS

"Every day may work a new beginning," continued Hypocrite. "You will see that the treasures over which you mourn are not worth the price of this anguish and sorrow; there is something better to be lived for. There are riches which time cannot tarnish nor steal."

"Position, friends, social prestige—all, all for which I have striven, are gone with this crash," answered Man-of-the-World.

"With their departure shall come a greater blessing," replied his friend.

Then I heard the Angel whisper within the soul of Man-of-the-World the words of Jesus:

"'What is a man profited, if he shall gain the whole world, and lose his own soul? or what shall a man give in exchange for his soul?'"

"Perhaps life is all an empty show," he said as if in reply.

PAINFUL AND DARK THE PATHWAY SEEMS

"Life is just what we make it, my friend. You and I began wrong, and a gracious God who corrects our follies has intercepted me; and it is He who in this loss of thine would save thee to higher life and enduring riches. I carry the scars of years wasted; and am indebted for light to Evangelist, who hath also sent thee his sympathy and prayers."

"Evangelist! Yes, we listened to his message that night at Longshore, as we sat in the beach pavilion," replied he.

"His message was then against the sin of covetousness and social wrong-doing. He gave to the multitude the teachings of Jesus, and pointed to the Cross. We thought his preaching foolishness," rejoined Hypocrite.

"I saw him once after that, by the Sea of Social Swirl. I saw his form, as in the evening he walked among the wrecks along the shore," added Man-of-the-World.

"Yes, and it was his friend who saved thy life when the Whirlpool of Wine was sucking thee down to perdition," continued Hypocrite.

Reflection is the first sign-board pointing to the Valley of the Cross; and now, by the reminiscence recalled through the words of Hypocrite, Man-of-the-World began to gather into thought the record of the past years.

As the Angel and Hypocrite left him, I heard him say: "I should like to talk with Evangelist."

"We shall ask him to visit thee; for he always beareth comfort for such as thee."

Satan and Deception were in hiding as Hypocrite conversed with Man-of-the-World, and with disgust written upon their faces at Man-of-the-World's last words, I saw them leave in haste, and hastily enter the castle grounds.

"What think ye caused the crack in the wall?" asked Deception of Satan, as they stood near the damaged castle.

The Archfiend was not in the mood to discuss material affairs, for the possible loss of a soul was in his mind; but one of the castle guards, joining them, said: "That damage was done the night of the terrible storm, when the thunders of Jehovah held the castle in their grasp."

"The thunders of the Resurrection were indeed let loose that night," admitted Deception. "The crack extends from the roof to the ground."

"The interior is damaged as well," added the fiend.

MASTER, SPEAK! I KNEEL BEFORE THEE

As Hypocrite knelt at his evening devotions, I saw the Good Angel standing by his side, and noticed that to the eye of faith she was revealing the scars within the feet and hands and side of Him who upon the Cross died to redeem mankind.

"Seest thou these marks?" she inquired.

"I discern them clearly," he replied.

"These He suffered for thee; and yet He wears them by the Throne."

"I will wear my scars for Him," was the reply as the vision passed.

CHAPTER XX

THE GOOD ANGEL'S PITY

"He that hath given alms to the poor, takes Jesus by the hand; he that patiently endures injuries and affronts, helps him to bear his cross; he that comforts his brother in affliction, gives an amiable kiss of peace to Jesus; he that bathes his own and his neighbor's sin in tears of penance and compassion, washes his Master's feet." —*Bishop Jeremy Taylor.*

I LAY upon the cushions in my tent in the early morning of a new day, and meditated deeply upon what had been shown and told to me since the night I stood beside the Bridge of Sighs and first beheld the Guardian Angel, and heard her hurl defiance at the Enemy of Souls. My mind dwelt much upon her gracious ministry on earth, and, as I mused, all around me faded into shadows, and I saw her radiant and fearless presence once more, but girded and shod as for a journey.

"Tell me, kind spirit," I entreated, "is thine errand to the dwellers in the valley completed?"

THE ANGEL TELLS OF HER VISION

"Nay," she replied. "I shall return for there is more work for the Master to be done here. But there are other regions where the hearts of the men and women are yet cold to the friendless poor—those whom stern necessity holds in galling chains. A piteous cry has arisen to Heaven, and I am commanded to go in the name of the King of Heaven and bear His infinite pity and succor in response to the appeal. These were the words of the Lord to me:

"Go thou in the name of thy God; for the spirit of the Lord God is upon thee: go thou to these my children: bind up the broken-hearted, proclaim liberty to the captive, and open the prison doors to such as are bound: comfort such as mourn, give unto them beauty for ashes, and the oil of joy for mourning, the garment of praise for the spirit of heaviness."

"This portends more antagonism to our cause," said the Archfiend to Deception. "She goes forth to establish some new centre of disturbance. We shall have to be both sagacious and alert."

"The sympathy of the heavenly world accorded her is a matter of grave concern to me," replied the latter, "for it evidences the interest of Jehovah in the Angel's undertaking."

THE BREATH OF SELFISHNESS

"She goeth forth to instil a spirit of mercy in the heart of mankind, a mission exactly the reverse of ours," explained a fiend who had just arrived at the castle, and now joined the Archfiend.

"Ha! a new plan of operation! Well, we shall regard it as a challenge"; and so saying, Satan commissioned a number of his most subtle liegemen to hold themselves in readiness and to oppose, with all diligence, the work of the Angel.

Then I saw that the Archfiend taught them how to use a vile exhalation, termed by him "The Breath of Selfishness," which vapor, acting upon the heart of mankind, chilled it to all generous impulses.

"Haste ye," he enjoined them, "and where ye discover the Angel kindling the fires of commiseration within the human soul, there breathe as I have bidden you, until each spark is extinguished. Desecrate each altar upon which mercy burns; for mercy, like truth, worketh us most dire mischief."

Following the course of the Angel, these servants of Satan went forth vowing to hinder her work wherever possible. Assurance of success possessed their souls, and the satisfaction of defeating the work of the Angel lighted their faces with a gleam of joy.

They dogged her steps in whatever realm she went, and sought by the vapor of their vile breaths to quench the fires of mercy which love was kindling.

PRAYER IS THE CHRISTIAN'S VITAL BREATH

The Angel, detecting their presence, guarded her work by an atmosphere of prayer, which repelled the breath of these satanic miscreants; and thus, to their dismay, confounded their purpose, while before their envious eyes she kindled fires of compassion which continued to burn upon the altar of the world's heart.

Kindness, with the kindred sympathies of love and mercy, glorified the nature of all to whom her ministry was given, until everywhere the name of Jesus was proclaimed, and his teachings followed. The hard and harsh elements of self-love and apathy began to be consumed, and instead, the grace of Christian brotherhood adorned the heart of discipleship with the charm of Heaven.

CONFUSION WORSE CONFOUNDED

Discomfited and chagrined, the emissaries of Satan withdrew for conference; and I saw that the fires of fury burned with desperation in their souls.

"What can this defeat of our efforts signify?" asked one.

"To me it remains unanswerable," added a second.

"Perhaps it is the fault of the breath," answered a third.

"This cannot be," replied the first fiend, "for with it I have nearly frozen the hearts of the unguarded."

"Think you, then, our failure lies in the power of the Angel to resist our influence?" asked the second.

"So it seems. She is possessed of the art of divine enchantment, and in spite of our assiduous labors to hinder, she hath lighted the fires of compassion within thousands of souls," replied the first fiend.

AN EXECRABLE DEMON ADVISES EXTINCTION

There was with this satanic band one of a peculiarly defiant spirit who suggested that extreme measures be resorted to for the destruction of the Angel.

"Instant extinction; this is my solution of the matter," said he, as he stamped furiously about the cave wherein their conference was being held.

"She is not mortal. You cannot destroy a spirit," explained a fiend.

Then, looking out of the cave's mouth, they saw the luminous form of the Angel, and upon her countenance glowed the righteous defiance of the Almighty. Poised in mid-air I saw her form, and pointing a finger of derision at the band, the more confused because of their discovery, she held them captive.

Reverberating thunder shook the hills, and to these vassals of the Pit the sound was the voice of retribution and doom. Flashes of lightning alternated light with darkness, while within the cave, pinioned by palsying fright, the servants of the Archfiend huddled together in wild confusion.

SO FAREWELL HOPE

"To thy doom, satanic wretches who defy the omnipotence of Jehovah! No longer shall thy vile forms plague the earth with thy venomous breath!"

A moment's silence seemed to rest within the very bosom of the furious storm. Then, from out the dark heavens, a sulphurous flash pierced the cave and rent the rocks asunder, entombing the forms of the hideous fiends.

IN A SERVICE THAT THY LOVE APPOINTS

The good word of the Angel's success was borne to the interested company which frequently gathered for conference in the home of Miss Sincere. There I beheld them.

THERE ARE NO FAILURES IN GOD'S PLAN

"What a power of resurrection lies concealed in the love of Jesus," said the prophet; "for love bequeaths both purpose and energy to the human heart; and while love such as the Angel breathes abounds, there the Kingdom has dawned with a power which the Enemy is impotent to disturb. Heat cannot melt it, nor cold chill it, nor can the winds of winter drive it away. Love in her hands softens the clods of indifference and scatters blessings which tire the eternities to exhaust."

"Ah," replied Determination, "the gentleness of her hands lighteth fires within souls when the clumsiness of human touch closes life to the light of love. We fail because of the crudeness of our humanity."

"We must follow where the Angel opens the path; and then in our frailty and weakness God will yet ordain power," answered the minister.

"Thou hast thought truly," replied Evangelist. "As one has said to her, 'The whiteness of her heavenly robes reflects a light from the face of God.' We must be children of the light; for the lives of angels and men blend with the thought of the Master, in the achievement of His purpose to kindle the fires of divine pity within the lives of mankind."

"So shall it be with them," added Minister Good, and I saw them depart after they had knelt in a prayer of devout thanksgiving for the crowning work of the Angel along the paths which later their own feet should take.

RUIN UPON RUIN, ROUT UPON ROUT

The mighty crashing of the storm that buried the fiends within the cave had widened the gap in the castle wall, and standing before it, the Archfiend blasphemed the name and memory of all that was righteous and good, as he learned of the extinction of the fiends having the poisoned breath.

Fear and cowardice somewhat tinged his outburst of wrath; and remembering the words of retributive justice which had once sounded within his ears in the garden, he ventured not forth, but sought solace in the companionship of his trusted fiends, Belial and Deception.

Deception quaked in spirit when he saw the demolition of the wall, and looked through the opening breach over the ravine toward the Valley of the Cross.

"Another such storm and our lives are imperilled. Look! the rent has widened!"

"'T is not an hour for the consideration of the walls," said Satan in anger.

"The fire of His refining burst upon the City of Worldliness."

"The Almighty is hurling defiance at the very seat of our power. This is surely a matter of grave import," said Deception, with an air of resentment.

"We had better roam the earth as vagabonds and yet succeed in quenching the fires of compassion and love, than dwell here and suffer defeat in every undertaking," answered the Archfiend.

"But our equipment," added Deception. "We are impotence itself apart from it. The rent in the wall has already damaged the Bureau of Lies, and fear racks the spirit of those who work in that corridor."

LOVE CANNOT BE CONQUERED

Somewhat calmed, Satan replied: "The condition of the wall is dangerous, and who knows when the shafts of the Almighty may strike it again. It shall be repaired; but first our every effort must be bent to defeat the work of the Angel. She hath appealed to the Church of Christendom for a compassionate heart; and everywhere her spirit goeth forth to ameliorate the condition of men. This must not proceed further. Our grasp upon the souls of the degenerate and those who know not of mercy must be tightened."

"Why do you so fear the compassionate heart?" asked Deception.

"Because it encourages in the recipient a spirit of love in response; and love hath never yet been fully vanquished," he replied.

"I have often mixed love with hate, and so confounded its purpose," persisted Deception.

"Thou hast been to me a valued servant," said Satan, "and thine arts have won many to our cause, but these times demand subtleties with which the age is not familiar."

"Generations pass," replied Deception, "and the tricks of the past, though old to us, are as novelties to those of a new age."

"But God abideth," answered the Enemy, "and during thousands of years has marked our schemes to destroy souls. He remembereth and sends forth those under His instructions who have power to foil past policies. Bestir thyself for new conceptions of attack."

MANY WATERS CANNOT QUENCH LOVE

"He worketh by the same methods," said Deception.

"Yes," replied Satan, "the same methods only modified and adjusted to each new age. His one purpose is to build the unquenchable fires of love within the human heart."

"This is an exacting age, I know," continued Deception, "and the Angel whom He hath sent seems amply able to undo our best work."

"She is an untiring foe," replied Satan, "for through her activities love immediately changes the environment of life, and where this is accomplished our best conceived art is powerless to restore old-time conditions. We must watch her progress. We must thwart it. When compassionate love turns millions of gold towards the betterment of the slums, and charity ministers to the lot of the poor, it is time for most serious opposition."

"Aimeth the Angel toward this?" anxiously inquired Deception.

"She hath accomplished it in many places by awakening the Church; and old Evangelist—curse him!—with his exhortations concerning consecrated wealth hath influenced hundreds to invest in what is called 'the Lord's Cause,'" answered the Archfiend.

"And he still labors?" asked Deception.

"He labors without cessation, and is at this time in league and sympathy with the Angel in kindling the fires of love in the human heart."

"Thou hast persuaded me of the necessity of immediate and vigorous action," replied Deception. And so saying, I saw the two hurry along the corridor for conference with Belial and Heresy.

SEE THAT GLORY-BEAMING STAR

Then I beheld the Angel return with joy from her pilgrimage, and take her way to the home of Minister Good, where she soon gathered with her the little company of the Lord's faithful workers. For their encouragement she related how she had inspired souls with feelings of mercy, and gladdened their hearts by the signs of promise which, throughout the Christian world, portended the dawning of the brotherhood of mankind.

"This is most blessed news," said the minister.

The fires of compassion were kindled in the soul of Hypocrite, who was present, for he had read of the One who, traveling through Galilee, had been gracious to the poor and downtrodden.

WHAT I HAVE, O LORD, I OFFER THEE

He had once heard the prophet read from the works of one of God's illustrious servants these words, which had mightily touched him; and he felt as though the Christ were beseeching the gift of his substance to the poor and wayfaring.

"Our life requires to be broken in two each day and replanted, that it may spring up again from sleep as new blossoms out of the soil. We are buried every night for a resurrection of each morning; and thus our life is not a continuous line unbroken, but a series of lives and deaths, of deaths and births.

"Thus shall I break my life for Him, as Mary of old did the ointment; and in the new life of His love, will I bring my wealth that I may minister to His name in the reclaiming of souls."

"Thus thou shalt kindle more fires than thou dreamest of," added Evangelist, "and where love consecrates its treasure, there the Enemy of Mankind trembles with alarming fears."

"I shall do it for Him," was Hypocrite's reply.

WHO COULD THERE REFRAIN FROM WEEPING?

Not long after, Whole-soul, journeying in a field near the Cross, happened upon a strange-appearing tree, and from its boughs gathered a peculiar seed having a pleasant fragrance. Wondering what it might be, he brought it to the city, and sought information concerning its name and nature from the prophet.

"We shall seek the Angel, that we may learn of its virtue."

Together I saw the two approach and enter the home of Miss Sincere, where tarried the Angel, and of her seek to know the name of the seed, the fragrance of which filled the room.

As she took it, I heard her ask, "Where found ye this seed?"

"Upon a tree in a field near to the Cross," answered Whole-soul.

"When?" she inquired.

"To-day," replied Whole-soul.

"Thou hast discovered a rare seed, which comes from a tree an angel planted on the day of the Saviour's crucifixion.

THE SEED MUST BE PLANTED

"It is the tree called Pity, and these are the seeds which it hath been caused to bear. They must be gathered by the faithful, and planted within the soul of the Church of Christ."

"'T is most wondrous!" exclaimed Evangelist. "Wilt thou not tell us of this angel and for what reason and intent she planted the seed from which the tree sprang?"

"I will, for until now the record of this deed hath been known to none but God. There stood near the Cross that day, one whose soul had been healed of a deep sorrow by the compassion of the Crucified; and as she beheld Him in His agony, and marked the stolid and heartless gaze of the multitude, her heart sorrowed for Him even to weeping, and a tear, hot with the intensity of her pity, fell to earth where she stood. That tear, shed for the sorrows of her Saviour, became the seed which, taking root within the hallowed soil, germinated and grew to reproduce itself for replanting within this wondrous age."

"It is strange to me that seed so precious should have been entrusted to one so unworthy as I."

"It is to those of thy name that the Lord commits His precious gifts," replied the Angel to Whole-soul. Then to all gathered around her she commanded:

SOW IN THE MORN THY SEED

"Go ye all by the ways which I, in my ministry, have lighted, and sow the seed of pity in the souls of the children of God; and may the care and blessing of the Triune Father be with you."

Then I beheld them go forth upon their mission, and noticed that Whole-soul led the way, after giving to each a quantity of the seed which the Angel herself had helped him gather from the Tree of Pity near the Cross of the Crucified.

Then in my dream I beheld a great company, whom Evangelist and his friends had influenced, take up the work and carry it on until throughout the whole Christian world the seed of pity was planted in receptive soil; and in turn the earth was filled with the beauty of the Lord. God gave to the seed sown an atmosphere of love in which each plant thrived and speedily bore fruit.

"The day of promise of which the Angel spoke has dawned, and the dayspring portends the greater glories of that noontide of blessing which this age may usher in," said the aged prophet, as he saw throughout the land the betterment of social conditions, and beheld consecrated wealth rearing orphanages and asylums, hospitals and homes for the poor.

"Thus hath pity wrought the miracle of a human brotherhood, which actualizes the thought of Christ in His divine purpose of saving the world," said the Angel, as she rejoiced with Evangelist over the blessed accomplishment.

The anger of Satan was frightful to behold when he learned of the tree he might have blasted; but now an host of shining guards surrounded it, and with drawn swords threatened all save the Lord's anointed who ventured near. Remembering the day when the Angel dropped the tear by the Cross, the Archfiend cursed himself for not having tempted her away.

"'T is too late to mourn over so trivial a matter," spoke Deception, consolingly.

"True, 't is too late, and our lack of vigilance has suffered the seed of the tree to be discovered by one of the Angel's company. Oh! the woes of these lost days."

"Speak not so," replied Deception, "for we may yet blast these seeds in their growth, and thus destroy the hope of harvest."

"Ah, but the heart has been warmed for their coming, and the past has shown us unequal to a contest with the Almighty," answered Satan.

The two withdrew from my vision, and then I saw Determination turn the Lamp of Truth upon the place on earth where there was marked resistance in men's hearts to the spirit of pity.

"Thou canst discern the cause?" he asked Evangelist.

"Truly I do," answered the prophet, as he studied the human heart under the light of truth. "It is love of self and ignorance which chill the heart. The light of truth within the hearts of those of thy spirit can alone know human nature and render it susceptible to the seed of compassion and pity."

LOVE TRANSFORMS HUMANITY

Then I beheld that everywhere throughout the Christian world where the Angel's path had led, and where those of God's children at His command had gone with the fragrant seed, the fruit appeared in human hearts.

The blossom and bloom of a fragrant love sweetened the world. The mission of mercy had softened the heart of mankind. Burdens began to lighten, darkness lifted, cares that grew out of distress took wings; and upon the face of Christendom, love's blest enchantment was working the miracle of a transformed humanity; for the touch of the compassionate heart was felt and seen.

LOVE OF GOD! SO PURE AND CHANGELESS

The hordes of the Archfiend found their work onerous and discouraging, for wherever Deception led his forces they were repelled by the fragrance of the flowers of pity. Men who aforetimes were attracted by their arts were now impossible to reach, and their spirits quailed as they breathed the air of love which everywhere impregnated the atmosphere of human lives.

"Satan was right," said Deception, as he led his assistants back into the grounds about the castle. "This is a new age, and old methods of approach seem out of vogue. The hold of the Infinite One upon life is growing more intense, and it is to me a problem what tactics to advise."

DETERMINATION CONFOUNDS DECEPTION

"The regions where the Angel has been are unbearable. We are powerless to work in the atmosphere she has created," added one of the helpers.

As the fiendish band thus conferred, a sound "as of a rushing mighty wind" was heard about them, and a voice in accents of authority spoke:

"Love everywhere is answering the longings and aspirations of the race, and within the restlessness of the human spirit, the Almighty, through His servants, hath set the dawn of a new era, in which truth and pity shall shine forth to baptize the whole earth with the beauty of Heaven."

Determination, in passing that way, had detected Deception and his band, and from the roadway of the King, which skirted the mountain, thus addressed them. Passing on, they saw him not.

"Thou hast confounded the host of the Archfiend with thy courageous words," said the Angel as she met Determination later upon the road. "Go thou forth, servant of Jesus, speak the words of truth without fear; and may the power of our God be thy garment."

Thus did Determination approach the city with joy, and to Evangelist he related the confounding of Deception, and revealed to the prophet the message of the Angel.

"It shall be even so with thee as she hath said," replied the prophet.

Everywhere the children of God were busy, and where they wrought, the impassionate heart relented; and within it the graces of commiseration and pity began to abound.

SATAN SEES THE FUTURE

Then in my vision I beheld Satan in the garden of the castle, and saw that in his hands he held a glass, called the Glass of Futurity, through which he peered in all directions into the mists of the ages to come. I noticed his dismay as he gazed into the regions whither the Angel and those of her guidance had gone. There the work of love was advancing with mighty purpose, and he beheld the walls and roofs and towers of innumerable buildings.

He was worried at the vision. The glass was telling him the sad fact of his defeat; and he dared not doubt its revelation. He saw how the touch of the compassionate heart had written God's name on the hearts of men, and that everywhere, touched

THE GOOD ANGEL'S PITY

with pity, they were giving the means by which the buildings of his vision were reared, in which a host of children were being gathered to find shelter and instruction.

FOR THE TRESPASS OF THIS NATION

Above the scene of his vision, Satan beheld the Hill of Calvary, and from the Cross, made the more radiant by the living Christ of the ages, he beheld a dazzling light which blazed out over the whole earth and fell with a benediction upon every agency operated for the redemption of the race.

Laying aside the glass, I saw him stand with bowed head as though engaged in deep thought. Then the fires of his wrath were kindled and the surrounding hills resounded with his rage, as he began to curse the memory of the woman whose tears of pity at the Crucifixion had become seed in the soil by the Cross and produced the Tree of Pity.

Pacing to and fro in the garden, he spent his rage upon those whom his hideous blasphemy had no power to disturb.

"Curse—!" The sentence was not finished, for above him a cloud heavy in its folds parted, and out of its midst came a flood of dazzling light, and in its searching glory I saw the Archfiend tremble.

"This is the glory which shall flood the years with unending peace, and all darkness shall pass forever in the shining sun of righteousness." Thus did a company of angelic beings speak from the cloud.

Torn in soul by the prophetic words, the Archfiend hastened within the castle.

ON THE CROSS OF CHRIST RELYING

"Never to be discouraged, but to live and love and trust, thus do we gather the promises of God from the harvest fields of hope," said Evangelist, as he and Minister Good stood by the Cross, whither they had come for an hour's communion.

From this retreat they beheld in spirit the triumph of their Lord, and bathed their souls in the foregleam of a day soon to appear, when love and pity should find in all human hearts a perfect and lasting experience.

"It is from this spot," added Evangelist, "that the world's hope arose."

"And the world's hope shall never set, until the arms of the Christ who was crucified are clasped about a ransomed and redeemed race," answered the minister.

"We have already touched that day," he added.

With face aglow with rapture, I saw Evangelist look upon the Cross, and then turning, as though with an eye of limitless faith he were sweeping the expanse of centuries, I heard him say:

"The world grows better; the day grows brighter; the kingdom of darkness wanes.

"'Everywhere His glory shineth;
God is wisdom, God is love.'"

CHAPTER XXI

Man-of-the-World Under the Lights

"The virtue of prosperity is temperance, the virtue of adversity is fortitude; which in morals is the more heroical virtue. Prosperity is the blessing of the Old Testament, adversity is the blessing of the New: which carrieth the greater benediction, and the clearer revelation of God's favor." —*Francis Bacon, "Essays."*

"TIMES have changed with us, wife," said Man-of-the-World, as he looked into her eyes and saw tears there.

"Yes, indeed," she replied, "and it is painful to be pinched by such poverty. Society seems to have done with us," and so saying she buried her face in her hands and wept.

Man-of-the-World's marble mansion had passed into the hands of his creditors, and he and his wife were occupying a modest but comfortable house in an entirely different part of the city.

"Better times are in store for us," he replied, in an attempt to console his wife. "Hypocrite says 'the best is yet to come.'"

LET US BE PATIENT

"But think of what we have lost!"

"How can I help thinking of it?" he replied.

Then a silence of some minutes followed, which was interrupted by the entrance of Evangelist.

"Peace be to thee, and His blessing upon thy home," was his salutation.

The prophet's call was very gracious, and came at a time when Man-of-the-World was seeking to gather up the broken fragments of his life; although he knew not how to use them. Agitated and perplexed, he needed the help of a higher intelligence to give him moral inspiration for the task. This he found in the coming of the prophet. Man-of-the-World had reached the hour when he was prepared to see God.

"I have come by thy invitation," began the prophet.

"And it is well thou hast come. We have waited for thee," answered Man-of-the-World.

I saw that his wife was won to the prophet by his kindly face and gentleness of manner.

The three sat in silence; it was one of those hours when souls feel deeply what they hesitate openly to utter; and I noticed that the Angel was in the midst of the little company.

CHANGE AND DECAY IN ALL AROUND I SEE

"Thou hast seen much of change in the world during thy life," said Man-of-the-World, at last.

"A great deal," answered Evangelist. "Vicissitude and sorrow characterize the earthly sojourn. In this world we are sure of having tribulation."

"Thou too hast had sorrow?" inquired Man-of-the-World.

"Yes, and even Jesus, the Son of God, had it. It was He who said, 'Have faith.' Faith is the victory which overcometh the world."

"To live on, patiently, though life is robbed of its old-time comforts; to take a new hold of the higher intimations which every future holds, is the will of God," whispered the Angel.

"Perhaps I have been actuated by wrong motives," answered Man-of-the-World. "Perhaps I am reaping what I have sown. It is hard to understand. Perhaps my friend Hypocrite hath chosen the better way after all."

"Not as I will," answered the prophet.

UNDER THE LIGHTS

Then I saw that Evangelist placed three lights upon Man-of-the-World, and that in turn the light from each fell upon him; and by the help of these he saw strange and wonderful things.

"What are these?" he asked.

"These are the three lights by which men see the Past, the Present, and the Future. These are the lights of Experience, Truth, and Faith," answered the prophet.

Then the Angel, with one sweep of her hand, chased away the mists which hung before the eyes of Man-of-the-World, as Evangelist bade him look down the years of his life by the aid of the Light of Experience.

"What dost thou see?" asked the prophet.

"My past life," answered Man-of-the-World.

"How doth it appear?"

Man-of-the-World made no reply, but looked intently upon the panorama of wasted years. There lay his ambitions, his hopes, his plans, his gains, and there the culmination of it all.

"A strange medley, indeed," replied he.

"Thou hast never viewed thy past as a whole before," said the prophet.

"It lies in dull colors: its glory has vanished," was the reply.

"It lies in the colors in which it was painted," answered Evangelist.

"And can it not be changed?" inquired Man-of-the-World.

"It can only be forgiven," replied the prophet.

Then it was that into the soul of Man-of-the-World, as he turned from viewing the past, the Angel said:

"'I, even I, am he that blotteth out thy transgressions for mine own sake, and will not remember thy sins.'"

"Look thou here," said the prophet, and he gave him the Light of Truth. In its searching rays Man-of-the-World saw the waste and emptiness of many years; and of it all there was nothing left but a new beginning.

THE GATE OF OPPORTUNITY

"What dost thou now behold?" asked the prophet.

"Nothing! nothing!" was the reply.

"Nothing left from all of the years?"

"For a thousand years thou shalt await the day of thy doom."

"Nothing from all of the years!" said the sorrowful man.

"Seest thou not that here is a place for a new beginning?" asked Evangelist.

"I see but dimly an open gate."

"That is the Gate of Opportunity," explained the prophet. "'T is God's hand which opens it to thee."

"Whither leads the path beyond the gate?" inquired Man-of-the-World.

Then I saw Evangelist turn the Light of Faith upon the path which led through the gateway, and bid Man-of-the-World look again.

"I behold a long road leading direct across valleys and over hills to a city which stands upon a distant plain," said he.

"That is the King's Highway, which was opened for such as thee by the King's Son," explained the prophet.

"This is the way of the Lord, walk ye in it," interposed the Angel.

"Seest thou a Cross upon a lonely hill just beyond the gate?" asked the prophet.

"I cannot see it," answered Man-of-the-World.

Then the prophet turned the Light of Faith upon the path again.

"I behold the Cross!" cried out Man-of-the-World excitedly.

"That is the Cross upon which He died, that the sins of your past might be forgiven."

"I have heard it told, but have never seen till now."

"Now thou seest by faith," replied the prophet.

"This is all new to me," Man-of-the-World remarked.

"Thou hast yet much to learn, but God is gracious," said the prophet. "Dost thou see near the Cross a tree of fair proportions?"

"Yes, I behold a tree in a field near the Cross."

"That," replied Evangelist, "is the Tree of Pity, of whose seed Hypocrite informed thee. It was planted there when the Redeemer was crucified."

Moments of silence followed, and within the depths of his soul Man-of-the-World heard the voice of the Angel pleading for him.

Placing his hand upon that of his wife, who also followed the words of Evangelist, I saw them kneel while the Angel stretched out her hands in blessing, as the prophet, through prayer, led the lives of the two into the love of God.

"It shall be a new beginning, for we have passed through the gate," said Man-of-the-World.

"And I will follow," said his wife.

As the prophet departed I saw the two standing side by side, rejoicing in the new hope which had been given them. The sorrow of penitence filled their souls, as the Angel of God, with the wooing of love, led them forward upon the blessed pathway which was to shine with increasing recognition of heavenly joys as they journeyed on.

THE HARD ROAD OF SACRIFICE

Following their footsteps, I saw that the Angel led them down a path till they came to a place where many, growing faint-hearted, had turned back. Her solicitude was tender and her care untiring; for she recognized the presence of the Arch-fiend and knew the malevolence of his design upon these two.

"What is the meaning of so much difficulty near the entrance gate of the new life?" asked Man-of-the-World, as he followed at much cost of strength.

"This is a stretch of the way known as the Hard Road of Sacrifice, and many have here despaired and returned to the old life," explained the Angel.

"It is difficult to walk in it," he added, "and why must we follow it?"

"Pilgrims here learn the insufficiency of their own strength, and are taught the lesson of trust. Didst thou not read the words above the gate to which the light of Evangelist pointed thee?" asked the Angel.

"We failed to note the words," replied Man-of-the-World.

"Ah, many others have done so," replied the Angel.

"The words are those of Him who opened the gate for mankind," she continued, and then recalled them: "'If any man will come after me, let him deny himself, and take up his cross, and follow me.'"

I AM THE WAY, THE TRUTH, AND THE LIFE

"Why bear a cross and stumble over a road like this, when life might be smooth and joyous?" whispered Satan.

Man-of-the-World, attracted by a voice he well knew, turned, and in so doing, his eyes fell upon the Cross.

"This is the way which leads to life; beyond the Cross there is a crown," said the Angel.

The Archfiend, dismayed at the determination of Man-of-the-World, cursed the Guardian Angel, as in his soul he planned some new method of appeal.

"Look ye here," said the Angel guide, and so saying, she pointed to the eye of their faith a number of foot-prints which lay as in adamant upon the path.

"What are these?" inquired Man-of-the-World.

THIS IS THE WAY, WALK YE IN IT

"These are the marks of the Saviour's feet. He passed this way bearing our cross, the burden of which caused these impressions to be made, which the iconoclastic instruments of centuries have been powerless to efface. Thou art but taking the path He trod," explained the Angel.

Man-of-the-World, grasping the truth of the Angel's teaching, turned to his wife, and I heard her say:

> "'T is not the things we have, you know,
> That count us good and true.'"

Then, with a spirit that had learned the secret of self-mastery, I beheld him look toward the Cross as he prayed:

"Lord Jesus, give unto us, Thy weak children, the power of which Thy Angel speaks, that together we may take this way with patience and self-denial, looking unto Thee, who art the author and finisher of our faith."

When Satan heard his former victim pray, he began to shoot arrows of doubt regarding its being answered, but the Angel, who knew the Archfiend's subtlety, whispered:

"Thy prayer shall receive an answer; for thy God hath promised that the petition of faith shall be honored. Faint thou not. The past is at an end, and a future of blessing has opened."

"And can no one hinder?"

"No one, if thou dost trust God and cling to God. He will not suffer thee to fail."

So I saw that both came over the Hard Road of Sacrifice into the Way of Peace and Trust, and that an abounding joy filled their souls as they went on.

As they journeyed on, they came to a small house by the road which had been built by the King. It stood upon a hill called Prospect; and at the word of the prophet they entered.

"This hath been erected for the help of all pilgrims passing this way," he explained.

"There is a goodly view from here," said Man-of-the-World; for in the distance could be seen the Hill-lands of Faith, and from all points of vision the Cross was in sight.

Entering the house, the prophet led the three to an upper room, from which opened a window through which pilgrims for centuries were wont to look. It was the Window of Revelation. Pushing aside the shutters, Evangelist said, "Behold the glories of the Heavenly Hill!"

THE GOLDEN THREAD OF THE PILGRIM PATH

Their hearts lacked the power of expressing their emotions. There lay the vast summits upon which the heavenly city rested, and to the eye of faith its loveliness was clearly revealed.

Wending between, lay the path of the pilgrim, like a golden thread; and upon it was a mighty throng ascending with songs of victory. Far beyond lay the river, upon which hung the fogs of death; but crossing it appeared the bridge across which the Angel had come, and over which they dimly traced the passage of a vast multitude.

"Now let the vision pass," said the prophet. "Ye have seen, by the eye of faith, the City of God, and how the path to which the word of the Angel directed leads thither. Pursue it, bearing thy cross, and ere long ye too shall enter and find rest."

WITH THE PAST BEHIND THEM

Life to them again assumed an earthly environment, and soon Man-of-the-World, with Hypocrite, the prophet, Determination, and Whole-soul, were working in the mission school of Miss Sincere.

"We must be witnesses of the things we have seen," said Hypocrite.

"Yes," said Man-of-the-World, "we must shelter these children from the temptations of Satan and guide their feet into the paths of truth. These must be taught to escape the sins which later bring failure, sorrow, and tears,

"'For future happiness depends
Upon the things we do.'"

THREE MODERN MARYS

Three untiring souls, the Marys of the new era—Miss Sincere, Mrs. Man-of-the-World, and Widow Faith—appeared before me in the vision, and above them in their work for the Master, I saw the Guardian Angel.

"Go ye to find her," I heard the Angel say.

Then I understood the sorrow I saw written upon the faces of the three. A lamb had wandered from the fold. A weak child, one much loved, had lost her way and fallen into sin.

Patiently they sought her, and when found in haunts where only such angelic spirits would go, I beheld them lead her back.

Tears of gladness stood within the eyes of the aged prophet as he marked their love and tenderness, and I heard him say:

"There shall be new joy in Heaven to-day, in that the faithful have saved a soul from the error of her way."

"Who would have believed it?" said Man-of-the-World as he saw the mother instinct of his wife, hallowed by the Christ love, clasp the magdalen in her arms and whisper in deep earnestness the message of a heart passionate to save.

"It is the indwelling love of God which worketh such miracles," replied Evangelist.

MAN-OF-THE-WORLD TAKES UP HIS WORK

Then I saw the beautiful law of Christian brotherhood unfold before my eyes. Hypocrite, now a new man in Christ Jesus, gave to Man-of-the-World, a place in his employ; and a part of his duties was to dispense the former's benevolence.

Besides this, he devoted his time to the rescue of those who needed a friend's counsel after enjoying the first swells of the Sea of Social Swirl.

"We shall help Man-of-the-World," said Hypocrite to Evangelist, "for those have forsaken him who once were his friends, and he needs the warmth of loyal companionship. We shall help bear his burdens also."

"That is the spirit of Him whom we serve. 'Give, and it shall be given unto you,'" answered the prophet.

Man-of-the-World, rejoicing in the blessings of the new life, went forth, and by such doors as could be opened, he entered to influence for Christ the lives of the young social set, if perchance by tender warnings against Satan's intrigues he might save them from the sorrows of later years.

"I have a message for such," he said to the prophet. "I have tasted the poisonous wine of society life, and through the same follies these are indulging in have lost all, and had it not been for thee and the Angel, my soul would have perished."

"What are your plans?" asked Hypocrite.

"I shall spend the summer in the Lord's work at Longshore. I shall seek also by the Sea of Social Swirl to save such as will hear the truth."

"I shall go with thee," said Hypocrite; and as they went forth to their work of rescue, I saw that Evangelist also accompanied them.

LEAD, KINDLY LIGHT

The season of Longshore was at its height, and a new generation, added to those who had long tasted of sin, were there in great multitudes, regaling themselves with the dissipations Satan had provided.

I saw the three standing in the evening twilight within the same pavilion where together, long before, they heard the message of Evangelist; and the sea with its incoming tides washed the very beach upon which the prophet delivered the message of God, which they were then not ready to hear.

Man-of-the-World interrupted the silence into which they had unconsciously entered.

"We are here as the witnesses of Christ, with lives scarred by the very sins to which this multitude has committed itself. The prophet hath spoken, and it is now our duty to tell the story of salvation as written in our lives; perhaps they will hear us."

"The Lord ever honors the efforts of His servants. Relying upon Him, let the message be spoken," rejoined Evangelist.

Taking their places upon the beach, Man-of-the-World prayed in silence:

"'Take my lips, and let them be
Filled with messages for Thee.'"

COUNTING EACH LOST AND MISSPENT DAY

Then in the twilight, with faces lighted up by the glow of the moon, which cast its sheen upon the waters, I heard Man-of-the-World and Hypocrite for the first time tell the story of their lives. The throng surged about them on every hand, and upon this dense mass of souls fell a great silence, for all were eager to hear.

The message was one of power in its appeal to the heart. The winds from the sea carried the words of these servants inward, until those who crowded the broad boardwalk could hear them distinctly. The Angel was there; and upon the message breathed a blessing which gave it peculiar power.

Thousands of men, women, and youth heard for the first time a confession of Christ from the lips of these two whom they once recognized as leaders among their own set.

Some laughed in derision, while others were skeptical of their sincerity; yet within many souls the Master spoke with warning against a profligate life.

Satan was moving among the multitude, and, flushed with anger, he marked the abiding impression for good left by the words of these servants of the Most High.

"Shall this opposition to my plans never end?" he asked of his soul.

"It shall never end until a sin-cursed world lies within the hands of Immanuel," whispered the Angel.

NOTHING BUT LEAVES

Upon the beach, lost in silent thought, I beheld Mr. Please-all looking wistfully out to sea. His soul, like the untiring bosom of the vast deep, was full of unrest; for the message of the evening had accused him, and conscience stirred his soul as the spirit of the Living God condemned him by reason of a withheld message.

As he passed toward home, I saw the abode of the sinful

whose slumbering consciences he had cajoled with pleasing words. The Angel was repeating within his soul the message of Almighty God.

" 'For the priest's lips should keep knowledge, and they should seek the law at his mouth: for he is the messenger of the Lord of hosts. But ye are departed out of the way; ye have caused many to stumble at the law; ye have corrupted the covenant of Levi, saith the Lord of hosts.' "

Before the eyes of his soul, Please-all saw the scene to which Man-of-the-World had pointed the sinning multitude for safety. He saw upon a lonely hill a Cross, on which hung in unutterable sorrow the Saviour of Mankind, and recalled how Hypocrite had pointed to the scars within His side, His hands, His feet. Redeeming love was appealing for new and fearless utterance of the divine truth. In sorrow, Mr. Please-all marked the failure of past years; for he had dishonored his Master in a desire to exalt himself.

Looking through his tears of contrition upon the Cross, he heard a voice saying:

" 'Take up the cross, and follow Me.' "

And as Evangelist and his friends at prayer remembered him at the Throne of Grace that very moment, I heard him say: "I will follow Thee. I will bear the Cross. I will henceforth declare the whole truth."

As my vision waned, the Angel was whispering these words to the three: "Contrite hearts find favor in the skies."

CHAPTER XXII

SAVED AS BY FIRE

"When God built the world, he did not build a palace complete with appointments. This is a drill world. Men were not dropped down upon it like manna, fit to be gathered and used as it fell; but like seeds, to whom the plow is father, the furrow mother, and on which iron and stone, sickle, flail, and mill, must act before they come to the loaf." —*Beecher*.

THE passions of the Pit had been poured by the Archfiend into the City of Worldliness, and a fever of extravagant wantonness throbbed within the pulses of its populace. Iniquity and shame, arrogant and sensual, had kindled the fire in which its boasted glory was to be consumed.

The message of the prophet had fallen upon dull ears, and now the hands upon the clock of time were pointing to the hour of doom.

The Almighty stood within the shadows, girt about with impenetrable silence.

"I fear the Lord may not save the city," said Minister Good to Evangelist.

STRICT TO MARK AND JUST TO RENDER

"With him all things are possible," replied the prophet.

"Perhaps He shall save it for the sake of the few righteous," continued the minister.

"He shall purge away the dross," whispered the Angel, "for the set time of His judgment hath come," and so saying I saw her beckon those of the household, as she led the way.

Then I saw in my dream that Determination, at the instance of the Angel, had gathered those of the household of faith, and that they all went outside of the city. It was evening. The sun had crossed the mountain, and by its touch of lingering light infused the vast banks of foamy clouds which lay above the valley with crimson and gold. A sense of peace pervaded Nature, and above the city the stars, one by one, were hung out by angel hands—lanterns along the roadways of the skies.

THE LITTLE COMPANY KNEEL IN PRAYER

I saw the company hasten on until they came to the brow of a hill above the city, and then I beheld them kneel in prayer.

Evangelist was in their midst, and around him were gathered those who with much toil and tears had labored for the redemption of the city. They were stationed as watchmen upon the battlements of the Kingdom, for their eyes were to witness wonderful things.

In the dying twilight I saw Man-of-the-World and Hypocrite standing together, with their eyes turned toward the Cross, which shone out in the darkness with an iridescent glory.

"Would the people of the city might behold the radiance of yonder Cross as we have come to see it," said Man-of-the-World.

THAT MAN IS BLEST WHO STANDS IN AWE

"The people shall come to behold the face of the anointed," answered the Angel, "but not until purified by the refining fire."

"The refining fire?" repeated Hypocrite.

"The dross must be removed, and then shall the silver and gold shine forth in their splendor," replied the Angel.

Widow Faith and Miss Sincere wept as they thought of those for whom they had striven and prayed; who yet remained indifferent to the pleadings of grace.

"Dry thy tears, for the Lord hath counted thy labors, and His arm stretcheth forth to save," said the Angel pityingly.

The voice of Evangelist announced the appearance of a strange light in the cloud beyond; and the eyes of all soon rested upon it.

"The Lord hath come; fear ye not, but behold the power of Jehovah; for His right arm hath been made bare to ransom the city from its waywardness and sin," said the Angel.

THE WONDERS OF HIS HAND

In the distance was heard the rumbling of thunder, like the rolling of many chariots, and this was followed by an illumination of the clouds.

"It is the day of the millennium. It dawns upon yon mountain, and the hosts of the Lord seek to usher in the age of righteousness," said Whole-soul.

"It records the beginning of the age for which the saints of the earth have prayed. The toil and sacrifice of the Lord's children shall soon be rewarded in a purified society, and the new Jerusalem which descendeth from Heaven shall appear, and be established on earth as was promised," replied the Angel.

Then the heavens opened and upon the clouds appeared the form of One like unto the Son of God.

"His eyes were as a flame of fire, and on his head were many crowns; and he had a name written, that no man knew, but he himself. And he was clothed with a vesture dipped in blood. . . . The armies which were in heaven followed him . . . And he hath on his vesture and on his thigh a name written, King of Kings, and Lord of Lords."

THE FIRE OF GOD'S REFINING

Then from the clouds descending, the fires of His refining burst upon the City of Worldliness, and a wail of sorrow filled the valley, as the Lord separated men from their pleasures and sins, and cast them into the fires of purification.

The company upon the hill stood aghast at the appalling scene; for the City of Worldliness upon which they looked, shone with the glow of a refiner's fire.

"This is the place of which God hath spoken," said the

Angel, as she pointed to the terrible scene enacted before their eyes; "for He hath declared, 'And it shall come to pass, that in all the land, . . . two parts therein shall be cut off and die; but the third shall be left therein. And I will bring the third part through the fire, and will refine them as silver is refined, and will try them as gold is tried: they shall call on my name, and I will hear them: I will say, It is my people: and they shall say, The Lord is my God.'"

THE PROPHET HAS A VISION

The patriarch, Evangelist, beholding the cleansing of the city, was moved with the voice of prophecy, and all near him gave heed to his words.

He spoke concerning the new day which had dawned, and interpreted the city's purification; for he had seen a vision.

"These," said he, "are the beginnings of the days of the Son of Man. The vision hath been God's answer to the people's reverent and obedient faith. The fires of purification have been those of the Holy Ghost, by whose chrism sin and its attendant evils are purged from the heart, that the people, instead, may offer unto the Lord an offering of righteousness.

BLEST ARE THE SONS OF PEACE

"Blessed are the eyes which see what ye have seen. Cast not away, therefore, your confidence, which hath great recompense of reward. For yet a little while, and He whom ye have

"The lowly home where the glorified Christ had deigned to come."

seen in the vision of the cloud 'will come, and will not tarry.' Ye have entered into the promises which many, dying in the faith, saw afar off. The city hath been saved by fire, and the Lord's children may behold His vision reflected within the crucible.''

"Evangelist hath seen the vision," said the Angel, "and his interpretation thereof is true. Betake yourselves hence to gather for the Lord at his appearing the souls purified by the refining fire."

"We shall obey," answered Determination. "The days yet call to labor, and we must go to do the will of Him who sent us." And so saying, the company of the faithful followed, and I beheld them enter the city where all things had been made new.

"Go ye forth to gather for the Lord his jewels," directed the Angel, "for the set time for the favoring of Zion hath appeared."

THIS NEW MANHOOD IN CITY AND TOWN

The new heaven and new earth baptized with a celestial glory shone on every hand, and as the faithful walked in its streets, the old curse of iniquity had been removed, and everywhere were recognized the signs of righteousness, which in lives redeemed were to advance the Kingdom of Love. Things which had offended were no longer seen, and truth and the will of God were operative in the hearts of the people.

Under the light of the Cross, which bathed the city, throughout, the touch of divine pity was everywhere manifest; and the people respected the teaching of the prophet, and began their ministrations to the poor, so that cries of want and suffering were no longer heard.

"Through the help of God, we have at last realized the ideal city, in which dwelleth righteousness," said Determination.

'And there are none to molest nor make us afraid," said Minister Good.

"These are wonderful times," observed Man-of-the-World, "for everywhere people are seeking to lay up their treasures in Heaven, 'where neither moth nor rust doth corrupt, and where thieves do not break through nor steal.'"

LADEN WITH GUILT AND FULL OF FEARS

Skulking about in the shadows beyond the city, the Archfiend found his approach arrested by an atmosphere of grace which he could not penetrate, and sorrowing grievously because his hopes were foiled, I saw him withdraw toward the wilderness, taking with him his attendant fiends.

"Thousands of years ago God decreed this doom; but never did I count it possible of fulfillment," said he. Oppressed by disturbing fears, he hastened on cautiously toward the castle, while his wild eyes burned with suspicion as he glanced right and left as though treading a path of doom.

As he reached the edge of the wilderness a strange light touched his feet. It startled him and he shrank back under shelter of the rocks, while the fiends huddled around him, each cursing the hour and its threatening terror.

"Whence came the light?" he asked, as he ventured forth and looked out toward the distant hill.

"It was from yonder cloud," answered one of the fiends.

"Nay, it was from the Cross upon the hill," insisted another.

The Archfiend writhed with inward agony, as he feigned outward boldness, and ventured again to utter words of defiance and blasphemy against the Almighty.

"The cloud parts!" shouted Determination, as he stood with Evangelist under shelter of the Cross.

"God worketh wonders," answered the patriarch.

From the distance came a sound like thunder, and its reverberation was heard throughout the neighboring ravine. Then silence brooded over the land.

"Behold! Behold!" shouted Determination. "Yonder upon the edge of the cloud standeth an Angel. What is that he holds in his hand?"

Evangelist, shielding his eyes with his hand, peered in the direction of the cloud. Then he spoke.

ETERNAL COUNSELS, DEEP DESIGNS

"I see an Angel coming down from Heaven having the keys of the bottomless Pit and a great chain in his hand.' He shall lay hold on the dragon, that old serpent, which is the Devil and Satan, and shall bind him a thousand years. He shall cast him into the bottomless Pit, and shut him up, and set a seal upon him, that he shall deceive the nations no more, till the thousand years shall be fulfilled; and after that he must be loosed a little season. Then he shall be cast into the lake of fire and brimstone, and shall be tormented day and night for ever and ever.''

The Cross was illumined with a radiance beatific, and within its glory Evangelist and his friends tarried to witness the descent of the Angel, who, in fulfillment of God's decree, had come to bind the Archfiend with inseverable chains.

Beyond them on the edge of the wilderness, the Avenging Angel intercepted Satan before the eyes of Evangelist and Determination. Relentlessly and with vehement rage, the Archfiend strove to overpower his opponent, but in vain. The clanking of chains was distinctly heard as the hand-to-hand combat continued.

SATAN IS CAPTURED AND BOUND

"Now," said Evangelist, "the chains are made secure; the Avenging Angel hath shackled the Enemy," and then the two knelt at the foot of the Cross and offered praise to Jehovah.

The Avenging Angel led forward his captive, while the other fiends in dismay and terror hurried toward the castle. Then the earth shivered as it was torn apart at God's command, and I could see a deep and hideous pit, bottomless as viewed by man's eyes, into which Satan, with dreadful groaning and curses, was cast; and where his chains were made secure. Above hung an impenetrable cloud.

"It is too terrible to behold; my soul shudders at the sight," cried out Determination, as he covered his face.

"Fear not, my son," replied the prophet. "The Lord is within the cloud. These are the days of fulfillment, in which the sons of God should greatly rejoice. But listen!"

"For a thousand years, for a thousand years, thou shalt await the day of thy doom." With these words did the Angel address Satan, and then, with a motion of his hand, he closed the bosom of earth and disappeared within the cloud.

THE PROPHECY IS FULFILLED

Then throughout the earth those things in nature occasioned by sin began to die, and instead of the thistle there sprang forth the fragrant rose; and everywhere souls filled with peace and blessing lifted anthems of rejoicing, in which the symphony of God's entire people was to blend.

WORTHY FOREVER IS THE LORD

Then I beheld in the dream that within the city redeemed there went up to God the shout of thanksgiving, and that everywhere earth and Heaven seemed one; for the will of God was being done on earth as in Heaven. Love with gentleness of perfection healed the deep wounds of the ages; while mercy perfected in the weak the blessings of the Most High. All loving the Lord were as one in Christ and lived beneath His smile; and life was spent in the delights of mutual benediction.

"At last the Lord hath answered the prayer of His Church, and within the blessings of the new age we shall join the choir invisible, whose music is the gladness of the world," said Evangelist.

Determination met the three as they entered the city, and together they sought Evangelist in the home of Miss Sincere with the news of the destruction of Satan's Castle of All Evil.

"So it hath fallen!" cried the prophet, with glad heart. "Its fall was the crash our ears heard when we beheld the Angel descend from the cloud. Nevermore shall its stones be set one upon another."

"Nevermore," answered Minister Good. "And now the Master Himself may soon appear. For this we must prepare."

"Yes, all must be ready for Him, for 'of that day and hour knoweth no man, no, not the angels of heaven, but my Father only,'" answered the prophet.

The Good Angel had undertaken a journey throughout the earth, and everywhere behind her the fires of purifying fell upon the people; everywhere the kingdom of Jesus upon its own foundation was being built up, and the glad day of His redeemed came in peace and power.

THE CASTLE OF THE ENEMY IS DESTROYED

Man-of-the-World with Hypocrite and Whole-soul, returning from a church service, came to the spot where it was told them by Evangelist that Satan had been entombed; and as they stood in their rejoicing with faces toward the Hill of the Cross, the eyes of the former glanced toward the castle, and lo! it was not there.

"What has befallen the castle?" cried he.

The eyes of the three turned toward the spot, and though they could trace the winding path up the mountain, none could see the castle of the Enemy of Souls.

"Let us go and behold what desolation hath been wrought," said Whole-soul.

Together I saw them climb the hill, and lo! when they reached the summit they beheld only the ruins of the Archfiend's stronghold.

"The Enemy in chains and his habitation demolished! Both have been wrought by the hand of our God!" cried Whole-soul.

"He hath gotten us the victory," assented Hypocrite.

"The victory through our Lord Jesus Christ, against whose kingdom the gates of hell were powerless to prevail," added Man-of-the-World.

CHAPTER XXIII

The Opening of the Heavenly Gates

> The heavenly chimes are ringing
>   From the Temple's tower afar,
> And the stars are candles shining
>   Through the Gates of Pearl ajar,
> Saying, "Come where souls find resting,
>   And earth's heartaches ever cease;
> Come toward Heaven, the Holy City,
>   Where the bells are chiming peace."

"THE light is breaking at last over the Hill of the Cross, and its glory is most gracious," said Minister Good.

"The promise is that, 'at evening time it shall be light,'" answered his wife.

"The Land of the Blessed, through all our years of service, has not been far away," he replied.

"Yes," responded his wife, "it has always been near; but at times the mists have obscured it."

Then in my vision I saw Evangèlist enter. Minister Good loved the old prophet, and had come to regard his words as

THE OPENING OF THE HEAVENLY GATES 441

inspired of the Lord. As the patriarch joined in the conversation it assumed a personal strain, for both of those servants of God were looking down vistas of happy memories.

The leading of God, and the work of the years, with all of the joy and sorrow they had held, were reviewed, and from the sunlit hills of blessed lives they spoke as dear friends sometimes do of those coming years which must witness the soul's transition into the land of the sinless and redeemed.

HOW SMALL THE HEAVY CROSS SHALL SEEM

"The human spirit grows homesick, at times, for the glories that await it," said the minister.

"Yes," answered Evangelist, "the end of our mission lies in the fruition which shall be reached after we have entered the Heavenly Gates. How small our heaviest cross shall then seem, when the vision of the crown appears."

"'Eye hath not seen, nor ear heard, neither have entered into the heart of man, the things which God hath prepared for them that love him,'" replied the minister.

"It is given to the Christian to near the gates of Heaven with a glad heart, if the work of life has been well done," rejoined the prophet.

"Yes, yes," continued Minister Good, "these years to us have been filled with toil and struggles for humanity. The future will bring its reward; and there will yet be more blessed ministries awaiting us upon reaching Heaven."

MINISTER GOOD IS CALLED TO HIGHER SERVICE

Not many days after, while returning from a ministry of mercy to one of God's children in sorrow, just as the setting sun from over the Hill of the Cross was gilding the path to be trod, the Master called for the higher services of Minister Good, and to human ears his spirit never spoke again. He had gone to join the choir invisible.

"It is a beautiful close of a blessed life," were Evangelist's words upon hearing that his friend's earthly ministrations were ended.

In a garden within sight of the Hill-lands of the Cross, Hypocrite purchased a plot of earth, and there the human form of Minister Good was tenderly laid to rest.

"Here," said the aged prophet, as the little company stood by the tomb, "we shall lay our brother and speak our tenderest words; here we shall let him rest, for he hath fallen asleep, and on the morning of the Resurrection this body shall rise again through the power of Jesus."

"He hath gone to his reward," said Whole-soul.

"He lived to bless us all," added Miss Sincere.

"God forgive us for aught of pain our sins of other days caused him," replied Hypocrite, "for he was our friend."

A light from the Cross fell upon the tomb with holy effulgence, as the Good Angel stood within the doorway of an old-time sepulchre close by, and extending her hands in benediction said:

"Sown in weakness, but raised in power, His spirit, victorious over death, hath crossed the Bridge, and for this servant of our God, the Gates of Pearl have opened."

A CROWN NEVER FADING, A KINGDOM OF GLORY

Again it was Easter morning, and as the Angel parted from them, the little company in reverent silence withdrew toward the city.

The songs of the Resurrection were everywhere rising throughout the world; and flowers, emblems of the risen life, having tossed aside the coverlet of winter, smiled with rejoicing, as the voices of God's children throughout this new age of Christendom burst forth in a chorus of praise to Him who from Joseph's sepulchre had brought life and immortality to light for mankind.

Man-of-the-World and Hypocrite walked through the redeemed city, and noted with delight the glories of the millennium which had dawned. Peace everywhere abounded, and humankind in bonds of perfect brotherhood fulfilled the laws of the Kingdom. Love constrained all hearts, and in mutual relations expressed the mind of Christ. Faith was far-reaching and genuine; for whatever was false and insincere had been cleansed from the world by the breath of the Spirit. Sorrows and troubles occasioned by misunderstanding and self-seeking were banished, and the King in His beauty everywhere held sway over the life of the age. Tears and heartaches were coming to an end, for the Archfiend was powerless to sow the seed from which they sprang. All things had become new.

HOW HARD TO REMEMBER

"These are wonderful times," said Hypocrite, as his keen sense of perception grasped the fulness of blessing which abounded on every hand.

"The Lord has been gracious in leading us into the blessedness of the redeemed life," replied Man-of-the-World.

"Would I could wipe from memory the wilful mistakes of my early life. They seem the more grievous as I view them by the light of the millennium," added Hypocrite.

"Yes, yes," answered Man-of-the-World, "would we might sweeten the past and cleanse it of the sorrows which our sins occasioned; but it lies beyond our recall. Oh! the sorrows of a misspent life."

"But all is forgiven; why should we suffer the remembrance of it to cast its shadow upon the gladness of these blessed years?" replied Hypocrite.

> "Threefold the stride of time from first to last.
> Loitering slow, the future creepeth—
> Arrow swift, the present sweepeth—
> And motionless forever stands the past,"

answered Man-of-the-World.

"Yes, the motionless past, soiled with our sin, lies where it has no power to harm."

"Yes," said Hypocrite, "it lies in the oblivion of God's mercy; we shall go forward, keeping the eye of faith upon the prize of our high calling of God in Christ Jesus."

THE OPENING OF THE HEAVENLY GATES 445

GLORIOUS TIDINGS, PLENTY

I saw them retrace their steps until they reached the home of Miss Sincere, where Evangelist stood in the doorway to greet them.

"Enter and be at peace," was the prophet's salutation, and then he told them the glad tidings he had received from the Angel, as he communed near the Cross that very day.

The aged prophet had gone to the little house on the Pilgrim's Road for rest and communion, and through the Window of Prayer had looked afar off toward the heavenly gates. He had stood silently gazing into the glories before him; and upon his benign face had rested the brightness of the Cross which shone through the window.

AND THE CITY LIETH FOURSQUARE

The clouds which hung in mid-air this side of the City of God had seemed a transparent veil through which he saw outlined the gates of pearl and the walls of precious stones, and beyond them the domes and towers of the Christian's home.

"The land of the blessed lies nearer than I have ever seen it before," said he to himself.

Closing the window he descended to the foot-path, and turning his eyes toward the Cross, he rejoiced to behold the approach of the Angel.

"I have good tidings for thee, thou servant of God," were her words of salutation.

"What revelation dost thou bear?" inquired the prophet.

"One that shall delight thy soul. The Christ hath come!"

"Whence?"

"He hath come from glory, to rule and reign within this age, as He promised upon His departure at Bethany. He hath appeared!"

"Blessed, blessed tidings! Where can we behold Him that our souls may bow down and worship?"

"He shall appear unto thee," was the reply.

"My heart longeth to behold the face of Him to whom through all these years my love and service have been given," declared Evangelist.

"He shall meet thee upon the road which leads down from the Cross. I saw Him there this day," answered the Angel.

EVANGELIST MEETS THE LIVING JESUS

Then did Evangelist relate what befell him after leaving the Angel, and the company burst into exultant song as the prophet told them of the return of their Lord.

> "'Again He comes! From place to place
> His holy foot-prints we can trace.
> He pauseth at our threshold—nay
> He enters—condescends to stay.
> Shall we not gladly raise the cry—
> Jesus of Nazareth passeth by?'"

"Listen, my children," continued the prophet, "for I would tell of our meeting."

"A meeting with the Christ! Lo, He hath come!" exclaimed Whole-soul.

THE OPENING OF THE HEAVENLY GATES

"Listen," urged Determination, who waited with intense interest to hear.

WHO IS THIS THAT COMETH UP?

"I will tell of our meeting," began Evangelist. "While in the way this side of the Cross, I beheld the approach of a stranger. From the Angel's description I discerned that it was our Lord; and hastening forward I fell at His feet in adoration. Oh, glorious moment!"

Thus did Evangelist speak, and a hush of reverent silence followed, in which none could utter a word.

"Beautiful face, radiant with heavenly light, which beamed upon me; beautiful hands, bearing the nail-prints, were then laid upon my head as I knelt at His feet; beautiful robes of white and crimson were those which touched me as I pressed against His form. Beautiful words, those with which my Lord addressed me as I looked into His eyes," continued the prophet.

"Then I feasted my soul until He parted from me, and I heard Him say, 'I shall see ye again.'"

"Would we might all behold Him face to face," exclaimed Whole-soul. "Would that we might know where He dwelleth and approach Him with our praise."

"The pure in heart everywhere behold Him. The prophet hath been privileged to see Him whose very presence is palpable to each; for everywhere His glory shineth," said Hypocrite.

"Yes," replied Evangelist, "He is not far off from any of us."

DO ALL THAT IS IN THINE HEART

So they parted to their tasks, and with them, though unseen, was the conquering Lord to bless each ministration and hallow it with His personal and sacred touch.

"Let us go and prepare the spot where the castle of Satan stood for the service of the Most High," said Determination to a band of earnest and valiant Christians.

"We are of one mind with thee in this matter," said they all.

Then in my vision I beheld them go forth, and saw them climbing the steep path toward the ruins of the castle. The ascent was difficult. A network of briars had hidden the path, and on the mountain side giant thistles and cacti clasped in their rough embrace the tangled undergrowth of shrubbery. The silence of death enveloped the hill, and nowhere was recognized the sign of a living thing.

"Behold the destruction the Almighty hath wrought," said Determination, as he and his faithful associates pressed their way to the summit. Standing at last upon the vast pile of stone, lying in disorder, where the proud castle once stood, I saw them look toward the Cross, whence, through the stern experience of the years, all inspiration and strength for service had come.

Standing upon the rocks of the dismembered castle these soldiers of Jesus looked down on the prison tomb of the Archfiend and burst forth in words of triumph and adoring praise:

" 'Thank be to God, which giveth us the victory through our Lord Jesus Christ.' "

"I saw that His hands were uplifted in benediction."

I WILL ORDAIN A PLACE

Days passed, and yet they labored and rejoiced the more by reason of their purpose to cleanse the spot and consecrate it to the service of God.

The hidden foundations of the castle were unearthed, and places long defiled by the presence and inspiration of evil were purified by the breath of prayer; and then arose the walls of a watch-tower, which, when completed, was dedicated to the service of the Most High. From it the prayers of the new Kingdom were to be noted and within the tower were stationed those who, by appointment of the Angel, were to record the onward sweep of the new age.

Many days after, Determination, with Man-of-the-World and Hypocrite, went up the mountain. A new clearing had been made and a broad path cut, by the sides of which clung the lowly myrtle, with here and there a rambling rose, laden with color, to adorn the way. Everywhere the face of nature had changed, and the breath of Heaven was in the air.

Reaching the tower, the three entered, and were greeted by the keepers. Determination carried with him the Lamp of Truth, and by its wonderful searching they looked throughout the world. The glory of the Cross near-by lighted up the distance, and they beheld what before had not been given mortal eyes to see. Each in turn beheld the same vision, and with mutual delight they rejoiced in the incomparable glories of the advancing age.

A NEW HEAVEN AND A NEW EARTH

"Turn the glass yonder," instructed the Angel who stood with them on the tower.

Determination obeyed.

"Thou art now looking in the direction of the Throne of Jehovah. What dost thou see?" she inquired.

"I behold, as it were a vast city coming downward toward the earth."

"Thou dost discern rightly," replied the Angel.

In turn Man-of-the-World and Hypocrite gazed through the glass upon the scene.

"Hath this vision a meaning which those of the world may understand?" asked Determination.

"It is not a vision thou beholdest, but a fulfillment of a vision seen of the disciple John long years ago while upon Patmos," the Angel explained, and so saying she repeated the language in which he had described it: 'And I John saw the holy city, the new Jerusalem, coming down from God out of heaven, prepared as a bride adorned for her husband.'"

BEHOLD, I MAKE ALL THINGS NEW

"What signifieth the sound like a voice which we heard while looking upon the city?" asked Man-of-the-World.

"That sound was the voice of one who spoke out of Heaven," replied the Angel.

"What was the message?" inquired Determination.

"'Behold, the tabernacle of God is with men, and He will dwell with them, and they shall be His people, and God Himself shall be with them, and be their God. And God shall wipe away all tears from their eyes; and there shall be no more death, neither sorrow, nor crying, neither shall there be any more pain: for the former things are passed away.'"

"What a wonderful message," exclaimed Man-of-the-World. "When shall these blessings be realized by mankind?"

"They have begun to realize them already; and with the reappearing of Jesus the day of a full redemption draweth nigh," answered the Angel. Then the three left the tower and directed their steps toward the city.

HE THAT OVERCOMETH SHALL INHERIT

"We have seen blessed things to-day," said Determination.

"We have stood upon the mount where to human hearts God revealed the wonders of His transfiguring touch," replied Man-of-the-World.

Then I beheld Evangelist and Whole-soul meet the three as they entered the valley; and to them the three told of the vision and the Angel's interpretation.

The aged prophet listened reverently to the message, and then broke forth in praise at hearing of the dawning age of blessedness, of which the voice out of Heaven had spoken.

"This is the day for which the people of all ages have waited and prayed. 'Many prophets and righteous men have desired to see those things which ye see, and have not seen them; and to hear those things which ye hear, and have not heard them,' " he declared.

" 'Blessed are your eyes, for they see: and your ears, for they hear,' " said the Angel.

AND THEY SHALL SEE HIS FACE

"We must hasten," said the prophet, "for we are to meet our Lord, returned, at the home of Widow Faith, at eventide."

Hurrying toward the city, they sought this poor woman's dwelling, and entered with reverence and rejoicing to behold again in the garment of flesh the Lord Jesus.

"He yet tarries with the lowly, and honors the poor with His presence," Miss Sincere had said to the prophet upon hearing of His visit.

"The Lord, no doubt, remembereth those who once welcomed Him in Galilee, and of those He spoke tenderly when to His Church He said: 'The poor always have ye with you,' " replied Evangelist.

"None are more worthy to receive the divine Lord than Widow Faith; for with great confidence she hath sacrificed much in order to minister unto the poor and homeless, through a long life," added Miss Sincere.

"Yes, she hath lived His life, and the beauty of the Lord has appeared on whatever her life has touched," said Hypocrite.

MY LORD AND MY GOD

Then I saw within the lowly home where the glorified Christ had deigned to come; and about Him in loving fellowship were

THE OPENING OF THE HEAVENLY GATES 453

gathered the little company. They looked upon His face, which beamed upon them with celestial light; and His voice of love, which had won the world, fell upon their ears as a melody divine. I saw them handle Him to be convinced; and with a tenderness that dissolved every doubt, He showed them the scars within His hands and upon His feet, as He said:

"These are the healed wounds from the nails of Calvary."

Adoring, Evangelist and the company fell before Him in exultation and praise; and I marked that the little room was ablaze with a glory that was heavenly. Throwing aside His garment, the Master pointed to a scar within His side.

"This," said He, "is where the spear of the soldier pierced my side after my death upon the Cross." And so saying, He added, "I am none other than He who died for the sins of the world, and of whom it was foretold that He should again appear."

Then, without their seeing, He disappeared, and amazed and wondering, left them to themselves and prayer.

The great day for which the Church of Christendom had waited long, and for the coming of which thousands had suffered the loss of all things, had at last dawned; and upon earth and in Heaven men and angels rejoiced in rapturous acclamations of praise, in honor of the all-conquering and triumphant Redeemer.

YE SHALL NOT TASTE DEATH

Upon the departure of Christ, the Angel entered the home of the Widow Faith.

"Life's day is far spent," said she. "Ye have seen the return of the Lord's Anointed; for whose coming ye have prepared the way. The time of your departure draweth nigh; and it is given unto you of His mercy not to taste of death."

So saying, the Angel beckoned the company to follow. Then I saw that the aged prophet arose and encouraged the others to obey the command.

THERE SHALL BE NO NIGHT THERE

Standing within the doorway with their guide, they beheld before them a cloud in which shone the glory of the world invisible, and within it were a host of celestial beings, chanting the song of the triumphant.

As I watched the wondrous phenomenon, I beheld the cloud move slowly before them as they advanced, with the Good Angel leading the way. As they passed the Cross, the angelic antiphone grew the more distinct as the heavenly choir drew nearer. Clad in robes of white, these pilgrims followed the cloud; and to my ears came the words of the song of the heavenly host. It was the *new, new* song.

A mighty chorus of voices sang: "'What are these which are arrayed in white robes? and whence came they?'" and was answered in marvellous tones by others: "'These are they which came out of great tribulation, and have washed their robes, and made them white in the blood of the Lamb.'"

Then I beheld the Angel as she approached the Bridge, and heard her say, "The victory is won"; and amid the music from angelic choirs assembled before the Gates of Pearl, on the farther side, Evangelist and the faithful band, over whom the Angel had kept guard for many years, mingled with the throng who were passing over; and I saw them no more.

HIM THAT LIVETH FOR EVER AND EVER

Ere the vision ceased, I beheld the All-conquering Saviour—once for mankind the Man of Many Sorrows, but now the world's acknowledged Redeemer, standing by the Bridge which spanned the river with hands uplifted in benediction, and upon His face, which was turned towards the Gates of Heaven, rested a gleam of glory from the City of Peace.

> "Welcomed at the pearly portal,
>   Evermore a welcome guest;
> Welcome to the life immortal,
>   To the mansions of the blest,
> Home, sweet home, our home forever;
>   All the pilgrim journey past;
> Welcome home to wander never,
>   Saved thro' Jesus—home at last."

LAST WORD.

Dear Reader, the allegory is ended, but it has not been told in vain if, by means of it, you are going to defy the works of the Devil, in some larger degree, and become more imbued with the Christ-spirit as exemplified in Jesus, the apotheosis of humanity.

We have delved after sins entrenched in the human heart, and have pictured the path of sorrow to which they inevitably lead.

Sham has been fearlessly exposed and brought into striking contrast with what is genuine in life and character.

The strait path, which alone guides to goodness and God, crosses each page; and the finger-board of divine judgment has been set up at the cross-roads of sins common in the CHURCH, the HOME, and SOCIETY.

This plain and pointed message has its inspiration and source in the Word of God. It will do truth's work where souls are ready to hear truth's word.

YOU have read the book, heard what it has had to say, and you know that what it says is TRUE.

NOW, WHAT ARE YOU GOING TO DO ABOUT IT?

The light of the Cross still shines. The Angel yet meets you on the road of life. You are either right or wrong. The Bridge must soon be crossed; but the Gates of Pearl shall swing open to those only who to-day are traveling in the company of Jesus, with clean hands, pure hearts, and loyal endeavors.

I. Mench Chambers.

N. B.—There are 64 pp. of illus. in the volume, and not numbered. Adding same to pages of the book makes the total number of pages 520.